W9-CGO-011

POLITICAL PARTIES *and Constitutional Government*

INTERPRETING AMERICAN POLITICS

MICHAEL NELSON, *Series Editor*

POLITICAL
PARTIES
and
CONSTITUTIONAL
GOVERNMENT

Remaking American Democracy

Sidney M. Milkis

THE JOHNS HOPKINS UNIVERSITY PRESS
Baltimore and London

© 1999   THE JOHNS HOPKINS UNIVERSITY PRESS
All rights reserved. Published 1999
Printed in the United States of America on acid-free paper
2 4 6 8 9 7 5 3 1

The Johns Hopkins University Press
2715 North Charles Street
Baltimore, Maryland 21218-4363
www.press.jhu.edu

Library of Congress Cataloging-in-Publication Data will be found
at the end of this book.
A catalog record for this book is available from the British Library.

ISBN 0-8018-6194-2
ISBN 0-8018-6195-0 (pbk.)

CONTENTS

WITHDRAWN

SERIES EDITOR'S
FOREWORD

Only one thing about the framers of the Constitution is clearer than their disdain for political parties: namely, that the Constitution they framed cried out for political parties in order to make it work. James Madison, lumping parties in with "factions" in *Federalist* No. 10, treated them as at best a necessary evil. George Washington, leaving office after two terms as president, expressed the hope in his farewell address that, being evil, parties would not become necessary.

Yet political parties were already forming in Washington's America, and hardly a political scientist or historian can be found who will argue that it could have been otherwise. The traditional explanation (and no less accurate for being traditional) is that the nexus between parties and the Constitution is grounded in the system of "separate institutions sharing powers." Just as Article I, section 6, keeps the elected institutions of the national government separate ("no Person holding any [executive] Office under the United States, shall be a Member of either House [of Congress"], so does the rest of the Constitution specify that virtually no power of that government can be exercised by one branch without the support or acquiescence of the other. Yet what is to provide the bridge between the branches that will foster such cooperation if not loyalty by the president and members of Congress to a common political party?

Sidney M. Milkis, the foremost scholar of presidents and political parties, offers an additional Constitution-based reason for the development of parties. Milkis argues that parties were formed in the early nineteenth century as " localized political associations . . . connecting the personal relationships and provincial loyalties formed in localities and states with the national government." As such, parties were designed by the Jeffersonians and Jacksonians to "ensure that space the Founders created between the cup of power and the lips of the people would not become so great as to make representation impractical."

According to Milkis, the twentieth century has seen a deterioration in the ability of political parties to serve as constitutional bridges of any kind, whether among the branches in Washington or between Washington and the nation. The reason is that Franklin D. Roosevelt, bringing to fruition a transformation begun earlier in the century by Progressives who wanted to centralize governing power in national administrative institutions, replaced the traditional parties with a "national executive-dominated party system" centered on the president and the White House staff. FDR wrought this transformation on the assumption that future presidents would be in his image—that is, programmatic liberals aided by generally complaisant congresses.

Roosevelt's assumption, Milkis demonstrates, has been belied by recent experience. Conservative presidents have become the norm, as has divided partisan control of the elected branches of the national government. Liberals, no longer regarding a strong presidency as the safeguard of their entitlements-based policy agenda, have increasingly used the courts and the career bureaucracy—that is, the government's two unelected components—to thwart executive power and to safeguard liberal programs from elections and other forms of majority control. The result, at century's end, is that localized political parties have been enfeebled but that nothing has satisfactorily taken their place.

Milkis deplores the modern system of political parties and constitutional government. Enervated parties, ineffective government, and voters who feel disconnected from both are a formula for political futility, he argues. Although he does not offer a cure for our nation's political ills in this book, Milkis provides an equally valuable service: a perceptive diagnosis of what ails us.

Michael Nelson

PREFACE

As this book went into production, William Jefferson Clinton, a popular president, presiding over the most prosperous times in three decades, became the first elected president to be impeached by the House of Representatives (Andrew Johnson, the only other president to suffer such an indignity, inherited the executive office after the assassination of Lincoln). Mindful of Clinton's remarkable support among the public, the Senate acquitted the president on the impeachment charges. But the nation was left in a funk; scornful of the tawdry affair and virulent partisanship that led to this constitutional crisis, government officials, pundits, and the public decried the absence of responsible leadership in American democracy.

Although the historic proportions of this episode are startling, the underlying forces that gave rise to it point to deep-rooted, long-festering problems in America. The pages that follow attempt to take account of these problems by examining the origins and development of political parties in the United States. Parties were formed in the early part of the nineteenth century as part of a deliberate program of constitutional reform, one that sought to remedy the inadequate means provided in the Constitution for democratic participation. Almost from the beginning of the Republic, localized political parties became critical agents of popular rule, essential political associations that ameliorated the chronic difficulty of fulfilling the Constitution's promise to empower "We the People," to make democracy work on a grand scale. Yet economic and political developments would transform the United States from a decentralized republic to a mass democracy, in which the principles and political associations that were critical for the maintenance of an engaged citizenry would be undermined. Born of the first three decades of the twentieth century, progressive democracy did not destroy political parties but transformed them into national programmatic entities that lost their connection with the public. The spectacle of a popular but irresolute president fighting for his political life against the tide of virulent and petty partisanship while an

entertained but indignant public looked on offered dramatic testimony that
the experiment to form a national democracy had gone badly off course.

This is not to say that the nationalism of the twentieth century should be
reversed—the national state that emerged during the first half of the twentieth
century has done much good in ameliorating economic insecurity and invid-
ious discrimination at home and fighting tyranny abroad. Rather, the wayward
path of progressive democracy compels us to come to terms with a dilemma:
the development of a more active and better-equipped central government,
but one without adequate means of common deliberation and public judgment. Just as political parties were formed to correct the deficiencies of the
Constitution—its insufficient attention to an active and competent citizenry—so the weakening of political parties has exposed the fragile sense of
citizenship in American political life.

In sum, this book represents an attempt to explore the deep historical
roots of the "crisis of citizenship" that scholars and pundits routinely declare
in their examination of contemporary American politics. My argument is that
the rise and fall of political parties—as critical agents of political participation—shed light on the character of mass democracy in the United States and
its corrosive effect on America's civic culture.

I am deeply grateful to many people for the intellectual and moral support they provided me during the long germination of this book. Henry Tom
and Michael Nelson never lost faith in me as I missed deadline after deadline.
My strongest hope for this book is that it rewards them in some small way for
their extraordinary patience and understanding. With their encouragement,
critical commentary, and gentle nagging, Henry and Mike taught me valuable lessons about the meaning of colleague and friend.

I also want to acknowledge the extraordinary help of Wilson Carey
McWilliams, who reviewed the manuscript for the Johns Hopkins University
Press and offered generous commentary that encouraged me to think more
carefully and creatively about the history of political parties. At various stages
of writing, I also received stimulating and constructive suggestions from
Martha Derthick, Richard Harris, Mark Hulliung, Marc Landy, R. Shep Mel-
nick, and Daniel Tichenor. Brad Clarke, Daniel Klinghard, and Peter Uber-
taccio offered the most energetic and intelligent research support. Greg
Shesko provided critical financial succor through Brandeis University's Mazer
Fund. Finally, I am thankful for the thorough and candid copyediting of
Grace Buonocore, who rescued the text from many stylistic flaws that would
have pained me deeply had I been condemned to read them in print.

It is customary to thank one's family at the end of a preface, and I surely owe mine an enormous debt of gratitude. Carol, Lauren, David, and Jonathan tolerate my work habits with love and good humor. Even in their unhappiness with the time I spend in my "cocoon," they have taught me valuable lessons of perspective—not to take myself and my work too seriously. The members of my extended family have also offered tough and humorous love—my father, Howard, his wife Barbara, and my sisters, Viki and Abby, never fail to remind me that though political science might be my professional calling, first and foremost I am a Milkis.

This book is dedicated to the memory of my mother, Lucille, whose unfailing devotion taught me to believe in myself. I know she would have overlooked the flaws of this book; she would have been proud of her "perfect" son in spite of them.

Parties and American Democracy

This book attempts to shed light on the uneasy place of political parties in the United States. As Wilson Carey McWilliams has observed, "In the Constitution of the United States, political parties are like a scandal in polite society; they are alluded to but not discussed."[1] Indeed, James Madison's famous discussion of "factions" in *Federalist* 10 reveals the Framers' hope that the division and separation of powers, operating within a large commercial society, would transform vital party dialogue and conflict into muted competition among a multitude of diverse interests.[2] The "Constitution-against-Parties," as Richard Hofstadter calls it, embodied the Framers' fears that the "civic virtue" cultivated by local communities and militant political associations was but local prejudices that threatened to degenerate into anarchy, or worse, majority tyranny.[3]

As Harvey Mansfield has argued, it is essential not to forget the Framers' arguments against parties: "It is simple good sense to remember that parties may dangerously divide a free country," that during great contests of opinion, "they can make compromise difficult by organizing moderates under the domination of extremists and by fixing opinion into opposed categories equipped with slogans designed to raise heat rather than convince." Or, on the contrary, during quiet times, parties may spread corruption by engaging in deal making and paving the way for mediocre politicians. "The necessity of combining into parties," he claims, "detracts from the independence of mind required of both politicians and citizens in a free country."[4]

Still, political parties have played an essential part in American democracy. Even as Mansfield urges us to restrain partisanship, he acknowledges its critical importance, admitting that political parties do the "real work of American politics by organizing the majorities necessary to fill offices and adopt policies."[5] Indeed, it is difficult to imagine how representative government could work in a large complex society like our own without party politics. The two-party system has played a principal part in combining the separated institutions of constitutional government, thus centralizing government sufficiently for it to perform its essential duties. It has enabled voters to find their place as effective participants in the political process, thus making the very concept of popular sovereignty practical. Most significant, the party system has been virtually the only reliable source of collective identity in our rights-based culture. By linking private and public concerns, political parties have made it possible for individuals in a commercial republic to form bonds of civic affiliation, to become citizens who honor their obligations, even as they jealously guard their rights. As E. E. Schattschneider, one of the great defenders of political parties, wrote, "The political parties created modern democracy and modern democracy is unthinkable save in terms of parties."[6]

Beginning with Tocqueville, a view has prevailed among observers of American democracy that parties remained derivative of the Constitution even as they made it work, that the advent of parties under the Constitution was shaped by fundamental principles and institutional arrangements that constrained partisanship. Once the great contest between the Federalists and Republicans was resolved by the critical election of 1800, Tocqueville observed, "great" parties, that is, "those more attached to principles than to consequences, to generalities rather than to particular cases, to ideas rather than to personalities," disappeared. In their place arose "small" parties, sustained not by "political faith" but by personal ambitions and private interests. Thus, "public opinion [was] broken up ad infinitum about questions of detail," just as Madison prescribed. European nations were divided by polarizing class and religious conflict; in contrast, Tocqueville observed with both reverence and contempt, "Americans' domestic quarrels [seemed] at first glance either incomprehensible or puerile, and one does not know whether to pity a people that takes such trifles seriously or to envy the luck enabling it to do so."[7]

But Tocqueville, writing in the 1830s, could not have had in mind the extraordinary battles that subsequently divided the country, the partisan upheavals that occurred in the 1850s and 1930s which both revisited and redefined the fundamental principles of constitutional government in the United States. In truth, the "Revolution of 1800," as Jefferson referred to the great contest of opinion between the Federalists and Republicans, was but the first epic struggle for the soul of the Constitution. These contests, this book argues, reveal that political parties were not simply derivative of constitutional forms. Indeed, there is a real sense in which these episodes involve mass democracy in a surrogate constitutional convention; in truth, partisan realignments make the work of constitutional government far more democratic than the architects of the Constitution anticipated it would be.[8]

This democratic feature of constitutional government in the United States was not a matter of historical accident; rather, it was the result of deliberate constitutional reform. As formed during the first three decades of the nineteenth century, political parties reflected the concern first expressed by the Antifederalists, and later revised by Jefferson, that the Constitution provided inadequately for the cultivation of an active and competent citizenry. "Enlarge the circle" of political life as far as conceived by the Constitution, the antifederalist Cato warned, and "we lose the ties of acquaintance, habits, and fortune, and thus, by degrees, we lessen in our attachments, till, at length, we no more than acknowledge a sameness of species."[9]

The Antifederalists were not fond of partisanship, but like their Jeffersonian descendants they viewed political parties as the most practical remedy for the corrosion of confidence between rulers and ruled, indeed among citizens themselves, in a large regime. Formed during the early part of the nineteenth century, political parties were conceived as bulwarks of decentralization, as localized political associations that could provide a vital link between constitutional offices, especially the executive, and the people; they would do so by balancing state and local communities, championed by the Antifederalists as the true guardians of the people's rights, and the national government, strengthened by the Constitution of 1787.[10]

Significantly, Madison, the principal architect of the "Constitution-against-Parties," became a defender of parties and local self-government during the critical partisan battles between the Republicans and the Federalists. Alexander Hamilton's success as secretary of the treasury in the Washington administration in strengthening the executive led Madison to rethink his understanding of republican government, to recognize that the Antifederalists might have been more correct in their criticisms of the Constitution than he previously had thought. By the early 1790s, he joined Jefferson in opposition to the Federalists, in the formulation of a party program of government decentralization, which renewed the conflicts that had divided the Federalists and Antifederalists and, consequently, gave birth to the American party system.

To be sure, those who played the leading parts in legitimizing and building parties, in making them part of the "living Constitution" by the 1830s, were not "antifederalists." Even the Jacksonians, who embraced a more militant states' rights position than their Jeffersonian forebears, supported the idea that the Constitution beheld "a more perfect union." Jacksonian parties, in fact, found their strength principally in the political combat of presidential elections—a battleground that encouraged Democratic and Whig partisans to overlook their differences in the interest of victory. Moreover, the positions espoused during these campaigns were not words to be ignored but, as one Whig representative put it, "worth fighting for . . . the rules of action." The national quality and strength of the two parties were demonstrated by the impressive party cohesion that shaped the work of the federal government during the 1830s and 1840s.[11] Paradoxically, the Jacksonian party system established a national framework of principles and behavior which defied local differences even as it transformed the doctrine of local self-government into a national idea.

Nonetheless, the "critics" of the original Constitution feared that its institutional arrangements tended toward "consolidation," undermining the foundation of local self-government, which they sought to strengthen as the sentinels of liberty in American constitutional democracy. The Jeffersonians and Jacksonians sought a remedy for this political disease in partisan principles and practices that celebrated the decentralization of power.

Rooted in the states and localities, parties penetrated deeply into American society between the 1830s and the 1890s. During the twentieth century, however, the Constitution-against-Parties would become newly relevant. Localized parties represented a formidable obstacle to progressive reformers who considered the expansion of national administration essential to industrial reform. Aroused by antiparty sentiments, the Progressive movement tended to discredit rather than reform partisanship. Given the constitutional and political difficulties involved in establishing a national programmatic, let alone a social democratic, party in the United States, most progressives looked to revive the antipartyism of the original Constitution as an agent of reform. Progressives hoped, as Herbert Croly put it, "to give democratic meaning and

purpose to the Hamiltonian tradition and method."[12] Progressive democracy
glimpsed a national community, in which new political institutions such as
the direct primary, initiative, and referendum would forge a direct link
between public opinion and government representatives. It rested on the possibility of creating a "modern," independent executive who might become, as
Theodore Roosevelt put it, "the steward of the public welfare."[13]

Progressive democracy came into its own with the New Deal. Yet the
expansion of the central government's power which followed from the New
Deal realignment did not result in the formation of the national state progressive reformers such as Croly had anticipated, one that established national
regulations and welfare programs that were expressions of a shared understanding of principles. Rather, the reconstituted executive was hitched to a
plebiscitary politics that exposed the fragile sense of citizenship in American
political life.[14] In the final analysis, the limits of progressivism—the danger of
resurrecting Hamiltonian nationalism—point to the limits of the original
Constitution, the "Madisonian system" that Madison himself came to view as
defective. The greatest flaw of progressive democracy was that its principal
objective—creating democracy on a grand scale—seemed to be a chimera.

To be sure, the displacement of localized parties by progressive democracy has not meant the end of party conflict. The advance of progressive
democracy—and the erosion of old-style partisan politics—allowed a more
national and issue-oriented party system to develop, one that was more compatible with the "nationalized" electorate created by progressive reforms and
the mass media. Indeed, the Reagan "revolution" of the 1980s supported
efforts by Republicans in the national committee and congressional campaign organizations to restore some of the importance of political parties by
refashioning them into highly untraditional but politically potent national
organizations. But the emergence of more centralized parties strengthened
the national party organizations and allowed for more partisan discipline in
Congress, only to weaken further partisan loyalties in the electorate.

The growing strength of political parties within the Washington beltway
in the wake of the New Deal realignment occurred amid the declining influence of Democrats and Republicans on the perceptions and habits of the
American people. The decline of partisan loyalties became especially pronounced in the late 1960s as the McGovern-Fraser reforms, which expanded
the number of presidential primaries, and the rise of mass media politics led
to a greater emphasis on candidate-centered, rather than party, campaigns.
The 1992 presidential campaign of H. Ross Perot, whose 19 percent of the vote

was the most significant challenge to the two-party system since Theodore Roosevelt's Progressive party campaign of 1912, was dominated by thirty-minute commercials and hour-long appearances on talk shows which set a new standard for direct, plebiscitary appeal. Disdaining pleas to form a third party from those interested in party renewal, Perot required no nominating convention to launch his 1992 candidacy. Instead, he called his supporters to arms on the popular Cable News Network talk show *Larry King Live*.

With the rise of mass media politics, it has become routine for scholars and pundits to declare that a crisis of citizenship plagues contemporary American political life.[15] But the estrangement of the people from their government in the United States has deeper historical roots than the mass media; a big part of the problem is inherent in the nature of the political system.[16] Just as political parties were formed to make constitutional government in the United States safe for democracy—to ameliorate the Constitution's insufficient attention to the cultivation of an active and competent citizenry—so the weakening of political parties has corroded civic attachments in the United States.

Viewing the traditional party system as an obstacle to the realization of a national community, progressive reformers failed to appreciate the purpose that it had served as an effective agent of democratic participation. Rooted in neighborhood organizations and local newspapers, traditional party organizations persuaded individuals that political participation was an extension of their private concerns. Just as important, highly decentralized party organizations ensured that national campaigns and controversies echoed in townships, wards, and cities, thus "encouraging the voter to see himself as a member of a well defined community rather than as an unimportant figure lost in a sea of electors."[17] Drawn into political associations by the promise of entertainment and personal gain, Americans also were lured into dealing with complex national issues such as slavery. Party politics thus combined passion and reason, provincial interests and nationalism, so that Americans might become citizens.

Not all progressives were indifferent to the role parties played in linking private and public concerns. "A democracy must be alive to the core," the municipal reformer Mary Simkhovitch cautioned her fellow progressives, and thus it was dangerous for reformers to risk the spread of indifference that might follow from their desire "to supersede the solid masonry of the old parties." For a majority of citizens, she warned, politics was alive in the world of particular personalities and provincial loyalties, not of principles. The reformer was well advised, therefore, to seek influence within, rather than stand aloof from, party politics. "The political party was a hard school, often subject to ignorant and domineering teachers," Simkhovitch admitted; but, she continued, "if one can keep one's heart and head, the battle is indeed worth while."[18]

But most reformers dismissed such tolerance of party politics as hopelessly romantic. The development of a more purposeful national government, they insisted, required that politics and government be emancipated from the constrictive grip of localized democracy. As Croly argued, progressive democracy's commitment to expanding the programmatic responsibilities of the national government "particularly need[ed] an increase of administrative authority and efficiency." Yet the American party system was established as an institution to control administrative authority—it "bestowed upon the divided Federal government a certain unity of control, while at the same time it prevented the increased efficiency of the Federal system from being obnoxious to local interests." The consequent weakening of administrative authority, although rooted in the "pioneer" conditions of the nineteenth century, Croly argued, was an essential and incorrigible aspect of the two-party system. Thus, "under American conditions, a strong responsible and efficient administration of the law and public business would be fatal to partisan responsibility."[19]

Croly's recognition of the tension between party politics and national administrative power has been confirmed by political developments of the twentieth century. His prescience reminds us that there is no easy solution to the crisis of citizenship in the United States. This book, certainly, does not attempt to call the American people back to some "golden age" of parties. Indeed, any project to restore parties should be informed by the historical need to weaken them in the first place. Progressive reformers had sound reasons for treating localized parties and the provincial liberties they upheld as an impediment to economic, social, and political justice. Inasmuch as they were molded from principles that were inhospitable to a strong national government, parties inhibited the development of a central power capable of undertaking the domestic and international responsibilities that all advanced industrial democracies assume. In the final analysis, examining the rise and decline of political parties in the United States demands that we come to terms with a legacy that yields a more active and better-equipped national state—the national resolve to tackle problems such as forced segregation at home and communism abroad—but one without adequate means of common deliberation and public judgment, the very practices that nurture a civic culture.

The chapters that follow probe the philosophical and historical roots of America's struggle to create democracy on a grand scale. This investigation takes the form of an extended essay that makes a case for the constitutional significance of political parties. Chapter 2 examines the constitutional program of the Jeffersonians and Jacksonians which established a formal two-party system as an integral part of representative government in the United States. By the 1840s, political parties, drawing strength from their alliance with the tradition of local self-government, would become the leading agent of popular rule in the United States. Thus, although the Federalists won the contest over the ratification of the Constitution, Antifederalist concerns would "find a reflection in American political parties."[20]

Chapter 3 examines the antiparty sentiment of the Progressive Era. The origins and organizing principles of the American party system established it as a force against the creation of the "modern" state. Progressive reformers' commitment to building such a state—that is, to the creation of a national political power with expansive programmatic responsibilities—meant that the party system had to be either weakened or reconstructed. In truth, progressive democracy both diminished and transformed partisanship. The logic of building popular support for progressive principles and programs required reformers to create new partisan organizations. As Barry Karl has observed about the Progressive party campaign of 1912, however, it was as much an assault on the very idea of a party system as it was an effort to form a militant reform party that could advance a program of national reconstruction.[21] Likewise, the New Deal Democratic party aroused militant partisanship in the service of principles and institutional reforms that represented a full-scale assault on party politics. The New Deal, like its successor the Great Society in the 1960s, was less a partisan program than an exercise in expanding both the president's power and the nonpartisan administration of the affairs of state. Understood within the context of the progressive tradition, the New Deal is appropriately viewed as the completion of a realignment to make future partisan realignments unnecessary.

Still, the profound shift in regime norms and practices represented by progressivism did not entail a straightforward evolution from localized to administrative politics. It is not accurate to characterize progressive reformers simply as "state builders," dedicated merely to emancipating national administrative power from the constraints of localized parties. Indeed, progressives such as Woodrow Wilson, hoping to combine progressive reform and grassroots democracy, looked to the transformation rather than the demise of the party system. He called for the creation of a more national and programmatic party system capable of carrying out platforms and proposals presented to the people during the course of an election. Chapter 4 examines Wilson's understanding of "responsible political parties" and its legacy for twentieth-century politics and government. It shows how Wilson's doctrine of responsible party government had a strong influence on Franklin Roosevelt, whose extraordinary party leadership both anticipated and influenced the advocates of party government during the 1940s and 1950s. More than any other critical period of party development, the New Deal era reveals the possibilities and limits of party government in the United States. Although FDR wanted to change the character of the Democratic party, and thereby also bring about a change in the American party system, he concluded ultimately that the public good and practical politics demanded that partisan politics be deemphasized rather than restructured. In particular, once the presidency and executive department were "modernized," some of the burden of party loyalty would be alleviated, freeing the chief executive, as leader of the whole people, to affect more directly the development of society and economy. As such, the New Deal directed the progressive animus against decentralized parties in a way that rejected party government and paved an alternative road to a stronger national government. The New Deal dedication to concentrating policy responsibility in a revamped executive resulted in institutional changes that rendered the struggle for party government a moot issue, at least for a time.

The New Deal realignment weakened but did not eliminate the deeply ingrained distrust of national administrative power in the United States. Indeed, the New Deal's institutional legacy made political accountability newly problematic in the United States. Administrative aggrandizement came at the expense of the more decentralizing institutions of constitutional government, such as Congress and local governments, which political parties had organized into effective representative bodies. As Karl has noted, "local government and community control," supported by the Constitution's federal structure and decentralized political parties, "remain at the heart of the most intuitive conceptions of American democracy, even though they may also represent bastions of political corruption and locally condoned injustice."[22] Consequently, the New Deal "threatened our sense of ourselves as citizens."[23]

Chapter 5 tells the story of how reformers during the 1960s and 1970s attempted to reinvigorate popular sovereignty in the United States. Hoping to reconcile national authority with the New Left's dedication to "participatory democracy," they rejected the New Deal practice of delegating power to the executive branch. These public interest advocates championed statutes and judicial rulings that would reduce the discretionary power of presidents and administrative agencies. Just as significant, reform activists played the principal part in revamping administrative law during the 1970s, so that liberal provisions were established for public participation in the bureaucratic process. Taking account of these changes, Samuel Beer noted at the end of the 1970s that "it would be difficult today to find a program involving regulation or delivery of services in such fields as health, education, welfare, and the environment that does not provide for 'community input.'"[24]

Although the reformers of the 1960s and 1970s set out to temper the "administrative state" and to revitalize self-government in the United States, the changes they brought continued, even increased, the dominance of political administration in the councils of government. The "institutional partnership" that liberals forged during the 1970s limited the administrative power of the president but involved Congress, the courts, and public interest groups in the details of administration. These institutional developments not only fixed the business of government more on administration than on politics but also accelerated the decline of political parties.

Indeed, the McGovern-Fraser reforms carried out in the wake of the 1968 Democratic convention, which virtually stripped party leaders of their authority to nominate presidential candidates, were the result of the same systemic forces that led to the reform of government during the 1970s. The reformers who took command of the Democratic party after the Chicago debacle followed the progressive tradition of emphasizing the candidate over the party— of desiring the emancipation of the presidency from the constrictive grip of partisan institutions. But they viewed the modern presidency as the *instrument* rather than the *steward* of the public welfare. Failing to address the question of the type of leadership or the type of executive which was desired, party reformers of the 1970s took for granted the general ideas current in the late 1960s and 1970s that presidential politics should be directed by popular movements.[25] At the end of the day, the reforms of the 1970s circumscribed the administrative power of the president but at the cost of making other government and political institutions—even the president's own staff—more bureaucratic in their organization and activities. As a result, the expansion of liberalism during the 1970s resulted in the enervation, rather than the surge, of popular rule.

Chapter 6 examines the "malaise" that afflicted the United States in the wake of this development. As Jimmy Carter observed in his notorious but prescient "malaise" speech of 1979, the American people had come to express a profound distrust of, indeed a "growing disrespect" for, government and its leaders. "Looking for a way out of this crisis, our people have turned to the Federal Government and found it isolated from the mainstream of the nation's life," he lamented.[26]

In the past, political parties had played a critical part in closing the distance between the nation's capital and society. During critical partisan realignments, America's "small" parties had gotten caught up in something big, thus jarring the Republic with uncharacteristic conflict over general principles and restoring the vigor of democratic politics. The Reagan "revolution," which appeared to culminate with the dramatic Republican triumph in the 1994 midterm election, led scholars and pundits to suggest that the nation might be on the threshold of still another critical partisan realignment.[27] But the American people had become alienated from both the Republican and Democratic parties by the 1990s, so much so that the renewal of partisan loyalties, let alone a full-scale partisan transformation, seemed unlikely. Instead, divided government—divided party control of the executive and legislature— has become a chronic condition of American democracy. Scholars have often characterized the tendency of growing numbers of voters to split their tickets as a form of "cognitive Madisonianism," a disinclination of the electorate "to place much faith in either party's leadership or direction."[28] It remains to be seen, however, whether the underlying factors that sustain separate partisan realms in American politics reinforce or corrode constitutional forms. "Without the parties and what they once did for the political nation, we have returned to where we began two centuries ago," the historian Joel Silbey warns. "We have empowered chaos, and given new meaning to such terms as fragmentation, factional warfare, and gridlock."[29] As the decline of voting which has been associated with the weakening of partisanship suggests, these features of contemporary politics may not be new symptoms of a historical political individualism; rather, they seem to indicate a serious weakening of the link between private and public concerns, a distressing deterioration of political life itself.

Chapter 7 concludes this volume by examining the prospects for revitalizing political parties. With the decline of traditional localized parties, there has arisen an administrative politics that belittles the efforts of Democrats and

Republicans alike to define a collective purpose with a past and a future and yields instead a partisanship joined to a form of politics which relegates electoral conflict to the intractable demands of policy advocates. In effect, political parties are much more focused on government than they once were, and to this extent, the new partisanship is consistent with the aspirations of progressive reformers. But a partisanship that emphasizes national administrative power in support of rights and entitlements has little chance to reach beyond Washington and win the loyalty of the American people. To be sure, the Democrats and Republicans consider elections important and have not despaired of extending their influence over them. But as "parties of administration," the Democrats and Republicans are hobbled in their efforts to form vital links with the public. This is the novel and pressing challenge for those who would take the idea of party renewal seriously as American democracy enters the twenty-first century.

Localism, Political Parties, and Democratic Participation

A substantial body of contemporary criticism singles out individualism, especially an obsession with rights, as the source of a contemporary crisis of citizenship in the United States. Yet individualism and rights discourse are as old as the Republic. "Telling Americans to improve democracy by sinking comfortably into a community, by losing themselves in a collective life, is calling into the wind," Robert Wiebe has written. "There has never been an American democracy without its powerful strand of individualism, and nothing suggests there ever will be."[1]

In truth, popular sovereignty in the United States has been bounded by the Declaration of Independence and its promise of natural rights, by a commitment to the democratic individual's right to pursue happiness. Collective obligation in the United States—the attachment of democratic individuals to their government—follows from the belief that government secures the rights of the People.

This chapter seeks to shed light on the fragile relationship between the American people and their government by revisiting the origins and history of political parties. Political parties were formed in the early part of the nineteenth century as a means of engaging the attention of ordinary citizens, and with localistic foundations that were critical for the maintenance of an engaged citizenry. The American tradition of local self-government, which preceded and was only partly modified by the "more perfect Union" formed in 1787, played a critical part in relating the private order to the public life of the United States. As Tocqueville observed in the 1830s, this tradition went well beyond the legal division between the national and state governments and left considerable discretion to counties and townships. The vitality of townships and counties depended on the well-established idea in the United States that "each man [was] the best judge of his own interest and best able to satisfy his private needs." The practice of leaving townships and counties in charge of their "special interests," in turn, cultivated civic attachments, by giving each individual "the same feeling for his country as one has for one's family." Happily, Tocqueville concluded, "a sort of selfishness makes [the individual] care for the state."[2]

Like Tocqueville, the Antifederalists and their Jeffersonian descendants viewed the states and localities as the schools of American democracy. But they were more concerned than Tocqueville seemed to be that the original Constitution provided inadequate support for provincial institutions. By the same token, whereas democratic reformers had become unabashed champions of the localized party system by the 1830s, viewing it as an essential corrective to the Constitution's frail connection between representatives and their constituents, Tocqueville appeared unimpressed with, if not contemptuous of, American partisanship.[3] Although Tocqueville considered localized parties in the United States to be valuable political associations in which individuals learned the art of cooperation and became citizens, he found them relatively indifferent to broad moral questions and dedicated to the personal ambitions of their members.[4] What he missed amid the restlessness of Jacksonian democracy was how state and local Democratic party leaders, such as Martin Van Buren of New York, were building the first national party organization in the hope of connecting presidential politics and governance with a collective body that could constrain excessive personal or programmatic ambition. To be sure, this partisan project was not completely successful; but it went far enough to ensure that the executive and members of Congress were held accountable to state and local officials.

In effect, political parties embodied Antifederalist principles. Forged on the anvil of Jeffersonian and Jacksonian democracy, political parties were conceived as localized political associations that could provide a vital link between rights and community in the United States; they would do so by connecting the personal relationships and provincial loyalties formed in localities and states with the national government. In this way, traditional political parties reflected Jefferson's desire for a "graduation of authority," in which national unity would grow out of local wards.[5] As Jefferson wrote in a letter to Samuel Kercheval, "In government, as well as in every other business of life, it is by division and subdivision of duties alone, that all matters, great and small, can be managed to perfection. And the whole is cemented by giving to every citizen, personally, a part in the administration of public affairs."[6] Although cautious in his support of partisanship, Jefferson founded the Republican party as a necessary means to the end of civic obligation, as an institutional device that welded the personal and the public.[7] "Aristocracy," Tocqueville observed, "links everybody from peasant to king in one long chain. Democracy breaks that chain and frees each link." In the United States, political parties would attempt to reforge the chain, Wilson Carey McWilliams has written, "giving its metal a new democratic casting."[8]

Localized Parties and Constitutional Reform

"Many factors have influenced the historical development of federalism," states a report of the Advisory Commission on Intergovernmental Relations. "Among the most important of these was the decentralized, non-disciplined party system which, the historical record suggests, had a significant decentralizing influence on intergovernmental relations by providing an often powerful institutional link between local, state, and national offices."[9] The decentralizing influence of political parties in the United States does not simply reflect the federal structure of the Constitution. Rather, the origins and organizing principles of American political parties yielded a highly mobilized and highly competitive locally oriented democracy that subordinated the powers of the national government to the prerogatives of the states and localities. As V. O. Key explained in 1964, "Federalism in our formal governmental machinery includes a national element independent of the states, but in our party organization the independent and national element is missing. Party structure is more nearly *confederative* than *federal* in nature."[10]

The confederative form of parties seemed to defy the "more perfect Union" created by the Constitution of 1787. Indeed, even though the early development of party organizations emerged with the arousal of national electoral followings for presidential candidates, these political associations were shaped by institutions such as the nominating convention and patronage system which centered power in states and localities. That the traditional party

was rooted in the local community was no accident, nor was it merely a pragmatic adjustment to political events. The persistent, confederate form of political parties was owed to their creation as agents of constitutional reform. Political parties were founded as part of a program to modify the original
Constitution so that it would conform in practice to many of the principles of
antifederalism. These political associations served the purposes of those who
shared the Antifederalist commitment to local self-government but joined Jefferson in accepting the Constitution as a work in progress, hoping to shape it
by amendment, interpretation, and practice.[11]

Ironically, one of the leaders of this revisionist project was James Madison, who played a critical part in writing and ratifying the Constitution. Donald Brand describes "Madison's philosophical and political about face from
the time he co-authored the *Federalist Papers* to the time he wrote pieces
more anti-federalist in spirit" as "one of the most perplexing episodes in the
American Founding period."[12] Madison's statements about property and
majority rule at the time of the Constitution gave no hint that he saw the need
for strong political associations to cultivate an active and competent citizenry.
To the contrary, he celebrated the Constitution for the way it separated the
cup of power from the lips of the people. In the normal course of events, the
majority would be indifferent, if not avowedly hostile, to the rights of property
and all too likely to carry out "wicked projects" that sought to distribute property equally and thus deny individuals the fruits of their own labor. Writing as
Publius, Madison argued in the *Federalist Papers* that the control of the majority lies in "enlarging the orbit" in which critical political relationships and
associations form, so that a majority would necessarily be composed of diverse
and narrow factions that would be unlikely to agree about much or for long.
As Madison wrote in a letter to Jefferson in October 1787—an extraordinary
postmortem on the Constitutional Convention—"Divide et impera, the
reprobated axiom of tyranny, is under certain qualifications, the only policy,
by which a republic can be administered on just principles."[13] Or, as Madison
put it somewhat more delicately in *Federalist* 51, "In the extended republic of
the United States, and among the great variety of interests, parties, and sects
which it embraces, a coalition of a majority of the whole could seldom take
place on any other principles than those of justice and the general good."[14]
Within this scheme of government, the states and localities were to play an
important role, but they were to be transformed from the principal sites of
political authority into mere interests, which added to the variety and diversity

of factionalism. The state legislatures would effectively defend "local inter-ests," Alexander Hamilton observed, and could be relied on "to erect barriers against the encroachments of the national authorities."[15] As Madison put it in *Federalist* 51:

> In a single republic, all the power surrendered by the people is submit-ted to the administration of a single government; and the usurpations are guarded against by a division of government into distinct and separate departments. In the *compound republic* of America, the power surren-dered by the people is first divided between two distinct governments, and then the portion allotted to each subdivided among distinct and sep-arate divisions. Hence a *double security arises to the rights of the people.* The different governments will control each other, at the same time that each will be controlled by itself.[16]

Given their collaboration on the *Federalist Papers,* and given Madison's brilliant efforts to create a new national regime capable of remedying the "mortal diseases of popular government," Hamilton had good reasons to believe that Madison would support his efforts as secretary of the treasury in the Washington administration to seize the governing initiative. Hamilton's reports of 1790–91 called on Congress to assume the war debts of the states, to create a national bank, and to enact a system of tariffs to protect infant indus-tries in the United States. In defining a long-term program for achieving eco-nomic development and national power under the guidance of an ambitious executive, these programs appeared to parallel the principles of Publius. Indeed, Hamilton's project to strengthen executive power was anticipated by his defense of a unitary executive in *Federalist* 70 and was designed precisely to provide the energetic leadership that was necessary to assuage the centrifu-gal forces encouraged by the new Constitution. Yet, by the winter of 1791–92, Madison was becoming the philosophical and congressional leader of an opposition group that would soon harden into the Jeffersonian Republican party, a group Hamilton and his political allies dismissed derisively as repre-senting a recrudescence of antifederalism.

Hamilton's program required a liberal—"elastic"—interpretation of the national government's authority, and some discretion for the judiciary in drawing the boundary between the state and national power, which antici-pated a significant extension of executive power. The power of the more decentralizing institutions—Congress and state governments—was necessarily subordinated in this enterprise. More than the policies themselves, Hamilton's interpretation of the Constitution persuaded Madison that he had underestimated the warnings of the Antifederalists that the original constitutional design portended a unitary system that would destroy the delicate balance that his understanding of federalism envisioned. As Marvin Meyers has written, Madison's "particular objections to Hamiltonian measures—to funding, for example, or debt assumption—seemed limited and moderate," but "a growing suspicion of the motives and consequences of the whole Hamiltonian system led him to see a fundamental attack on republican principles and national interests."[17]

Madison's suspicion was confirmed by the Washington administration's response to the war between Britain and France that broke out in 1793. Fearing that America's alliance with France, established by a 1778 treaty, would provoke renewed hostility with Britain, Washington abrogated the terms of that alliance by issuing a neutrality proclamation. The proclamation pledged the United States to be impartial between the two belligerents and proscribed Americans from aiding, abetting, or delivering contraband to either one.

The Neutrality Proclamation of 1793 greatly aggravated a rift that had been developing between Jefferson and the rest of the administration. Jefferson criticized the president's action on two grounds. First, he believed such a unilateral action to be unconstitutional—a declaration of neutrality was, in effect, a declaration that there would be no war, a decision that rightfully belonged to Congress. Second, he pointed out that, according to the 1778 treaty, the United States was obliged to provide for France any necessities of war which had to be brought across the Atlantic. Jefferson had supported Washington's efforts to exert control over the executive branch, but he could not abide this effort to carve out a special sphere of presidential power in foreign affairs.

Madison shared Jefferson's antipathy to administrative aggrandizement. In the aftermath of Washington's Neutrality Proclamation in 1793, which was issued without consulting the Congress, Madison wrote a letter to Jefferson, in June 1793, which expressed a far less sanguine view of the Constitution than he had expressed in the Federalist Papers. "I must own my surprise that such a prerogative should have been exercised," he stated. "Perhaps I may have not attended to some parts of the Constitution with sufficient care, or may have misapprehended its meaning."[18]

At Jefferson's urging, Madison decided, albeit reluctantly, to bring his case against the proclamation before the public. Madison's reluctance eventually gave way to alarm after reading Hamilton's effective defense of the administration's policy. Writing under the pseudonym Pacificus, Hamilton put forth a sweeping justification of discretionary presidential power. Hamilton claimed that neither the enumerated powers granted to Congress in Article I nor the principle of the separation of powers embodied in the institutional arrangements of the Constitution hindered the executive in matters of foreign policy, which "naturally" were the domain of the president. Indeed, Hamilton set forth a theory of presidential power which not only delegated to the chief executive nearly absolute discretion in the conduct of foreign affairs but also proposed a broad conception of prerogative power which later presidents, particularly those in the twentieth century, would generously draw upon.[19]

"Nobody answers [Hamilton]," Jefferson warned his friend, "and his doctrines will therefore be taken for confessed." Pleading in terms that Madison found impossible to resist, Jefferson wrote, "For God sakes my dear Sir, take up your pen, select the most striking heresies and cut him to pieces in face of the public."[20]

Writing under the pseudonym of Helvidius, Madison denied that foreign policy was "naturally" an executive power. In foreign as in domestic matters, Madison argued, republican government required that the president's power be confined to the execution of the law. The tasks of foreign policy—to declare war, to conclude peace, and to form alliances—were among the "highest acts of sovereignty." The Constitution granted such sovereign authority to the legislative branch, relegating the president to the subservient position of executor of such decisions. To suggest, as Hamilton did, that foreign policy was within the proper definition of executive power was to imply that the executive branch had a legislative power. Such an argument was "in theory an absurdity—in practice a tyranny." In the final analysis, Madison believed, democracy, even a refined and enlarged republican version, required public debate and judgment that could only take place in the legislature. To relegate the highest acts of sovereignty to executive decree was to destroy self-government.[21]

Madison's essays in the *National Gazette*, which were written during the critical period of partisan maneuvers in 1791 and 1792, reveal that his revised thoughts on the original Constitution—his fear that it provided inadequately for executive accountability—had caused him to reformulate the arguments of *Federalist* 10.[22] Whereas Madison originally feared that the security of liberty would be violated by a majority faction bent on a misconceived notion of economic justice, requiring institutional arrangements that divided and filtered the voice of the people, his concern about Hamilton's program focused on the need to arouse a "common sentiment" among the states against government consolidation, a task that informed the creation of the Republican party.[23]

As such, Madison, the chief architect of the "Constitution-against-Parties," played a leading role in founding the first majority party, a popular party dedicated to strengthening the decentralizing, and therefore supposedly more popular, institutions of the Constitution—the legislature and the states—against the encroachments of national administrative power. In the *Federalist Papers*, Madison defended the Constitution's strengthening of the national government as necessary to "break and control the violence of faction." His revised understanding of government and society championed *political* centralization, that is, a consolidation of public opinion under the banner of the Republican party, as a way of defending state and local interests against *governmental* centralization. Combining political centralization and governmental decentralization, Madison argued, was the "proper object" to unite former Antifederalists—"those who are most jealously attached to the separate authority reserved to the states"—and the more ardent republicans of the Federalists—"those who may be more inclined to contemplate the people of America in light of one nation":

> Let the former continue to watch against every encroachment, which might lead to a gradual consolidation of the states into one government. Let the latter employ their utmost zeal, by eradicating local prejudices and mistaken rivalships, to consolidate the affairs of the states into one harmonious interest; and let it be the patriotic study of all, to maintain the various authorities established by our complicated system, each with its respective constitutional sphere; and to erect over the whole, one paramount Empire of reason, benevolence, and brotherly affection.[24]

Hitherto united as Publius in the *Federalist Papers*, Madison and Hamilton were estranged by the 1790s, thus reopening some fundamental questions seemingly settled by the ratification of the Constitution. Madison believed

that the multifactioned extended republic he hoped for at the time of the
founding of the Constitution had been thwarted by the emergence of a struggle between the many and the few. Just as the Federalist party was "antirepub-
lican," so the Republicans would "naturally find their account in burying all
antecedent questions, in banishing every other distinction than that between
enemies and friends to republican government."[25]

The republicanism of the 1790s faced its greatest danger and found its
greatest opportunity in the resistance to the Alien and Sedition Acts, which
were passed and administered by the Federalists to stifle the criticisms of the
Jeffersonian press. In his report on the 1799 Virginia Resolutions, Madison
appealed "to the intermediate existence of the state governments between the
people and [the national government], to the vigilance with which they
would decry the first symptoms of usurpation, and to the promptitude with
which they would sound the alarm to the public."[26] As if to underscore the
defects of the arguments of the *Federalist Papers*, Madison defended the right
of the Virginia assembly to declare the Alien and Sedition Acts unconstitutional, but only as a matter of "opinion"—to "excite reflection" among the
people in the various states and to encourage their cooperation in resisting the
offensive statutes. Just as the judiciary's rulings "enforced the general will,"
Madison hoped the resistance of the states to the Federalist government might
"lead to a change in the legislative expression of the general will—possibly to
a change in the opinion of the judiciary."[27] The reference to a Rousseauan
general will was not frivolous; rather, it reflected Madison's revised understanding of the Constitution, in which government must rest not merely on
effective institutional arrangements but also on national opinion, cultivated
by civic associations in the states and localities.[28]

Madison's report figured prominently in the election of 1800, the "Revolution of 1800," as Jefferson called it, which featured a great contest of opinion
that reformed significantly the institutional arrangements Madison had
played such a central part in founding. He was now committed to a doctrine,
later set forth by Jefferson's first inaugural address, which celebrated "the state
governments in all their rights as the most competent administrations for our
domestic concerns and the surest bulwarks against anti-republican tendencies."[29] Madison's alliance with Jefferson helped to revitalize a tradition dedicated to local self-government, thus ensuring that federalism—the interplay
between one nation and many local communities—would be a central feature in the dynamic of American constitutional government.

Jacksonian Democracy and the Creation of a Party System

"Out of the original clash," between the Federalists and the Republicans, James Piereson has written, "there developed in America the tension between party politics, on the one hand, and governmental centralization and bureaucracy, on the other."[30] Similarly, the emergence of open party conflict altered the Constitution, which was now joined to a doctrine of local self-government. But Jefferson and Madison were dedicated to transforming government, not necessarily to establishing a permanent, formal two-party system. Although it was a party that cultivated popular support for republican principles and reforms, Jefferson and Madison appeared to hope that this task would be short term, that the flaws of the original constitutional design might prove to be temporary. Once the Federalists and their program of executive aggrandizement were defeated, they hoped, the Republican party could safely wither away, restoring the nonpartisan character of the Constitution. The country, Jefferson assured an anxious political ally, would see a "rapid return of general harmony," and its countrymen would "[move] in phalanx in the paths of regular liberty, order, and sacrosanct adherence to the constitution."[31]

Madison was not so sure that the spirit of party was ephemeral. As the partisan wars between the Republicans and Federalists were not fought over "occasional and transient subjects," Madison conceded, "parties seem[ed] to have a permanent foundation in the variance of political opinions in free states." Indeed, "the Constitution itself . . . must be an unfailing source of party distinctions." Still, like Jefferson, Madison did not expect the partisan distinctions of the 1790s to endure or to evolve into a system of competitive, ideologically divided parties that accepted the idea of a loyal opposition. Thus, even as he anticipated the recrudescence of partisanship, Madison hoped that effective measures might be taken to "divert [the spirit of party] from the more noxious channels." Moderating the indomitable spirit of party, he prescribed, required the "ascendent party" to ally itself with the Constitution, "to elucidate the policy which harmonizes jealous interests . . . and to give to the Constitution that just construction, which, with the aid of time and habit, may put an end to the more dangerous schisms otherwise growing out of it." Madison shared Jefferson's conviction that the Republican party had exercised such a "remedial power . . . over the spirit of party."[32] To a point, this shared conviction that the Republican party was an agent of national unity made partisanship an integral part of Jeffersonian democracy. The Constitution and the Supreme Court might eventually become the guardians of the people's rights. But until that occurred, the Republican party embodied the will of the people.[33] Unlike the Federalists, the Republicans were not merely a party, a faction that degraded the general harmony. As Jefferson declared in 1811, "the republicans [were] the *nation*."[34]

By the 1820s, Jefferson's claim that the Republicans embodied a new national consensus seemed justified. Indeed, the Federalists had grown so weak by 1816 that they had stopped fielding national tickets; in 1820, the Republican president, James Monroe, was reelected without opposition. The complete triumph of the Republicans over their Federalist rivals, ushering in the so-called Era of Good Feelings, appeared to restore the nonpartisan character of the Constitution, albeit on terms favored by the Republicans. The Republican party did not wither away, the historian Roger Sharpe has written, but it "became bloated and shapeless."[35] With the demise of the Federalists, the motivation for Republicans to unite behind a single national ticket was greatly reduced; moreover, the centralized party organization of the Republicans coexisted uneasily with their commitment to local self-government. Consequently, the national party structure they formed, dominated by the congressional caucus, broke down by 1824, when four major candidates ran for the presidency, each representing not only his own ambitions for office but also the aspirations of a sectional constituency. The presidential choice of the Republican caucus, William Crawford of Georgia, finished third in electoral votes behind Andrew Jackson of Tennessee and John Quincy Adams of Massachusetts, both of whom had been nominated by their state legislatures. The powerful Speaker of the House, Henry Clay, came in fourth. Party politics had been displaced by narrow factionalism.

The task of transforming party politics into a formal institution fell after the 1824 election to militant Republicans, such as Martin Van Buren of New York and Thomas Ritchie of Virginia. The outcome of this election, in which John Quincy Adams was selected by the House of Representatives, even though Jackson had more popular and electoral votes, persuaded Jacksonian reformers that the Constitution's vulnerability to centralized administration had not been corrected by Jeffersonian democracy. The controversy stirred by the election was further aroused by its aftermath: Adams' selection of Henry Clay, who orchestrated his victory in the House, as secretary of state; and the president's first State of the Union address, which proposed an active role for the federal government in the economy and society. With the weakening of the national party structure, Van Buren lamented, a system of personal and local factions displaced the "common sentiment" that had upheld republican principles, thus favoring champions of "consolidation."

Adams' ascendance to the White House was abetted by James Monroe's policy of conciliation—the president's effort to complete the triumph of the Republicans over the Federalists by persuading moderate Federalists to join his administration. Adams was one of the more prominent of these converts. His position as secretary of state in the Monroe administration advanced the cause of so-called National Republicans who sought to challenge orthodox republican commitments. Van Buren considered Monroe's policy of national unification a disaster; by abandoning militant partisanship for impartiality, the president made a revival of federalism possible. The spectacle of a fragmented and apathetic electorate allowing the House to select the neo-Federalist Adams as president revealed the need to establish political parties as permanent institutions.[36]

The Jacksonian ambition to revitalize partisanship gave rise to the Democratic party. Styling themselves as orthodox Jeffersonians, Democratic party leaders, as Van Buren put it, sought "to draw anew and . . . reestablish the old party lines."[37] Whereas the Federalists, dedicated to strengthening national power and proscribing popular rule, did not need a popular party to advance their program, the Republicans, and their heirs, the Jacksonian Democrats, stood in need of "an extraneous force to secure harmony in its ranks." The Federalist ambition to create an administrative republic did not require an elaborate party apparatus rooted in the states and localities; rather, the Federalists sought to center government responsibility in the executive, which would cultivate and maintain the support of commercial interests through the disbursement of bounties, licenses, and tariffs. In this way, the executive would wed commercial interests to state power—and develop, in turn, a stable commercial republic. In contrast, the task of the Jacksonian Democrats was to organize public opinion in support of government decentralization. Dedicated to the tradition of local self-government, and to the provincial liberties that supported it, the Republicans were successful, Van Buren counseled, as long as they were "wise enough to employ the caucus system . . . and to use in good faith the influence it is capable of imparting to the popular cause."[38]

As the leader of the Republican caucus, Van Buren (the junior senator from New York) supported Crawford in 1824. But the collapse of the caucus required that Van Buren turn to Jackson, hoping to link the Tennessean's personal popularity with a new party organization. In truth, Van Buren considered Jackson's great personal popularity to be both a threat and an opportunity. As he put it to Ritchie, the great task was to "substitute party principle for personal preference."[39] The success of this partisan project ensured that Jackson's appeal to the people was not entirely direct; instead, his election campaigns and policy fights would be waged through the new Democratic party, which called for a return to the principles set forth in Jefferson's first inaugural address.

The Jeffersonians had merely tolerated the Republican party as a temporary agent to advance the doctrine of local self-government; by the mid-1820s, Jacksonian reformers began to defend parties as indispensable allies of local democracy. "Although this is a mere party consideration, it is not on that account less likely to be effectual," Van Buren wrote in calling for Jackson's candidacy to be linked with the emergence of a new party; "considerations of this character not infrequently operate as effectively as those which bear upon the most important questions of constitutional doctrine."[40] By the 1830s, Jacksonians were defending political parties, indeed, a party *system*, as constitutional doctrine. Although a formal party system appeared to threaten the original constitutional design, a Jacksonian newspaper argued, it was not to be scorned, for only such an institution could cultivate a strong attachment between the people and the fundamental law:

> [Political parties] are the schools of political science, and no principle can be safely incorporated into the fabric of national law until it has been digested, limited, and defined by the earnest discussions of contending parties. They are the agents of political reform, and no great advance can be secured in the science of civil government but through their instrumentality. Such is the present constitution of all free states, that no reform can be successful until it has received the sanction of a party; and none can be proposed without rallying a party around it. . . . [Parties] diffuse knowledge, cultivate the popular mind, and as they tend to give the people larger liberties, prepare them for enjoyment.[41]

Just as Jeffersonian democracy gave rise to a party that established a formidable wall between the national government and the states, so Jacksonian democracy fortified this barrier. Similarly, the alliance between the Constitution and local self-government was strengthened. The Jacksonians' ambition to make partisanship part of the "living Constitution" was embodied by the

Democratic party, which organized voters on the basis of principles that were militantly decentralizing, as was the very process of party politics they established. Jacksonian democracy had established the "confederate" form of political organization which became the distinguishing feature of representative government in the United States. The Jeffersonian emphasis on political centralization comported with national parties, which rested on the nomination of presidential tickets by the congressional caucus. As this national structure weakened, state party organizations emerged as key actors in national, as well as state and local, politics. The Jacksonian political reforms institutionalized this political devolution. With the collapse of "King Caucus" after 1824, presidential tickets soon were nominated by national conventions, which were dominated by state party organizations. "The proponents of the convention system in the Democratic party, Van Buren being foremost among them, thought of the convention as merely a substitute for the caucus in which instructions would continue to be handed out from Washington," James Ceaser has written. "But they soon discovered the federalizing influence of the new institution, an influence that exceeded even their own republican principle of limiting the powers of the Washington establishment."[42]

That the decentralizing thrust of their movement sometimes went further than Jacksonian leaders preferred is not in doubt; however, the Jacksonian political philosophy, rooted in the understanding that "consolidation" was a chronic problem, encouraged a much bolder assault on national institutions and programs than the Jeffersonians had undertaken. After his election in 1828, Jackson withdrew the federal government from the realm of internal improvements. Military power, especially the army, was kept to a minimum. Jackson's fiscal policy was to hold down expenditures. Most significant, the Bank of the United States, which Jeffersonians had learned to live with, was dismantled, and its deposits were reinvested in selected state banks. As such, the strengthening of the presidency during Jackson's stay in the White House, as Marvin Meyers has written, "mobilized the powers of government for what was essentially a dismantling operation."[43]

In light of the ardent Jacksonian commitment to constraining national power, the political decentralization brought by the revitalized party system could hardly have been unanticipated, or unwanted. As Jackson pointed out in his veto of legislation that would have renewed the national bank's charter, Democrats believed that the "true strength" of the Union consisted "in leaving individuals and States as much as possible to themselves—in making itself

felt, not in its power, but in its beneficence; not in its control, but in its protection; not in binding the States more closely to the center, but leaving each
to move unobstructed in its proper orbit."[44] Viewed through the lens of contemporary mass democracy, this dismantling operation might appear to have
served a radical concept of individualism. In fact, the Jacksonian assault on
the national government was intended to preserve the integrity of local communities, thought to be the home of popular collective action, of collective
assertions against the rich and powerful who threatened the economic and
political independence of the democratic individual.[45]

So dominant had this doctrine of local self-government become by the
end of Jackson's presidency that even the Whig (former National Republican)
opposition, led by Adams and Clay, dedicated to expanding the economic and
social responsibilities of the national government, imitated the Jacksonian
brand of national politics. By 1840, the Whigs subscribed to the Jacksonian
style of democracy, shaped by the convention system and widely disbursed
patronage appointments, which held the national councils of power accountable to the states and localities. In part, the Whigs' acceptance of Jacksonian
politics was strategic, an acceptance of popular campaigns and practices so as
to avoid the fate of the Federalists. "The cry of aristocracy takes with certain
folks," John C. Spencer wrote to Thurlow Weed in 1831, "and there is no way
to meet it but to clamor louder than our adversaries."[46]

Just as significant, however, the Whigs, no less than the Democrats, had
an appreciation of the importance of local self-government in the tradition of
popular rule in the United States. The Massachusetts Whig statesman
Edward Everett gave voice to this understanding in his review of Tocqueville's
Democracy in America, in which he reserved special praise for Tocqueville's
recognition of New England town meetings as the "primary schools" of liberty. "On the whole," Everett wrote in hearty agreement, "no element of
American liberty is more essential than the unobtrusive, humble, domestic,
municipal organization. Everything is done by the neighbors; by the people,
whose interest and comfort are to be promoted. It is the curse of *centralization,* that it puts power into the hands of those who know not Joseph."[47]

Paradoxically, the celebration of local self-government in the 1830s and
1840s was joined to an ardent defense of the Union. Although Jackson
defended states' rights, he also personified and defended the sovereignty of the
nation, never more so than in the nullification crisis that arose near the end of
his first term. In an effort to compel the federal government to accede to its

demands for a lower tariff, South Carolina's legislature summoned a state convention on November 24, 1832, to declare the new 1832 tariff law "null and void." South Carolina cited John C. Calhoun's nullification doctrine, which held that a state could declare any federal law that it deemed unconstitutional to be inapplicable within its borders. The ordinance of nullification that the South Carolina convention passed forbade federal officials to collect custom duties in the state after February 1, 1833, and threatened that the state would secede from the United States if the federal government responded by attempting to blockade Charleston or otherwise use force.

Calhoun took Jefferson's defense of states' rights to its logical extreme. As noted, Jefferson and Madison had defended the right of states to declare acts of Congress unconstitutional, but only as a matter of "opinion." Even Jefferson, who was less cautious in his defense of state interposition than Madison, never counseled secession. But the logic of the Jeffersonian theory of states' rights, as Lance Banning argues, "could be extended far too easily" to the conclusion "that any of the parties to the [Union] could legitimately judge a federal act to be a violation of the terms on which it had assented to the Constitution and, accordingly, not law, but an assertion of an illegitimate authority that might be justifiably resisted."[48]

In the face of this threat to the Union, Jackson issued a ringing proclamation that vigorously rejected South Carolina's claim of a right to disobey a federal statute. For a state to presume to annul a law of the United States, the president argued, was "incompatible with the existence of the Union, contradicted expressly by the letter of the Constitution, unauthorized by its spirit, inconsistent with every principle on which it was founded, and destructive of the great object for which it was formed."[49] In 1861, Lincoln based his own response to southern secession on the same argument.

In contrast to Jefferson's defense of legislative supremacy, Jackson placed the responsibility to defend the Union squarely on the president's shoulders. It was the people, acting through the ratifying conventions, who formed the Union, and the president—not the Congress or the states—embodied the will of the people. Jackson thus gave voice in a new age to the rising spirit of democratic nationalism, which sustained and strengthened the Union in the face of serious sectional conflicts over the tariff and slavery.[50]

Nonetheless, the "tribune" of the people espoused a political doctrine that strictly interpreted the powers of the national government. In his farewell address, Jackson insisted that the nation's identity rested on its local foundations:

From the extent of our country, its diversified interests, different pursuits, and different habits, it is too obvious for argument that a single consolidated government would be wholly inadequate to watch over and protect its interests; and every friend of our free institutions should be always prepared to maintain unimpaired and in full vigor the rights and sovereignty of the States and to confine the action of the General Government strictly to the sphere of its appropriate duties.[51]

The Jacksonian party was an institutional elaboration of this spirited, but circumspect, idea of democratic nationalism. Implicit in the idea of the national convention was that the delegates' authority sprang directly from the rank and file, that they came, as Jackson put it, "fresh from the people."[52] But the Democrats and Whigs were not merely loose coalitions of state and local organizations. Although their organizational structure and practices were decentralized, the two parties orchestrated national campaigns; and their representatives in Congress tended to eschew sectional or local interests in supporting party policies.[53] Indeed, the hope of Whig leaders that Jackson's opposition to the national bank would founder on the rock of sectionalism was sorely disappointed. Henry Clay, the Whigs' likely nominee for president in 1832, expected that when Jackson vetoed the bill to recharter the bank, Democrats from the more commercial states, such as Pennsylvania and New York, would abandon him, thereby weakening the president's prospects for reelection. Instead, the 1832 election was a national partisan contest that appeared to uphold Jackson's veto of the bank bill. Jackson's overwhelming defeat of Clay, which was fought in large measure over the bank issue, convinced even his political opponents, the weekly *Niles' Register* reluctantly reported after the election, "that when the president cast himself upon the support of the people against the acts of both houses of Congress," he had been "fully maintained."[54] Jackson's triumph transformed the Democratic doctrine of states' rights into a national creed.

The Democratic and Whig parties were national organizations, but they celebrated a national idea that complemented a deep and abiding respect for localized politics and governance. In truth, the Jacksonian theory of governance was not one of states' rights per se but of local community. To be sure, Democrats believed that local rights were best guaranteed in national politics by states' rights. As Tocqueville recognized, however, the power of state governments was challenged by reformist aspirations that sought to devolve power to counties and townships.[55] New York governor Horatio Seymour proclaimed this doctrine of local self-government in a widely distributed July 4 oration in 1856, delivered in Springfield, Massachusetts. "The democratic theory takes away control from central points and distributes it to the various localities that are most interested in its wise and honest exercise," he observed. "It keeps at every man's home the greatest share of political power that concerns him individually. It yields it to the remoter legislative bodies in diminishing proportions as they recede from the direct influence and action of the people." Such a system of local self-government, Seymour instructed, was not based on a naive view of "the people's wisdom and patriotism"; rather, it was dedicated to the proposition that republican government rested on right opinion, which was nurtured by "the great theory of local self-government" and the parties that made it effective:

> This system [of local self-government] not only secures good government for each locality; but it also brings home to each individual a sense of his rights and responsibilities; it elevates his character as a man; he is taught self-reliance; he learns that the performance of his duty as a citizen, is the best corrective for the evils of society, and is not led to place a vague, unfounded dependence upon legislative wisdom and inspirations. The principle of local and distributed jurisdiction, not only makes good Government, but also makes good manhood.[56]

Seymour's defense of local self-government was not empty rhetoric. The decentralizing spirit of Jacksonian democracy influenced reform not only at the national level but also in the states. By the 1840s, constitutional reform had spread to most of the states, including most of those in the South, and devolved considerable power from the state capitals to the counties and townships. In New York, for example, the constitutional convention of 1846 created small electoral districts to give better representation to local patches of opinion; made most state and local positions, hitherto appointed by either the governor or legislature, elective offices; and decentralized patronage. Before these changes, the Democratic reformer Jabez Hammond wrote, the "central power [of the state] reached every county, and was felt by every town in the state. The convention of 1846 [has] wholly annihilated this terrible power."[57]

Such action did not go unchallenged. As Ceaser suggests, many Democratic leaders, including Van Buren, were somewhat taken aback by the radical devolution loosed by Jacksonian democracy. At the New York constitutional convention of 1821, in fact, Van Buren had opposed the direct election of jus-

tices of the peace, powerful officials whose patronage he thought essential to
the New York Democratic party's dominance. When taunted by his political
enemy DeWitt Clinton for not trusting the people, Van Buren replied that
direct popular election would give the opposition, minority faction in New
York control over as many as half of the state's justices of the peace. More penetratingly, Van Buren believed that the Democratic party had the special
function of protecting the principle "first formally avowed by Rousseau that
the right to exercise sovereignty belongs inalienably to the people."[58] Subject-
ing all offices to direct election favored wealthy figures of reputation, such as
Clinton, Van Buren argued; majority rule and the rights of the average citizen
required the support of a disciplined state party organization that could exercise firm control over public opinion and government action. The humble
members of society—the farmers, the mechanics, the laborers—required a
disciplined party organization to achieve unity and to make their will effective
in the councils of government. Thus, as John Casais has written, "While it
possessed a legislative majority the [New York Democratic party] would rule,
protecting the common man from his own enemies, and, in a Rousseauan
way, from his own folly."[59]

The Anglo-American devotion to provincial liberties, as Tocqueville
observed, would not easily abide such a centralized instrument of the "general will." Indeed, Van Buren's party suffered the consequences for challenging the sovereignty of local opinion in the state elections of 1824, which
returned Clinton and his allies to power. Two years later, an amendment was
added to the 1821 constitution giving "the people in their several towns, at their
annual elections," the power to choose justices of the peace.[60] Thereafter, Van
Buren's ideal of a rigorously disciplined, united party as a guide to public
opinion had to be modified, acquiescing to popular aspirations for the direct
election of local officials. The Regency, as the New York Democratic party
was known, led the fight at the 1846 state convention for reforms that would
subject all judicial offices to popular election. At the same time, this recognition of local self-government enabled the Democratic party to endure as an
important intermediary between government and society and thus to remain
an essential agent of popular rule.

The Whig press charged that Jacksonian reforms went too far, investing
"a revolutionary, fickle and radical spirit in politics" which undermined the
republican character of the state constitution. "Our judges are to be chosen
directly by the people!" lamented the *American Review*, a Whig journal, in the
wake of New York's 1846 constitutional convention. "And that serene and ele-

vated region, which the winds and waves of political excitement have, till this time, respected, is to be thrown open to their utmost violence."[61]

Tocqueville shared the Whig concerns about the popular, decentralizing thrust of the Democratic party. Although he admired the Americans' "taste for local freedom," considering it a critical corrective to their excessive attention to private concerns, Tocqueville feared that Jacksonian democracy might make it impossible for the national government to attend to those few, critical matters "important enough to attract its attention." He praised American democracy for achieving government centralization, which involved the government in such matters as foreign policy and national commerce, even as it avoided administrative centralization, involving the national government in "secondary concerns," better left to states and localities. And yet, militant Jacksonian reformers would have destroyed this balance between government centralization and administrative decentralization. Jackson himself, according to Tocqueville, was a popular but not a strong leader—"the majority's slave"—who threatened to deprive the federal government of that limited government centralization, without which a nation could not "live, much less prosper." In attacking the Bank of the United States, Jackson merely flattered the "provincial jealousies" and "*decentralizing* passions" that had brought him to power.[62]

But Jacksonian Democrats defended the political reforms of the 1830s and 1840s as necessary to prevent the consolidation that they considered a threat to constitutional government in the United States. Jackson was no slave of the majority, they claimed. Indeed, there was no popular demand to kill the bank; Jackson, through the medium of the party organization and press, convinced the people that this relic of Hamiltonian nationalism was not only bad public policy but also unconstitutional. Moreover, as his stand against John Calhoun in the nullification crisis of 1832 revealed, Jackson's commitment to devolution was hitched to the rising spirit of democratic nationalism. As a review of *Democracy in America* which appeared in the Jacksonian press, written by John O'Sullivan, argued, the president did not "shrink from responsibility; on the contrary, . . . by the freedom and firmness with which he used his legislative veto, and asserted his right to act upon the Constitution, as he understood it, [he] developed the energies of government in a point where they had been previously dormant, and thus left it more efficient than he found it."[63] What Tocqueville did not appreciate, Jackson's Senate ally Thomas Hart Benton alleged in his memoirs, was that the president's attack on the bank was rooted in Jeffersonian principles, that it meant "going back to the constitution and the foundation of party on principle."[64] The renewal of party conflict did not weaken federal authority but linked it vitally with the public.

Whereas Tocqueville feared that the American celebration of local self-government might become excessive, corroding representative institutions and making even the most limited objectives of government centralization profoundly difficult, the Jacksonians viewed it as a fragile obstacle to Hamiltonian nationalism, made dangerously seductive by the Whigs. Indeed, American political culture may not have been as hostile to centralized administration as Tocqueville claimed. The honor that most Americans accorded the commercial spirit demanded in some sense a national state that would cultivate economic integration and protect interstate commerce from local government interference. Tocqueville underestimated, his Jacksonian critics charged, how far the Constitution proscribed popular rule, how it might foster, if shaped by Federalist or Whig doctrine, a national state that would protect vested, commercial interests at the expense of equal opportunity.

Tocqueville feared the instability of America's laws and political institutions; Jacksonians claimed that nearly the opposite was the case. As O'Sullivan observed in his review of *Democracy in America*, Tocqueville invoked the *Federalist Papers* in lamenting the mutability of laws in the United States. But Publius's observations on the instability of laws "alluded to the unsettled state of things between the close of the war and the adoption of the Federal Constitution." Publius's observations about the instability of law in the United States could not be taken as criticism of existing political institutions, O'Sullivan averred; rather, they were offered in defense of the Constitution, which had largely satisfied the Federalist authors' hope for greater political stability. Indeed, O'Sullivan argued, the Constitution went too far in tempering the democratic taste for innovation. "In fact, we have rather reason to regret that aversion even to improvement, which has hitherto so materially retarded the still progressive amelioration of our institutions," he wrote. "Being, as a mass, actively industrious people, we are generally willing to make great concessions of convenience, and even sometimes of principle, for the sake of tranquility and regularity of the old habit; and it requires, indeed, a strong stimulus of great interests and principles at stake to overcome this moral *vis inertia*, and induce us to apply the hand of reform of any institution or system extensively connected with the general business of the country."[65]

The Jacksonians did not see themselves as dishonoring the free enterprise system—they were not civic republicans who rejected private interests.

Rather, they denied that free enterprise, properly understood, was linked to energetic government. Jacksonian Democrats hoped to unleash the commercial spirit from government-created monopolies, such as the national bank. Only then would commercialism conform to a "natural rights" republicanism whose clarion call of "equal rights to all and special privileges to none" promised political and economic independence to the producing "bone and sinew" of the country.[66] This independence required local self-government, a deep and abiding effort, as Governor Seymour put it, "to distribute each particular power to those who have the greatest interest in its wise and faithful exercise."[67]

The localized parties of Jacksonian democracy gave political effect to this decentralized polity, linking it to public causes and national developments. As noted, with the transition from the age of Hamilton and Jefferson to Jackson, Tocqueville believed that "great" parties, based on the leading principles of government, ceased to exist. They were replaced by "small" parties that eschewed principles for material and provincial interests. "This had been a great gain in happiness but not in morality," he concluded.[68] But, as George Pierson observes, Tocqueville may have failed to appreciate how these diminutive parties could engage Americans in public deliberation and judgment.[69] To be sure, the Jacksonian concept of "the people" was limited; it did not apply to African Americans, women, or American Indians. Nor did the localized party system, animated by patronage practices and entertaining partisan displays such as torchlight parades, cultivate political debate that reached the highest note on the scale. But the limitations of this popular revolution should not blind us to the fact, as Robert Wiebe argues, that "something profoundly important occurred in nineteenth century America that acquired the name democracy."[70] Once established, it penetrated deeply into American society, dominating the political perceptions and voting habits of the people. Thereafter, calls for justice, indeed demands for rights, would have to come to terms with the "tenacity of this highly mobilized, highly competitive, and locally oriented democracy."[71]

Conclusion: Party Politics and the Struggle for National Community

The confederate form of party organization which was legitimized during the Jacksonian era endured well into the twentieth century. Even the rise of the Republican party in the 1850s as a result of the slavery controversy, and the

decline of the Whigs, did not alter the essential characteristics of the party system in the United States; and these characteristics—decentralized organization and hostility to centralization of power—ultimately short-circuited the
efforts of radical Republicans to complete their program of Reconstruction
after the Civil War.

In truth, like their Whig forebears, Republicans were diffident in their
opposition to the Democratic doctrine of local self-government. Senator
Stephen Douglas, the author of the 1854 Kansas-Nebraska Act, justified northern Democrats' defense of "popular sovereignty" in the territories on the basis
of this theory of government, proclaiming in his 1858 debates with Abraham
Lincoln that government in the United States was "formed on the principle of
diversity in the local institutions and laws, and not on that of uniformity."
"Each locality," Douglas continued, "having different interests, a different cli-
mate and different surroundings, required different local laws, local policy
and local institutions, adapted to the wants of the locality."[72] To Republicans,
this marked the triumph of petty particularism over the principles of the Declaration, rightly understood. Still, Lincoln pledged not to interfere with slavery where it was already established, a promise he reiterated in his first inaugural address, in which he disavowed "any purpose, directly or indirectly, to
interfere with the institution of slavery in the states where it exists."[73]

Although Lincoln's respect for the limits imposed by the Constitution
and local self-government deterred him from attacking the existence of slavery in the southern states, he was not willing to tolerate slavery's extension into
the territories. To do so would create a crisis by depriving the Constitution of
its moral foundation. Drawing on a verse in the Book of Proverbs—"A Word
Fitly Spoken is like apples of gold in pictures of silver"—Lincoln praised the
Declaration's principle of "liberty to all" as the measure of political life in the
United States. "The assertion of this principle, at that time," he wrote, "was
the word 'fitly spoken' which has proved an 'apple of gold' to us. The Union,
and the Constitution, are the pictures of silver, subsequently framed around
it. The picture was made, not to conceal, or destroy the apple; but to adorn
and preserve it."[74]

Lincoln's invocation of the Declaration as the nation's founding document was not an original contribution to American political thought. It had
been an important part of the Whigs' program and became, with the arousal
of the slavery controversy, the animating principle of the Republican party.[75]
In fact, the very name they chose for their party represented the Republicans'
identification with Jefferson, the Declaration's author. As Albert Bovay, one of

the founders of the new party, explained, "Jefferson called his party 'Republican'—never Democrat—but the name was dropped after his day, and the party claiming still to be the same, assumed the Democratic name."[76] But in tolerating the expansion of slavery, in linking popular sovereignty with the infamous Kansas-Nebraska Act, the Democrats had forsaken their Jeffersonian heritage. Indeed, Lincoln insisted that Jefferson had given form to the Framers' opposition to the expansion of slavery into the territories by drafting the Northwest Ordinance of 1787, which banned slavery in the five states— Ohio, Michigan, Indiana, Wisconsin, and Lincoln's own Illinois—which composed the Northwest Territory. As such, prohibiting the expansion of slavery in the territories was true to principles of the Declaration of Independence, as well as to the proper understanding of the Constitution. Equally important, with the enactment of the Missouri Compromise in 1820, which prohibited the expansion of slavery in the northern part of the Louisiana Territory, this policy became a matter of party doctrine and thus a public philosophy shared by a majority of Americans.

In repealing the Missouri Compromise, Lincoln argued, in opening new territory to slavery, the Kansas-Nebraska Act violated the Founders' understanding that slavery was a "necessary evil" that must be contained and allowed to die a "natural death." This constitutional impropriety was compounded in 1857 by the Dred Scott decision, authored by the militant Jacksonian Chief Justice Roger Taney, in which the Supreme Court declared unconstitutional any act to abolish slavery by Congress or the territorial legislatures. Most insidious, as a matter of Democratic party doctrine, this perversion of the founding principles had penetrated public opinion, giving currency to the proposition "that the Negro had no share in the National Declaration of Independence."[77] The doctrines preached by Douglas and Taney, Lincoln feared, threatened to transform slavery from a necessary evil into a positive good, a moral right, and thus risked "a gradual and steady debauching of public opinion." In a nation like the United States, in which popular sovereignty was everything, the consequences of such a change in the public mind would be devastating.[78]

The importance Lincoln and his political allies accorded public opinion focused their attention on party politics. The Democrats' enactment of the Kansas-Nebraska Act converted the party founded by Jefferson into an "overshadowing pro-slavery organization," Bovay proclaimed, requiring the creation of a new, Republican party, "a great anti-slavery party to antagonize it" and thereby purify Jefferson's legacy. In forming such a partisan coalition, which grew out of local protest meetings and political organizations, the Republicans did not choose to reject local democracy but to appeal to it—to restore, indeed fortify, the moral principles that made local principalities part of the nation. "The Republican remedy for the decayed and obsolescent state of the old parties was not to condemn the party system as such but to form and justify a new party which was portrayed from the outset as ready to take its place among the great parties of the American political tradition," Richard Hofstadter has written. "They stressed the current 'degeneracy' of the Democratic party and set up the Republican party as the legitimate inheritor of the best principles of *both* the old parties—a rationale appropriate to a new party that was recruiting both ex-Democrats and ex-Whigs."[79]

The Republicans' tepid opposition to local self-government, then, did not reveal moral indifference; rather, it acknowledged the importance of public opinion, as well as of the decentralized political parties that were the principal agents of it. Just as the Jacksonians saw parties as an antidote to the natural political indolence of individuals in a commercial republic, so the Republicans viewed ardent partisanship essential to overcome the immoral neutrality prescribed by Douglas in the face of the slavery controversy. New York's William H. Seward, a leading spokesman for the new party, gave voice to this view in defending the organization of the anti–Kansas-Nebraska movement as a party:

> Where there are no great parties, there are either many small factions, or no parties or factions whatever. A state that surrenders itself to the confused contests of small parties or factions, is sinking inevitably toward despotism. A state that has no parties or factions at all is a despotism already. . . . [A] healthy and vigorous republic . . . cannot last long . . . [in] the absence of a firm and decided majority to direct its course. . . . This condition is one which tolerates two firm and enduring parties, no less and no more.[80]

Vigorous partisan competition, a great contest of opinion over the slavery controversy, would divide the nation but also bring a multitude of citizens together in the service of a cause toward which they might otherwise have remained indifferent. Like the Jacksonian Democrats, Republicans viewed parties as the enemy of indifference and thus an ally of political freedom.[81]

Lincoln never gave systematic expression to the place of political parties in American constitutional government, but he was a loyal partisan throughout his active life. He was among those who formulated Republican party principles, and as president, "he used the patronage system with the virtuoso skill of an inveterate spoilsman, and became instrumental in the most sweeping removal of federal office holders up to that time in American history."[82] Amid these partisan maneuvers, however, Lincoln did not lose sight of his party's responsibility to cultivate a new public philosophy in the country. It was at his insistence that Republicans made the Thirteenth Amendment—the emancipation amendment—the "key stone of the party platform" for the 1864 election.

Reelected by large majorities, Lincoln and Republican leaders pressed the amendment through a reluctant Congress in 1864 and 1865. Once the measure had passed, Congress, which was persuaded by a combination of the president's exalted rhetoric and his deft horse trading, sent it to Lincoln for his signature. The Constitution does not require presidents to sign constitutional amendments, but legislative leaders somehow forgot that Lincoln's was not needed.[83] This oversight, whether or not deliberate, testifies to the importance of Lincoln as a popular leader, as the head of a popular collective organization with a past and a future. That this amendment, which was ratified in 1865, was drafted as a pastiche of the Northwest Ordinance must have given Lincoln special satisfaction, because he had been pointing to that document since 1854 as a symbol of hostility to slavery by the Framers of the Constitution.[84] Just as surely, the Thirteenth Amendment, sanctified by an emerging majority party in a popular election, vindicated Lincoln's position that the Republicans, and not the Democrats, were the true heirs of Jeffersonian democracy.

The Republicans' indictment of slavery, and the changes in the Constitution which followed from it, brought forth a new, more positive view of liberty, in which the government had the affirmative obligation to ensure equality under the law. Lincoln's celebration of the Declaration was embodied in the Civil War amendments to the Constitution, which not only abolished slavery but also promised blacks the right to vote (the Fifteenth Amendment) and guaranteed to all Americans the "privileges and immunities" of citizenship, "due process," and "equal protection of the law" (the Fourteenth Amendment). These amendments changed the course of constitutional development: whereas eleven of the first twelve amendments to the Constitution had limited the powers of the national government, six of the next seven expanded those powers at the expense of the states and localities.[85]

Yet there were limits to the constitutional change brought by the Republicans; indeed, the Republican party's identification with Jeffersonian principles circumscribed the party's mission. Lincoln's understanding of the equality that was guaranteed by the Declaration was modest when compared with the collective aspirations of twentieth-century reform presidents such as Theodore Roosevelt, Franklin Roosevelt, and Lyndon Johnson. The Republican program was tightly bounded by the nation's longstanding commitment to private property, limited government, and administrative decentralization. Allied to local self-government, Republicans could not sanction the constant presence of the national government in the society and economy. Their contribution was to free local democracy from the taint of slavery and, thereby, to establish the moral obligation of the federal government to ensure "a fair chance in the race of life."[86] This more positive view of liberty obligated the national government to eliminate forced servitude and to uphold, even advance, the cause of free labor through policies such as the Homestead Act of 1862. But as the failure of Reconstruction revealed, this understanding of liberty stopped well short of championing the expansion of national administrative power.

Indeed, Republicans were no less opposed to centralized administration than Democrats and thus saw little purpose in dismantling the localized party system. Rather, to the dismay of twentieth-century progressive reformers such as Herbert Croly, they more or less took "over the system of partisan organization and discipline originated by the Jacksonian Democrats." As Croly would put it in *Progressive Democracy*, this party system "bestowed upon the divided Federal government a certain unity of control, while at the same time it prevented increased efficiency of the Federal system from being obnoxious to local interests."[87] As such, the decentralized party system was an obstacle to progressives' programmatic ambitions. Their reform zeal aimed, above all else, at the concentration of wealth, specifically at the giant trusts, which, according to reformers, constituted uncontrolled and irresponsible units of power in American society. These industrial combinations created the perception that opportunity had become less equal in the United States, that growing corporate power threatened the freedom of individuals to earn a living. This threat to equal opportunity posed a severe challenge to the doctrine of local self-government, as reformers had good reasons to believe that the great business interests, represented by newly formed associations such as the National Civic Federation, had captured and corrupted state legislatures and local officials for their own profit. Party leaders—both Democrats and Republicans—were viewed as irresponsible "bosses" who did the bidding of "special interests."

As we will see in the next chapter, progressives saw little possibility of converting the existing party machinery into an instrument for the realization of their national program. Their goal was to restore the national character of the Constitution, to emancipate national administration from the constraints and corruption of localized parties. This position was anticipated by reformers at the end of the nineteenth century—the so-called Mugwumps—whose challenge to the legitimacy of parties set an important example for twentieth-century politics in the United States.[88] "No serious impression can ever be made on [the evils of political corruption]," the late-nineteenth-century reformer Henry Adams wrote, "until they are attacked at their source; not until the nation is ready to go back to the early practice of the government and to restore to the constitutional organs those powers which have been torn from them by the party organizations for the purposes of party aggrandizement."[89]

These words were penned in 1876 at the height of the party system's dominance over American democracy. Adams did not express considerable hopefulness about the prospects for "purifying the political system," nor did he dismiss lightly the close relationship that had formed between the party system and the Constitution during the nineteenth century. The ostensible villain of his novel *Democracy*, published in 1880, Senator Silas Ratliff, is a formidable, if unprincipled, statesman whose partisan loyalty gives him a certain dignity. As Ratliff tells the refined Madeline Lightfoot Lee, the cause of party justified the "vice" sometimes required of a politician:

> I was a Senator of the United States. I was also a trusted member of a great political party which I looked upon as identical with the nation. In both capacities I owed duties to my constituents, to the government, to the people. I might interpret these duties narrowly or broadly. I might say: Perish the government, perish the Union, perish this people, rather than that I should soil my hands! Or I might say, as I did, and as I might say again: Be my fate what it may, this glorious Union, the last hope of suffering humanity, shall be preserved.

Ratliff's appeal to party was self-serving, to be sure. But this appeal to what is obviously the Republican party's past also had some merit. Although the Grand Old Party's glory had dimmed considerably by the end of the nineteenth century, Adams recognized that it was no longer possible to stand "outside of politics," to aspire, as Washington had, to be a patriot king. Although Mrs. Lee's disdain for partisanship leads her to reject Ratliff's marriage proposal, he remains powerful in politics, indeed, a leading candidate to become the next president. The aloofness of reformers in *Democracy* leaves them powerless. "The bitterest part of all this horrid story," Mrs. Lee laments, in the final words of the novel, "is that nine out of ten of our countrymen would say I had made a mistake."[90]

The critical role political parties played in America's democracy at the end of the nineteenth century, Adams believed, "arose not so much from the intrinsic strength of the parties whose wealth and power are to be attacked, as from the extent to which they have twisted their roots around and among the organs of the Constitution itself." With this entanglement came legitimacy and fierce loyalties. But Adams prophesied the animating force of twentieth-century reform politics. Like Adams, progressives above all believed that the influence of parties on constitutional government had to be reduced, that "the relation between the party system and the constitutional framework" had to be "reversed."[91] Thus, progressive democracy sought its justification in a campaign to restore the Constitution-against-Parties.

3

Progressivism and Direct Democracy

The Revival of the Constitution-against-Parties

No event so aroused the idealism of reformers during the early part of the twentieth century as the nationwide celebration, in 1909, of the one hundredth anniversary of the birth of Abraham Lincoln. As an editorial in the progressive journal the *Arena* rejoiced, "Coming as it did in the flood-tide of the most dangerous and determined reaction from fundamental democratic ideals and principles that have marked our history, it has given a new inspiration and hope to thousands who were all but despairing of the success of popular rule in the presence of the aggressive, determined and powerful march of feudalism and privileged wealth, operating through political bosses and money-controlled machines, and the pliant tools of predatory wealth in state, press, school, and church."

Yet this celebration of Lincoln went hand in hand with a militant attack on the party system that he had supported so strongly. Forgetting that Lincoln and his Republican brethren had defended localized parties as critical agents in preserving "government of the people, by the people, and for the people," progressives scorned party leaders as "the handymen of the interests, the usurpers of powers not granted by the constitution."[1]

Viewing parties as the linchpin of corruption and injustice, progressives championed, as one reformer put it, "government at first-hand: government *of the People directly by the People.*"[2] Indeed, in their attack on intermediary

42

associations such as political parties and interest groups, reformers of the early twentieth century issued a battle cry that enlisted popular support not only for woman suffrage, primaries, and direct election of senators but also for methods of "pure democracy," such as initiative, referendum, and recall. Especially controversial was the progressives' program to subject constitutional questions to direct popular control, including proposals for an easier method to amend the Constitution and referenda on laws that the state courts declared unconstitutional. This commitment to direct democracy became the centerpiece of the Progressive party campaign of 1912, which was sanctified as a "covenant with the people," a deep and abiding pledge to make the people "masters of their constitution."

Like the Populists of the late nineteenth century, the Progressives invoked the preamble of the Constitution to assert their purpose of making "We the People" effective in strengthening the federal government's authority to regulate the society and economy. But Progressives sought to hitch the will of the people to a strengthened national administrative power, which was anathema to the Populists. The Populists were animated by a radical agrarianism that celebrated the Jeffersonian and Jacksonian assault on monopolistic power; their concept of national democracy rested on the hope of arousing the states and Congress for an assault on the centralizing, unholy alliance between national parties and the trusts. Similarly, the Populists hoped to reform rather than destroy the localized democracy organized by the two-party system. To be sure, like the Republican party of the 1850s, the Populists hoped to form a movement strong enough to break through the existing two-party system. But they had no particular objection to party as a political institution.

In contrast, the Progressives set out to reduce drastically the influence of party organizations in politics and government. They championed national administrative power—a "new nationalism" that could not abide the localized democracy of the nineteenth century. For Progressives, public opinion would reach fulfillment with the formation of an independent executive power, freed from the provincial, special, and corrupt influence of political parties and commercial interests. Thus, unlike their Populist forebears, Progressives invested little hope in reforming the party system. Dedicated to Jeffersonian principles, political parties in the United States were wedded to constitutional arrangements that impeded the expansion of national administrative power in the name of the people's economic welfare. The origins and organizing principles of the American party system established it as a force against the creation of a "modern state." The Progressive reformers' commitment to building such a state—that is, to the creation of a national political power with expansive programmatic responsibilities—meant that the party system had to be either weakened or reconstructed. As Barry Karl has noted, the Progressive party campaign of 1912 was as much "an attack on the whole concept of political parties as it was an effort to create a single party whose doctrinal clarity and moral purity would represent the true interest of the nation as a whole."[3]

The Meaning of Progressive Democracy

The Progressive campaign against parties represented a critical historical moment in the transformation of the United States from a decentralized republic to a mass democracy. "While fully admitting that the transition may not be as abrupt as it seems," Herbert Croly wrote in the wake of the 1912 election, "we have apparently been witnessing during the past year or two the end of one epoch and the beginning of another."[4] Political scientists and historians have tended to confirm Croly's belief that the 1912 election was a barometer of fundamental changes taking place during the Progressive Era. "In several respects, the election of 1912 was the first 'modern' presidential contest in American history," Arthur Link and Richard McCormick wrote in 1983. "The use of direct primaries, the challenge to traditional party loyalties, the candidates' issue orientation, and the prevalence of interest-group political activities all make the election of 1912 look more like 1980 than that of 1896."[5]

Although a number of works attribute importance to the changes brought by the Progressive Era, scholars continue to disagree about the character of these changes and their legacy for twentieth- and twenty-first-century American politics. Indeed, for the past quarter century, the scholarly effort to define progressivism or to identify principles and organizational forms of the Progressive movement has been under full-scale attack. Peter Filene, for example, has argued that the Progressive movement is an intellectual construct, a mere semantic, which never existed.[6] Although not going this far, Daniel Rogers acknowledges that "the trouble with comprehending 'progressivism' as a list of beliefs is that progressives did not share a common creed or a string of common values." This era, he suggests, exemplified a new fragmented and issue-oriented politics, in which often contradictory reform movements sought to capitalize on the declining influence of traditional party control over politics and government. After all, Rogers notes, "those whom historians had labelled progressives shared no common party or organization."[7]

There was a Progressive party, of course, but its brief, albeit significant,

existence underscores the powerful centrifugal forces of progressive democracy. With the celebrated former president Theodore Roosevelt as its candidate, the Bull Moose party won 27.4 percent of the popular vote and eighty-
eight electoral votes from six states in 1912. This was extraordinary for a third
party; in fact, no third-party candidate for the presidency—before or after
1912—has received so large a percentage of popular vote or as many electoral
votes as did Theodore Roosevelt. Despite its remarkable showing in 1912, however, the Progressive party was forlorn four years later, its fate inseparable from
the dynamic leader who embodied its cause. The old saw of historical literature on the Progressive Era is that the Progressive party was essentially a personal vehicle for Theodore Roosevelt, an organization relegated to serving his
own political ambitions. TR's bolt from the Republican convention in 1912,
the argument goes, was born of his party's rejection of his designs, after a brief
retirement from politics, to return to power. Accordingly, the Progressive party
was not invested with a collective mission and organization that could survive
his return to the Republican party in 1916. At the end of the day, it had brought
neither an ongoing multiparty system nor a fundamental party transformation,
pitting progressives against conservatives, for which many participants in the
Bull Moose campaign had expressed hope.

Arguably, however, the Progressive party lies at the very heart of fundamental changes in American politics—changes that were initially, if only par-
tially, negotiated during the Progressive Era.[8] The personalistic quality of Roosevelt's campaign was part and parcel of these changes, but they went much
deeper than his desire to regain past political mastery. The Progressive party,
with its leader-centered organization, accommodated and embodied an array
of reformers—insurgent Republican officeholders, disaffected Democrats,
crusading journalists, academics, social workers, and other activists—who
hoped that the new party coalition would realize their common goal of
expanding the responsibilities of the federal government and making it more
responsive to popular economic, social, and political demands.

The Progressives' pledge to rescue the government from the throes of corporate capitalism resembled the Jacksonians' hatred of the "monster bank." In
truth, however, most Progressives were avowedly hostile to Jacksonian democracy—dubbed derisively by Croly as "pioneer democracy." As Martin Shefter
has written:

> For each of the major institutional reforms in the Jacksonian era, the Pro-
> gressives sponsored an equal and opposite reform. The Jacksonians had

increased the number of executive offices subject to popular election; the Progressives sought to reduce that number and to create the position of chief executive through such reforms as the short ballot and the strong mayor plan of municipal government. . . . The Jacksonians extended the franchise; the Progressives contracted it through registration, literacy, and citizenship requirements. The Jacksonians established party conventions to nominate candidates for elective office; the Progressives replaced them with primary elections. The Jacksonians created a hierarchical structure of party committees to manage the electorate; the Progressives sought to destroy these party organizations or at least render their tasks more difficult through such reforms as the nonpartisan municipal government, and the separation of local, state, and national elections. Finally, the Jacksonians established a party press and accorded influence to the political editor; the Progressive movement was linked to the emergence of a self-consciously independent press (magazines as well as newspapers) and with muckraking journalists.[9]

Still, the profound shift in regime norms and practices represented by progressivism did not entail a straightforward evolution from partisan to administrative politics. Indeed, the Progressive party crusade was badly crippled by fundamental disagreements among its supporters over issues that betrayed an acute sensitivity, if not attachment, to the commitment in the country to local self-government. The party was deeply divided over civil rights, leading to bitter struggles at the Progressive party convention over delegate selection rules and the platform which turned on whether the party should confront the shame of Jim Crow. In the end, it did not, accepting the right of states and localities to resolve the matter of race relations. Moreover, Progressive delegates waged an enervating struggle at the party convention over whether an interstate trade commission, with considerable administrative discretion, or militant antitrust policy was the appropriate method to tame the trusts. New Nationalists, led by Roosevelt, prevailed, pledging the party to regulate, rather than attempt to dismantle, corporate power; however, this disagreement carried over to the general election as the Democrats, under the tutelage of their candidate for president, Woodrow Wilson, and his advisor, Louis Brandeis, embraced a New Freedom version of progressive reform, which emphasized antitrust measures and state regulations as an alternative to the expansion of national administrative power.

The split between New Nationalism and New Freedom progressives

threatened the creation of the modern state. The progressive program, presupposing a more activist national government, "foreshadowed administrative
aggrandizement," Croly acknowledged. Yet progressives could not agree on
how administrative power should be used; indeed, the conflict between New
Nationalism and New Freedom progressives revealed that many reformers
were profoundly uneasy about the prospect of expanding national administrative power. Woodrow Wilson gave expression to this concern in a series of lec-
tures he delivered at Columbia University in 1907:

> Moral and social questions originally left to the several States for settle-
> ment can be drawn into the field of federal authority only at the expense
> of the self-dependence and efficiency of the several communities of
> which our complex body politic is made up. Paternal morals, morals
> enforced by judgment and choices of central authority at Washington,
> do not and cannot create vital moral habits or methods of life unless sus-
> tained by local opinion and purpose, local prejudice and conve-
> nience,—unless supported by local convenience and interest; and only
> communities capable of taking care of themselves will, taken together,
> constitute a nation capable of vital action and control.[10]

Wilson's respect for provincial liberties made him reluctant to join the
progressive assault on political parties. "Students of our politics," he warned,
"have not always sufficiently recognized the extraordinary part political parties
have played in making a national life which might otherwise have been loose
and diverse almost to the point of being inorganic a thing of definite coherence and common purpose." National parties had played the critical part in
forging a country out of America's local communities and sectional interests,
even as these organizations recognized the legitimacy of provincial concerns.
In words that were reminiscent of Van Buren's belief that parties were essential agents in securing harmony in the ranks of the people, Wilson defended
partisanship as a vital link between private and public interests. "It has been
nothing less than a marvel how the network of parties has taken up and broken
the restless strain of contest and jealousy, like an invisible network of kindly oil
upon the disordered waters of the sea," he enthused. "It is in this vital sense
that our national parties have been our veritable body politic."[11] Brandeis
shared Wilson's admiration for parties, expressing special appreciation for the
way political associations transformed opinions into political action. "The
more I see our American government," he confided to a friend, "the more I

appreciate the necessity for these great fundamental machines to start up the people and formulate through public opinion."[12]

Respectful of the role traditional partisan organizations and practices had played in constraining the unhealthy aggrandizement of administrative power, Wilson and Brandeis hoped to reform, rather than dismantle, the two-party system. This hope was encouraged by the greater sympathy for progressivism in the Democratic party than could be found in the GOP. William Jennings Bryan was the most dominant Democrat during the first decade of the twentieth century, and his influence led the party to embrace many features of progressive democracy. Indeed, Wilson's nomination in 1912 was due largely to Bryan's dramatic intervention at the Democratic National Convention in Baltimore. Fearful that his party would follow the Republican example of spurning reform, Bryan prevailed upon the delegates to support a resolution that condemned Democrats, such as Thomas F. Ryan of Virginia and August Belmont of New York, who had close ties to business. The enactment of this resolution against members of "the privilege-hunting and favor-seeking class" proved to be the turning point in the convention, leading ultimately to Wilson's nomination on the forty-sixth ballot.[13] Moreover, the Democratic platform, also greatly influenced by Bryan, supported progressive measures, such as the direct primary, which were scorned by the Republican convention.

To be sure, there were important differences between Bryan and Wilson. Bryan's idea of progressive democracy was heavily influenced by the populist fear of executive power, especially its use in foreign affairs. Thus, the Democratic platform prescribed a constitutional amendment that would limit presidents to a single term. Wilson would abandon this pledge as soon as he was elected, committing himself to the progressive cause of popular presidential leadership. As he wrote to his attorney general, Alexander Mitchell Palmer, in February 1913, progressives "are seeking in every way to extend the power of the people, but in the matter of the Presidency we fear and distrust the people and seek to bind them hand and foot by rigid constitutional provision." Hoping to deflate support for a single term, Wilson proposed a national presidential primary that would make more democratic, rather than diminish, the exercise of executive power.[14]

As the next chapter shows, Wilson would find it difficult to reconcile his commitment to progressivism and his loyalty to the Democratic party. Nonetheless, unlike Roosevelt, Wilson did not believe that the two-party system was an insurmountable obstacle to his personal and programmatic ambition. Indeed, Wilson heralded the New Freedom as an understanding of progressive reform which was rooted in the antistatist tradition of the Democratic party.

Wilson agreed with Roosevelt that the president must direct more attention to national problems, but he believed that executive leadership would be ineffective or dangerous unless the president's role as party leader was strengthened. Whereas TR had bridled against the constraints of party and championed direct presidential leadership of public opinion in an effort to strengthen national administrative power and the president's control over the executive branch, Wilson believed that the high purpose of the modern executive was one of rhetoric rather than administration. As Wilson argued in his essays on constitutional government, TR, as president, had been all too inclined to act in defiance of his party and to appeal to the people over the heads of Congress. A better strategy, Wilson insisted, would be to break down the barriers between president and Congress by making the president a strong party leader. In this way, constitutional government's various parts would work in concert but without violating the principles and institutions that protected the nation from an unhealthy aggrandizement of executive power. The president could "dominate his party by being spokesman for the real sentiment and purpose of the country," Wilson insisted, "by giving the country at once the information and the statements of policy which will enable it to form its judgments alike of parties and men." Rejecting TR's sweeping defense of executive power as portending a dangerous consolidation of administrative power, Wilson called for a diminution of the president's executive duties. Presidents must regard themselves "as less and less executive officers and more and more directors of affairs and leaders of the nation—men of counsel and of the sort of action that makes for enlightenment."[15]

Wilson's celebration of popular leadership shows that the reluctance of many progressive reformers to embrace centralized administration did not represent a commitment to local self-government, at least as it was then practiced in the United States. The "complex republic," as James Madison called it, was shaped in the nineteenth century by party organizations and legal doctrines that formed a wall of separation between government and society. New Freedom progressives wanted to expand the responsibilities of the national government but hoped to find nonbureaucratic and noncentralized solutions to the ills that plagued the political economy. Reconciling government centralization and administrative decentralization involved, in part, building on measures such as the Sherman Act, enacted in 1890, which would rely on competition and law, rather than administrative tribunals, to curb the abuses of big business. Just as significant, New Freedom progressives hoped to cultivate local forums of public discussion and debate which would "buttress the foundations of democracy." For example, Wilson and Brandeis were active in the social centers movement that sought to make use of school buildings for neighborhood forums on the leading issues of the day. This movement, which began early in the twentieth century with local experiments in cities such as Rochester, New York, had emerged as a national association by the eve of the 1912 election. Its ambition, as George M. Forbes, the president of Rochester's board of education, announced at the National Conference on Civic and Social Center Development, was to form local institutions through which the people in the community could gain an understanding of civic obligation:

> We are now intensely occupied in forging the tools of democracy, the direct primary, the initiative, the referendum, the recall, the short ballot, commission government. But in our enthusiasm we do not seem to be aware that these tools will be worthless unless they are used by those who are aflame with the sense of brotherhood. If action of a democracy is to be but the resultant of a clash of selfish interests, it is hardly worth battling for. . . . The idea [of the social centers movement is] to establish in each community an institution having a direct and vital relation to the welfare of the neighborhood, ward, or district, and also to the city as a whole. . . . [This] means that our public school buildings, consecrated to education, may become the instruments of that deepest and most fundamental education upon which the very existence of democracy depends.[16]

The movement for neighborhood organization was not entirely new, of course. As Tocqueville observed in the 1830s, the tradition of local self-government in the United States went well beyond the legal division between the national and state governments and left considerable discretion to counties and townships. The more populist progressives hoped to restore the "municipal spirit" that Tocqueville so admired and extend it into twentieth-century urban America. At the same time, they hoped to reconstruct the primary unit of political life as a more cosmopolitan sphere, as a place that could more easily dovetail with the nation, indeed, the international community. As the prominent progressive intellectual Mary Parker Follett put it, "The relation of neighbors one to another must be integrated into the substance of the [national] state. Politics must take democracy from its external expression of representation to the expression of that inner meaning hidden in the intermingling of all men."[17] This rather cryptic, idealistic aspiration found more concrete expression in the progressive hope for the neighborhood school, which, according to social centers activists, was the only "non-exclusive institution" in the United States.[18]

Ultimately, the progressive hope of strengthening self-government in the United States depended on transmuting local self-government into direct rule of the people, who would not have to suffer the interference of decentralizing associations and institutions. Only then could individuals participate in a national movement of public opinion that might cultivate a "more perfect Union." Wilson and Brandeis hoped a reformed party politics would abet the creation of a new national community. But most progressives saw party as "the worst obstacle to the advance of practical democratic participation."[19] Emancipated from the petty particularisms of partisanship, reformers hoped, the people would display their potential for broad-mindedness. "Truly, the voice of the people is the voice of God," wrote a progressive journalist in the early party of the twentieth century, echoing Andrew Jackson; "but that means the voice of the *whole* people."[20]

Just as surely as the progressive schism over the appropriate methods to reform the political economy betrayed fundamental disagreements in its ranks, so its program of direct government elicited a shared sense of endeavor. No less than New Freedom progressives, New Nationalist reformers championed institutions and practices that would nurture a democratic public. During the 1912 election campaign, in fact, TR joined Wilson in celebrating the use of schoolhouses as neighborhood headquarters for political discussion. Declaring his enthusiastic approval for the maxim "Public buildings for public uses," Roosevelt proposed that neighborhood schools be turned into a "senate of the people," where they could discuss the issues of the hour.[21]

Indeed, TR's bolt from the Republican party freed him to make a bolder, more consistent defense of "pure democracy" than Wilson, who, as the nominee of the Democrats, was necessarily more constrained by the structure and organizational practices of the traditional two-party system. The one doctrine that unified the disparate strands of the Progressive movement was its advocacy of "pure democracy," including support for measures such as the universal use of the direct primary; the initiative, referendum, and recall; and an easier method to amend the Constitution. Above all, the measures of direct government espoused by TR marked the Progressive party campaign as militantly reformist. "These . . . measures have been more widely discussed, more bitterly condemned, and more loyally praised than almost any other measures connected with the whole progressive movement," wrote Benjamin Park Dewitt.[22] Yet Roosevelt did not flinch in the face of this controversy. Sensing that popular rule was the glue that held together the movement he sought to lead, his defense of it became more bold throughout 1912. Indeed, Roosevelt announced toward the end of September, in a speech in Phoenix, Arizona, that he "would go even further than the Progressive Platform, applying the recall to everybody, including the President." TR "stands upon the bald doctrine of unrestricted majority rule," the *Nation* responded. "But it is just against the dangers threatened, by such majority rule, in those crises that try the temper of nations, that the safeguard of constitutional government as the outgrowth of the ages of experience has been erected."[23]

The more extreme measures of the program of direct democracy, such as the right of people to recall judicial decisions, alarmed not only conservatives, such as the incumbent Republican president, William Howard Taft, but also TR's progressive rivals in the Democratic and Republican parties: William Jennings Bryan, Robert La Follette, and Woodrow Wilson. Yet Roosevelt's campaign resonated with the American people. It stirred enthusiasm, indeed, a remarkable religiosity, which put on the defensive the Democrats and Republicans who attacked the Progressive party's program as too radical. Wilson received the nomination of his party, in fact, and won the general election, not only because of his "antistatism" but also because he was nearly as enthusiastic as Roosevelt in bowing to the court of public opinion. "What these critics never understood," John Dewey wrote in his penetrating eulogy of TR, "was the admiring affection and unbounded faith with which the American people repaid one who never spoke save to make them sharers in his ideas and to appeal to them as final judges."[24]

Roosevelt's appeal to the people was helped considerably by the press. Before the 1890s, public debate was dominated by the decentralized party press, which had prevailed since the Jacksonian era. But the elimination of patronage that supported the "party organ" style of journalism combined with technological advances to bring about a new medium by the beginning of the twentieth century. The challenge to traditional partisan politics and the development of inexpensive and rapid forms of manufacture made possible "a *mass* market beyond the confines of one faction, party, or following."[25] Indeed, it was the press itself that led the reform assault against party organizations around the country. Political leaders like La Follette and Roosevelt used newspapers to go over the heads of party leaders and establish their own direct links with the public.

One group of journalists, the so-called muckrakers—the label was original with Roosevelt—occupied an especially important place in early-twentieth-century politics. They wrote mainly for new and low-priced mass-circulation magazines such as the *Arena* and *McClure's*, monthly publications whose influence on public opinion was hardly less important than that of Roosevelt himself. As TR's Progressive party ally Albert Beveridge wrote in 1910, "Party lines all over the country have pretty well disappeared." The cause was clearly "the cheaper magazines which are circulating among the people and which have become the people's literature [producing] almost a mental and moral revolution among the people."[26]

Roosevelt and his progressive allies did not embrace the muckrakers without reservations. By fixing their gaze almost exclusively on the "vile and debasing" aspects of political life, he feared, they neglected the achievements of the constructive elements of society.[27] As Croly observed, muckrakers encouraged neither the "searching diagnosis" of political and economic problems nor the enactment of "effective remedial measures" that progressives claimed to value; their influence was to stir resentment against machines and trusts. Nevertheless, TR was not averse to taking advantage of this literature of exposure, which brought discredit upon the "special interests" he opposed. Partly by inspiring intimates in the press to write articles and partly through the force of his personality and ideas, TR, as the journalist Mark Sullivan noted, "kept the pages of the popular magazines glowing with support for his crusades."[28]

In 1912, the popular press supported Roosevelt's "Stand at Armageddon," his "battle for the Lord," which above all was a crusade for "pure" democracy. As he put it in his "Confession of Faith" speech at the Progressive party convention, "The first essential of the Progressive program was the right of the people to rule." Significantly, the 1912 presidential election became the first in history in which direct primaries were an important factor. Roosevelt had been denied the GOP nomination by party leaders, even though he had demonstrated considerable support in the twelve states that had selected convention delegates by popular vote. That TR won most of these contests, even thrashing Taft in the incumbent president's home state of Ohio, gave moral force to his insurgency. By ignoring the results of these contests, TR and his

supporters claimed, Republican "bosses" showed the need for more comprehensive reform. Progressives' celebration of "the right of the people to rule
themselves," through measures such as the direct primary, the initiative, the
referendum, and recall, summoned a militant and diverse group of reformers
to Chicago who viewed the Progressive party as "a party against parties," as a
movement of "We the People" which no party loyalty or advantage should
compromise.[29]

The reform-minded delegates who came to Chicago championed the
direct rule of the people with a fresh enthusiasm that delighted the progressive
journalists who reported the proceedings of the new party's convention. After
observing an evening of reformist speeches, punctuated by the singing of
hymns, "which burst forth at the first flash of every demonstration," a reporter
for the San Francisco Examiner, which was owned by the progressive pub-
lisher William Randolph Hearst, marveled that the convention "was more like
a religious revival than a political gathering."[30] In the religiosity of the delegates, in their repeated singing of "Onward Christian Soldiers" and "The Battle Hymn of the Republic," the Examiner detected a political revolution: an
assault on the partisan practices that had dominated the American political
process for nearly a century. Indeed, TR's very presence at the Progressive
party convention signified the beginning of a new political era. Marking a
novel departure in the proceedings of national conventions, Roosevelt and his
running mate, California governor Hiram Johnson, immediately were notified of their nomination, and in the midst of deafening cheers they appeared
before the delegates to voice their acceptance and to pledge their best efforts
in the coming campaign. In the past, party nominees had stayed away from the
convention, waiting to be notified officially of their nomination. TR's personal
appearance at the Progressive convention gave dramatic testimony to his dominance of the proceedings. More significant, it gave evidence of an important
historical change, of presidential campaigns being conducted less by parties
than by individual candidates who appealed directly for the support of the
electorate.[31]

Although the Progressive party did not win the 1912 election, its strong
showing signaled the significant advance, if not the triumph, of the progressive
idea of democracy. "Newspapers that belittle the Roosevelt movement and
believe that they can obtain results with insincere criticism and sneers will be
disappointed," the Examiner predicted. "The People of this country are ready
for something new, something different from the old machine routine." The

Progressive party's platform, its support of measures that would establish the right of the people to choose their representatives and influence the councils of government without suffering the interference of political parties, would surely "have the attentive hearing" of the American public.[32]

The general election campaign of 1912 confirmed the *Examiner*'s prescience as well as the influence of the new mass media on American politics. The support of the press and his national prominence gave TR, as the reform journalist William Kittle wrote, "a far-reaching megaphone-like Voice raucous and strident indeed, but of high purpose like that of the prophets of old."[33] Although the Progressive party campaign did not educate public opinion, Croly admitted, it capped an era of muckraking that aroused "the American conscience against malefaction in high places." "The agitation," he concluded, "was a complete success."[34] Indeed, it was neither the Democrats nor the Republicans but the Progressives who set the tone of the 1912 election. The Progressive party platform proposed the most extensive reforms during the campaign, but, as Eldon Eisenach notes, "all three major parties, in varying degrees and with differing emphasis, urged Progressive measures."[35] The Progressive public doctrine, promising the end of party dominance and the more direct influence of public opinion on politics and government, appeared to be victorious.

No one was more impressed with, or dejected by, this triumph than William Howard Taft. In 1911, he had sought to raise the postal rates on popular magazines, indignant that the government was subsidizing journalists who presumed "to be controllers of public opinion and occupy a disinterested position."[36] But Taft failed to dent the image of these magazines as "the agents of Heaven in establishing virtue"; unable to persuade Congress to challenge the special political position of independent journalists, he consoled himself with the hope that there soon would "be a sickening of the popular stomach with this assumption of pure disinterestedness and of attacks on indefinite persons scheming against the public weal without specification or proof."[37] Yet, by 1912, the power of the "disinterested" press had grown, and the alliance between muckrakers and insurgent politicians had undermined the party basis of politics. Taft's stalwart defense of traditional party practices in the face of TR's insurgency ended in an immense electoral defeat—he won the support of but two states (Utah and Vermont) and only 23.2 percent of the popular vote. "The initiative, the referendum, and the recall, together with the complete adoption of the direct primary, as a means of selecting nominees, and an entire destruction of the convention system are now all made the *sine qua non* of a real reformer," he lamented, "and everyone who hesitates to follow all of these or any of them is regarded with suspicion and is denounced as an enemy of popular government and of the people."[38] Such denunciation, he was surprised to learn, found great sympathy from the people throughout the country.

Taft allowed himself to hope that Wilson's victory might simply represent "the normal political change from one party to another." Electoral competition between two great parties was "the sheet anchor of popular government"—fortification against petty and virulent interest group politics. Thus, he granted, the Democrats' victory might be good for the country, especially after the Republican party had been in power so long that "jealousies and factions in it [had] destroyed the discipline and the loyalty of its members and [had] injured its political prestige." But the success of the Progressive party, he warned—Roosevelt's strength as compared with the regular Republican ticket—might portend more dramatic change. "When a party like the Bull Moose party comes forward and proposes to utterly tear down all the checks and balances of a well-adjusted, democratic, constitutional, representative government, to destroy the limitations on executive and legislative power as between the majority and the minority, as between the majority and the individual, then the issue becomes a capital one, and it affects the permanence and continuance of our government."[39]

Although the progressives' faith in unmediated, national mass public opinion appeared to threaten valued traditions in the United States, such as federalism and the separation of powers, their celebration of the rights of the people resonated with the public at a time when industrial capitalism and urbanization threatened the integrity of local and state governments. The progressive defense of direct rule of the people, in fact, capitalized on the commitment to popular sovereignty in the tradition of local self-government, which, as we have shown in the previous chapter, coexisted uneasily with strong local and state party organizations. Arguably, the seeds of the celebration of the whole people, unmediated by either local institutions or political associations, were present in the constitutional reforms of the Jacksonian era, resisted by Van Buren, which provided for the direct popular election of state and local judges. The assault on judicial patronage during the Jacksonian era was frequently linked with a broader challenge to representation itself.[40] Indeed, one early progressive tract that defended direct government made this connection between the nineteenth-century concept of self-government and the progressive idea of democracy explicitly:

Direct Legislation is law-enacting by the electors themselves as distinguished from law-enacting by representatives or by some aristocratic body, or by a single ruler, such as the king, emperor, or czar. In small communities this is accomplished by electors meeting together voting on every law or ordinance by which they are to be governed. This is done in New England town meetings. . . . In communities too widespread or too numerous for the voters to meet together and decide on the laws by which they are to be governed, Direct Legislation is accomplished by the use of imperative petitions, through what is known as the Initiative and Referendum.[41]

In effect, some progressives hoped that the election or polling district, organizing the voter's immediate neighborhood, would replace the small village meeting as source of civic involvement. But progressive measures such as the initiative, referendum, and direct primary did not benefit from "the power of meeting" which was so central to Tocqueville's celebration of the New England town meeting; nor did these measures support the strong party organizations that Van Buren considered an imperative force to secure harmony in the ranks of the people. Rather, progressives dedicated themselves to political forms and associations that freed individuals from provincial concerns and partisan organizations in order to prepare them for participation in a more enlightened government. Even the social centers movement, committed to the use of public schools for political debate and civic forums, rested on an extraordinary faith in public enlightenment. "No social center can meet the present crisis in the history of democracy without an organization . . . in which every narrow interest of sect or party or class is swallowed up in the consciousness that the interests of the whole community are supreme," George Forbes insisted, "and that the effort to realize them in the spirit of brotherhood is the supreme function and the supreme satisfaction of citizenship."[42] Progressives preferred public opinion to localized parties, as one ardent reformer put it, "for the people are patriotic, they do not expect offices, they cannot be bribed, they are disinterested, they have an unbiased judgment and they are yet sound to the core."[43]

In condemning reformers for lacking a coherent set of principles, contemporary scholars point to the apparent contradiction between progressives' celebration of direct democracy and their hope to achieve more disinterested government, which seemed to demand a more powerful and independent bureaucracy. In truth, the progressive faith in public opinion was far from complete. Most progressives celebrated an idea of national community which did not include immigrants and African Americans.[44] Moreover, the commitment of New Nationalist reformers to forming an independent executive led to support for technical expertise that insulated government decisions from the vagaries of public opinion and elections. The most extreme version of this support for enlightened administration was the city manager form of government, which removed even the position of chief executive from direct popular election.[45] In this form, the movement to strengthen executive management mirrored the managerial reforms that Frederick W. Taylor and his followers were advocating for private industry. Like their political counterparts, proponents of Taylorism promoted efficiency, entailing more active and systematic—scientific—forms of management throughout the firm, from the head office to the shop floor.[46]

Progressives did not celebrate expertise for its own sake, however. Rather, they sought to strengthen national administrative power as an arm of presidential responsibility. "At present our administration is organized chiefly upon the principle that the executive shall not be permitted to do much good for fear that he will do harm," Herbert Croly lamented. "It ought to be organized on the principle that he shall have full power to do either well or ill, but that if he does ill, he will have no defense against punishment."[47] As Roosevelt described this concept of executive power, the president was "a steward of the people bound actively and affirmatively to do all he could for the people, and not content himself with the negative merit of keeping his talents undamaged in a napkin."[48] Significantly, TR's presidency marked the dividing line between the old commitment to party patronage in public affairs and the modern recognition that nonpolitical administration was a principal tool of governance. Progressives never carried the idea of nonpolitical service to the same lengths as the British; indeed, their celebration of the People testified to their diffident approach to state building. But by the end of Roosevelt's term in office, merit had begun to supplant spoils. Presidential leadership, previously dependent on patronage-seeking state and local party machines, now required careful attention to administrative management, sometimes to foster economy and efficiency and sometimes to bolster the power of the increasingly active federal government.[49]

The new challenge for the president was to take charge of the large and disparate administrative apparatus. As Stephen Skowronek has written, "A state building sequence that began with Roosevelt's determination to forge 'a more orderly system of control,' ended with the consolidation of a new governmental order defiant of all attempts at control."[50] Indeed, Wilson, Brandeis, and Bryan attacked the Progressive party's proposal to create an interstate trade commission precisely on these grounds, charging that such a provision threatened to exacerbate the problem of administrative responsibility. It would be all too easy, they warned, for the president to appoint commissioners who would rule by administrative fiat, without any responsibility to the people.[51]

Without denying that the Progressive movement was weakened by a tension between reforms that diminished democracy and those that sought to make democracy more direct, its central thrust was an attack on political parties and the creation of a more direct, programmatic link between government and the people. Progressives argued, not without reason, that the expansion of social welfare provisions and "pure democracy" were inextricably linked. Reforms such as the direct primary, as well as the initiative and referendum, were designed to overthrow the localized two-party system in the United States, which bestowed on the separated institutions of the federal government a certain unity of control while at the same time it restrained programmatic ambition and prevented the development of a stable and energetic administration of social policy. By the same token, the triumph of "progressive" over "pioneer" democracy, as Croly framed it, would put the American people directly in touch with the councils of power, thus strengthening the demand for government support and allow, indeed require, administrative agencies to play their proper role in the realization of progressive social welfare policy. "So our nascent, insurgent, still unfolded democracy, which unites many men in a common hostility to certain broad economic and political developments, is now passing over to a definite program," the progressive thinker Walter Weyl wrote hopefully in 1912. "It is becoming positive . . . and seeks to test its motives and ideals in relation to American history and conditions."[52]

Progressive Democracy, the Modern State, and the Constitution

The Progressive program seemed to challenge the very foundation of "republican" democracy in the United States: the idea underlying the Constitution that space created by institutional devices such as the separation of powers and federalism allowed representatives to govern competently and fairly. Likewise, the Progressive vision of democracy rejected party politics, at least as they worked in the early part of the twentieth century. Political parties might once have been "the best of all agencies of civic education," Delos Wilcox wrote in 1912. But, he continued, "the caucus and convention have come to be in large measure, mere schools of political trickery. Citizens who merely 'learn the game' do not thereby become properly educated."[53] More fundamentally, many reformers charged that political parties, no less than interest groups, denigrated the progressive idea of "pure democracy." As Croly wrote, "The two party system, like other forms of representative democracy, proposes to accomplish for the people a fundamental political task which they ought to accomplish themselves."[54]

The Progressive party's vision of democracy, which TR made the centerpiece of his reform program, created a campaign, George Mowry has written, which "was one of the most radical ever made by a major American political figure."[55] Not surprisingly, this campaign aroused strong opposition. Stand-pat Republicans and large industrial interests who long had appreciated TR's disdain for radical economic and political remedies rapidly abandoned the former president.[56] But the opposition to "pure democracy" went far beyond the embattled "stand-patters" of the Republican party. The Progressive party's attack on representative institutions also led moderate progressives, such as Taft, to fashion a new understanding of Republican conservatism which was rooted less in a militant defense of property rights and business than in the Whigs' defense of ordered liberty. Taft and like-minded moderates in the Republican party such as Henry Cabot Lodge and Elihu Root characterized their battle against insurgency as a struggle for the soul of the Constitution.

During the 1912 campaign, the burden of this fight fell most heavily on Taft. The incumbent president had supported the pragmatic progressive program TR had pursued while in office, when he cooperated with Republican party regulars to pass specific policies, such as the Hepburn Act. Now Taft found his own efforts to carry on that pragmatic tradition of reform the object of scorn and derision, the victim of TR's celebration of "pure democracy." Yet Taft found honor in his opposition to the Progressive party's political reforms. He could now "stand pat" in defense of the Constitution and argue that the Progressive idea of democracy would destroy it. "With the effort to make the selection of candidates, the enactment of legislation, and the decision of the courts to depend on the momentary passions of the people necessarily indifferently informed as to the issues presented, and without the opportunity to them for time and study and that deliberation that gives security and common sense to the government of the people, such extremists would hurry us into a condition which would find no parallel except in the French revolution, or in that bubbling anarchy that once characterized the South American Republics," the president warned his fellow Republicans at a Lincoln Day celebration in 1912. "Such extremists are not progressives—they are political emotionalists or neurotics—who have lost the sense of proportion, that clear and candid consideration of their own weakness as a whole, and that clear perception of the necessity for checks upon hasty popular action which made our people who fought the Revolution and who drafted the Federal Constitution, the greatest self-governing people the world ever knew."[57] Support for "pure democracy," Taft charged, encouraged the same "factional spirit" that Madison warned against in his famous discussion of republican government in *Federalist* 10, an unruly majority that would "sacrifice to its ruling passion or interest both the public good and the rights of other citizens."[58]

In resisting this temptation to flatter the whims and passions of the majority, the most sacred duty of true conservatives was to uphold the courts. As Taft told an audience in Boston, TR's defense of direct democracy "sent a thrill of alarm through all the members of the community who understood our constitutional principles and who feared the effect of the proposed changes upon the permanence of government."[59] It was unthinkable to the great majority of leaders in Congress and the states, and to the great mass of people as well, Taft argued, that Roosevelt should seriously propose to have a plebiscite on questions involving the construction of the Constitution. TR's audacity drew most clearly the fundamental issue that divided Republicans and Progressives:

> The Republican party, . . . respecting as it does the constitution . . . , the care with which the judicial clauses of that fundamental instrument were drawn to secure the independence of the judiciary, will never consent to an abatement of that independence to the slightest degree, and will stand with its face like flint against any constitutional changes in it to take away from the high priests upon which to administer to justice the independence that they must enjoy of influence of powerful individuals or of powerful majorities."[60]

In response to such criticisms, reformers insisted that the Progressive idea of democracy was not a radical rejection of the American constitutional tradition but an effort to restore it. State and local machines, they argued, had perverted the original design of the Constitution, which was dedicated to emancipating the American people from provincial and special interests, embodied by the Articles of Confederation. Whereas the Articles of Confederation read

"We the undersigned delegates of the States," the preamble to the Constitution of 1787 was declared by "We, the People." The change to "We, the People," claimed Theodore Gilman at a Progressive party rally in Yonkers, New York, "was made at the Federal Convention with the full understanding of the meaning and effect of the new form of words," signifying that the new Constitution represented the aspirations of one sovereign people to create a "more perfect union."[61] Political parties had preempted this original design, shifting power to states and localities in the service of "local self-government." Jeffersonian and Jacksonian reforms were necessary in the nineteenth century to thwart the "aristocratic" pretensions of the Federalists, but the problems thrown up by the industrial revolution demanded that progressives revisit the potential for national democracy in the Constitution. As Croly put it, "The nationalism of Hamilton with all its aristocratic leaning, was more democratic, because more constructively social, than the indiscriminate individualism of Jefferson."[62] Just as the original theory of the electoral college had been abandoned after the "Revolution of 1800," closing the space between presidential politics and popular choice, so Gilman claimed, "The people now propose to come into closer touch with their representatives by the abolition of the machine, and the substitution thereafter of the direct primary, the initiative, referendum, and recall. This is all one logical and irresistible movement in one direction, having as its object the restoration of our form of government to its original purity and ideal perfection, as a government under the control of 'We, the people,' who formed it."[63]

Gilman's defense of progressivism against the charge of radicalism received indirect support from social democrats, who were no less hostile to the progressive idea of democracy than were conservatives. Eugene Debs attacked the Progressive party as "a reactionary protest of the middle classes, built largely upon the personality of one man and not destined for permanence."[64] The Progressives' transience stemmed not just from TR's notoriety, Debs argued, but also from the flimsy doctrine that underlay it. Although supportive of political reform, Debs had long considered devices such as the referendum a very small part of the Socialist party program. "You will never be able, in my opinion, to organize any formidable movement upon [the referendum] or any other single issue," he wrote in 1895. "The battle is narrowing down to capitalism and socialism, and there can be no compromise or halfway ground. . . . Not until the workingman comprehends the trend of . . . economic development and is conscious of his class interests will he be fit to properly use the referendum, and when he has reached that point he will be a

Socialist."[65]

Given his view of progressivism, Debs was chagrined that TR "stole the red flag of socialism" to symbolize his fight for the rule of the people. That Roosevelt selected the crimson bandanna as the symbol for the Progressive party did not make socialism, which he had long denounced as anarchy, respectable. Rather, the Progressives' fight for the rule of the people deflected attention from the injustices of capitalism, Debs complained, which were truly the cause of the people's discontent.[66]

Some of Roosevelt's political allies, who hoped that TR's campaign might flower into a European-type social democratic party, were hardly less contemptuous than was Debs of the former president's obsession with "pure democracy." "I am weary to death of the Rule of the People and a millennium created by constant elections and never-ending suspicion of authority," the respected jurist Learned Hand wrote in the wake of the storm created by TR's democratic platform. "When will the day come that some courageous men will stand sponsors for a real programme of 'social justice' in the words of our leader?" Gazing enviously across the Atlantic at the progress of social democrats in England, Hand asked Felix Frankfurter plaintively, "Can you see a single man who would really dare to commit himself to any plan like the Fabians? Why have we nowhere any Fabians? Why aren't all of us Fabians?"[67]

In truth, the Progressive party's millennial celebration of direct rule of the people was not reactionary. It did, however, behold a program of reform which sought to preserve the dignity of the democratic individual. Emphasizing the candidate instead of the party, the Progressives deflected attention from class conflict. Seeking to build a welfare state within unified public opinion rather than through a social democratic party, it emphasized individual political action. The primary, referendum, and recall, after all, were devices that asked citizens to vote their individual consciences. Progressives were disdainful of collective organizations, such as the Democratic and Republican parties, formed on personal, family, or community attachments; similarly, they found repugnant the idea of sectarian partisanship in which "enlightened" voting decisions were submerged in class or racial conflicts.

To the extent that Progressive democracy was radical, it represented a distinctively American form of radicalism—one conceived to rescue American individualism from an emotive attachment to the Constitution, especially the designated "high priests" of the Constitution. "It is difficult for Englishmen to understand the extreme conservatism of my proposition as to the referendum to the people of certain judicial questions," TR wrote to a friend abroad; "and this difficulty arises from the fact that in England no human being dreams of permitting the court to decide such questions! In England no court can declare any legislative act unconstitutional." In actuality, TR claimed, he sought to avoid the delegation of policy to an unchecked legislature that might truly embody the sort of factionalism that plagued France and England and had worried the architects of the Constitution. Recognizing that factionalism was abetted by militant partisanship in government, he wrote: "I do not propose to make the legislature supreme over the court; I propose *merely* to allow the people . . . to decide whether to follow the legislature or the court."[68]

In the final analysis, the progressive faith in public opinion represented a compromise with the widespread fear of a centralized state in the United States, a willingness on the part of even the most nationalist of reformers to accommodate these fears even as they sought to strengthen national administrative power. As the militant New Nationalist Croly wrote in *Progressive Democracy*, many well-meaning social democrats in England or France, as well as the United States, favored the formation of a national programmatic party to bring about social and economic reform. Such devotees of a permanent social democratic party disdained direct popular government, Croly pointed out, because they expected that, at least in the near future, direct popular government, dependent on the vagaries of public opinion, would increase the difficulty of securing the adoption of many items in a desirable social program. Herein they were right, Croly acknowledged. But reformers of this sort attached too much importance to the accomplishment and maintenance of specific results and not enough to the permanent social welfare of democracy: "An authoritative representative government, particularly one which is associated with inherited leadership and a strong party system, carries with it an enormous prestige. It is frequently in a position either to ignore, to circumvent or to wear down popular opposition. But a social program purchased at such a price is not worth what it costs."[69]

The Progressive party dedicated itself to expanding the national government's responsibility to secure the economic welfare of the individual. At the same time, it stood for the proposition that any program of social control, social insurance, and a standardization of industry could not be adopted until it was well digested by public opinion. There was no prospect in the United States—where centralized administration was a cardinal vice—that the people would grant legitimacy to a welfare state that was not attuned to their preferences, even biases. The popularity of the direct primary in the United States, Croly noted, revealed that centralized and disciplined national parties went against the looser genius of American politics. To the extent that government became committed to a democratic program that was essentially social in character, the American people would find intolerable a two-party system that thwarted the advent of direct popular rule. As the prominent social reformer Jane Addams noted in a speech delivered at the Second Annual Lincoln Day dinner of the Progressive party, held in 1914, a fundamental principle of progressivism was that a welfare state could not be created in the United States "unless the power of direct legislation is placed in the hands of the people, in order that these changes may come, not as the centralized government [has] given them, from above down, but may come from the people up; that the people shall be the directing and controlling factors in this legislation."[70]

The short-lived existence of the Progressive party, then, is not attributable to the cult of TR's personality, or to disagreements over Jim Crow laws or trusts which divided its leaders, but followed instead from the almost hopeless task of reconciling loyalty to the progressive ideal with loyalty to a particular organization. "The logic of the progressive democratic principle was self destructive," Croly predicted. "Just in so far as a progressive political program is carried out, progressive social democracy will cease to need a national political party as an instrument."[71] Progressive democracy would reach its fulfillment in an alliance between public opinion and the autonomous political executive, now freed from the constraints of localized party organizations and practices.

Conclusion: The Wayward Path of Progressivism and the Crisis of Citizenship

The Progressive party's brief but significant existence anticipated a shift in which a political order defined by the differences between the Democrats and Republicans gave way to one defined by differences between progressives and conservatives in both parties. Before the 1912 election, one belonged to a party as one belonged to a family or church—and national politics was held accountable to state and local party leaders. Progressivism was advanced in 1912 in a way that began to weaken party loyalties; thereafter, the individual's relationship to the nation's capital and an expanding federal power rivaled his ties to party and place. This shift, one might say, was ratified by Woodrow Wilson's move toward positions and policies that accepted national administrative power. Most significant, Wilson eventually supported the idea of a regulatory commission with broad responsibilities for overseeing business practices, resulting in the creation of the Federal Trade Commission (FTC) in 1915. During the 1912 campaign, Wilson attacked the Progressive party for proposing to expand national administrative power. But Wilson's first term, the *New Republic* proclaimed, "waxed increasingly paternalistic, centralizing, and bureaucratic." In addition to the Federal Trade Commission, Wilson and the Democratic Congress also enacted the Federal Reserve Act in 1913, which established a board to oversee the national banking and currency system. The *New Republic*, under the editorial leadership of Herbert Croly, did not "nag" Wilson and the Democrats for their inconsistency; rather, it congratulated them on their readiness to abandon obsolete principles: "The whole record ignores and defies the Jeffersonian tradition. Its tendency is to use Hamiltonian administrative nationalism in the interest of a democratic social policy which is, of course, precisely what the Progressives proposed to do four years ago. The Progressive party is dead, but its principles are more alive than ever, because they are to a greater extent embodied in the official organization of the nation."[72]

To be sure, as the "return to normalcy" of the 1920s showed, Wilson's adoption of many elements of the Progressive party's program did not signal the triumph of New Nationalism. But it did mean that localized parties were no longer the principal agents of democracy and that the alliance between decentralization and democracy was gradually weakened in favor a relationship between the individual and the "state." The advance of the ideas and institutions of progressive democracy invariably followed. Robert La Follette's 1924 Progressive party campaign, which captured 16 percent of the popular vote, reveals that progressivism did not go into hibernation during the 1920s. Indeed, La Follette's independent campaign, lacking any semblance of a party organization, advanced further the progressive concept of direct democracy. That La Follette received such an impressive vote, despite a booming economy and the popularity of incumbent president Calvin Coolidge, testified to the growing fragility of the two-party system.[73] With the celebration of public opinion spawned by the Progressive party campaign of 1912, even conservatives like Coolidge were forced to go directly to the public to ensure support for themselves and their policies. Coolidge, in fact, was the first president to make use of a new medium, the radio, which he used effectively to enhance his image and to enlist support for his tax reform plan.[74] The "confederate" party system would endure as an important institution until the 1970s; yet it would never again be a bulwark of local self-government—"a wall of separation" between the national community and the many communities at the state and local level.[75]

Emancipated from the "wheelwork" of the two-party system, public policy came to betray more centrally the mores and biases of public opinion. Indeed, as Morton Keller reveals, the surges of progressivism sometimes brought policies that appeared reactionary.[76] Thus, woman suffrage, a principal cause of the Progressive party, triumphed, but so did immigration restriction and Prohibition, which many, if not a majority of, progressives supported in 1920. Similarly, the enactment of strict registration requirements and the Australian ballot reduced political corruption but also discouraged participation in elections.[77] More to the point, in their rejection of traditional constitutional remedies and their indifference to political associations, reformers risked the manipulation of progressive means for ends that badly fractured the Progressive movement, ends that some reformers abhorred. The mere fact that immigration restriction and Prohibition "were potentially or actively regressive does not mean that they were not progressive," Arthur Link argues. "On the contrary," he continues, "they superbly illustrated the repressive tendencies that inhered in progressivism precisely because it was grounded so much upon majoritarian principles."[78]

Because of this dedication to direct democracy and the way it cast discredit on the two-party system, the Progressive movement never clearly existed as a recognizable organization with common goals. Rather, it is better understood as a movement of public opinion which has been aroused episodically to our own time by powerful issues, domestic and international crises, and dynamic leaders. Just as progressivism advanced a new concept and practice of democracy, in which candidates and public officials would form more direct ties with the public, so progressivism corroded civic attachments in the United States. For all their failings, political parties had played a critical part in linking private and public concerns, as well as local loyalties and national purpose. "Without them and their activities, however, a critical element forging commitment, cohesion, and control was missing—and missed," Joel Silbey has written. "Without the road maps parties had provided, without their infrastructure promoting connection and coherence, the American political nation was now the setting of a very different, individualistic, and certainly more volatile political world."[79] Progressives' faith in the *whole* people betrayed them, Wilson Carey McWilliams has argued, for they ignored or slighted the implication that "we all begin in a world of particulars, from which the human spirit ascends, on any account only slowly and with diffi-culty."[80]

It was precisely on these grounds that the Antifederalists had warned that the Constitution would fail to create self-government on a grand scale. Enlarg-ing the sphere of political life as far as was conceived by the Constitution would weaken the ties of familiarity, custom, and shared endeavor and even-tually destroy civic attachments. The persistence of local self-government and decentralized political associations through the end of the nineteenth century postponed the question of whether the Founders' concept of "We the People" was viable. But with the Civil War, its aftermath, and the rise of industrial cap-italism, constitutional government in the United States entered a new phase. It fell to the progressives to confront the question of whether it was possible to reconcile democracy with an economy of greatly enlarged institutions and a society of growing diversity.

The test of this proposition in the Progressive Era appeared to validate the Antifederalist fears. "The long term danger of Progressivism," McWilliams observes, "points in the direction of the 'tyranny of the majority' and the sort of happy nihilism that is apt to be celebrated in our time."[81] As Tocqueville might have expected, this popular despotism is a soft one, based not on mob rule but bureaucratic torpor and endemic apathy. As it sucked much of the meaning from elections and party competition, "pure democracy" proved to be fool's gold that left the political process vulnerable to crass sensationalism and frac-tious interest group politics. As John Dewey conceded in 1927:

> The same forces which have brought about the forms of democratic gov-ernment, general suffrage, executives and legislatures chosen by major-ity vote, have also brought about conditions which halt the social and human ideals that demand the utilization of government as the genuine instrumentality of an inclusive and fraternally associated people. "The new age of human relationships" has no political agencies worthy of it. The democratic public is still largely inchoate and unorganized.[82]

In the final analysis, then, the failings of progressivism shed light on the limitations of the American constitutional order. Like the Antifederalists, pro-gressives rejected the Federalist view that institutional arrangements could be substituted for virtue. But progressives were unwilling to subordinate their vision of the nation's destiny to provincial liberties, even as many of them acknowledged the importance of localism. With John Dewey, progressives fell back on the vague hope that locality could be allied to larger loyalties by "free-ing and perfecting the processes of inquiry and of dissemination of their con-clusions." The dignity of the democratic individual, progressives held, had to shift from the emotive grounds of local ties to "the cumulative and transmitted intellectual wealth of the community." As Dewey put it optimistically, "the Great Community, in the sense of free and full intercommunication," would do "its final work in ordering the relations and enriching the experience of local associations."[83] By the eve of the Great Depression, Dewey's faint opti-mism would give way to a more confident prescription that progressivism re-create itself as a "new individualism"—one that did not celebrate a rugged individualism that abhorred state interference with private property but instead viewed the state as a guarantor of social and economic welfare. At the time, however, as Robert Wiebe has observed, "Dewey became just another voice in the chorus declaring a crisis in democracy."[84]

Thus, just as political parties were formed to make constitutional govern-ment in the United States safe for democracy—to ameliorate the Constitu-tion's insufficient attention to the cultivation of an active and competent citi-zenry—so the weakening of political parties had exposed the fragile sense of citizenship in American political life. Progressive reformers were not unmind-ful of the possibility that dismantling the parties would breed an apathetic public that was susceptible to plebiscitary appeals. But they believed that this risk had to be taken, lest government remain impotent in the face of the major changes taking place in the economy and society. In the event that the people failed to participate in progressive democracy, some reformers suggested, they should be, so to speak, forced to be free. "The people will *not* go to the pri-maries; that is settled," declared an editorial in the progressive journal the *Arena*. "If they will not do it voluntarily they should be compelled by law to do it and deposit there a ballot, and also at the general election, even though a blank, under the penalty of disenfranchisement and fine."[85]

There was no prospect, however, that the American people, dedicated to individualism, could be forced to be free. As Tocqueville understood, civic attachments in modern commercial republics would have to rely largely on associations and practices that encouraged "self-interest, rightly understood."[86]

In a sense, the wayward path of progressivism takes us back to the origins of the party system. Despairing of the constraints the "Revolution of 1800" threatened to impose on the national government, Hamilton urged in a letter to James A. Bayard, in April 1802, that there be "a systematic and persevering endeavor to establish the future of a great empire on foundations much firmer than have yet to be devised." Hoping to strengthen the "frail" system the Constitution proved to be in the hands of the Jeffersonians, Hamilton expressed approval of a proposal then before the House of Representatives to reform the electoral college by providing for discrimination between candidates for the presidency and vice presidency, as well as having electors chosen by the people under the direction of Congress. Hamilton supported the popular election of electors because he regarded as "sound principle, to let the Federal government rest as much as possible on the shoulders of the people, and as little as possible on those of the State Legislatures."[87] In Hamilton's view, a strong executive, linked directly to the support of the people, could become the linchpin of an "administrative republic." The dominance of executive leadership in the formulation and carrying out of policy was essential to resist the deterioration of republican government.[88]

Such a view was considered mischievous by the more ardent defenders of popular rule among the Founders, such as Jefferson and Madison, as well as their Jacksonian successors, who believed that republican government required more support for local self-government than could be found in the Constitution. This constitutional defect required political parties, which might arouse a common sentiment against "consolidation." Progressive reformers understood that the development of a more purposeful national government meant loosening the hold of traditional parties on the loyalties and voting habits of citizens. But they failed to appreciate the purpose these parties served as effective channels for democratic participation.[89] Political parties, which embodied the principle of local self-government, were critical agents in counteracting the tendency of citizens to shut themselves up in a limited circle of domestic concerns out of the reach of broader public causes. By enticing Americans into neighborhood organizations and patronage practices that were beyond their tiny private orbits, traditional party organizations helped to show individuals the connection between their private interests and public concerns. Similarly, highly decentralized party structures ensured that national campaigns and controversies focused on the partisan activities of townships, wards, and cities, thus cultivating a delicate balance between local and national community.[90] Drawn into political associations by the promise of social, economic, and political advantage, Americans might also learn the art of cooperation and form attachments to government institutions. As Tocqueville put it in a nice turn of phrase, "Public spirit in the Union is . . . only a summing up of provincial patriotism."[91]

Still, we must not allow the wayward path of progressivism to blind us to the shortcomings of the nineteenth-century polity—no "golden age" of parties ever existed. Progressive reformers had good reasons for viewing political parties and the provincial liberties they upheld as an obstacle to economic and political justice. The resurrection of Hamilton nationalism they favored, which required the weakening of political parties, yielded a stronger executive that became the principal agent for undertaking domestic and international responsibilities that must be assumed by all decent commercial republics. The nobility of the modern presidency comes, to use Woodrow Wilson's phrase, from its "extraordinary isolation," which provides great opportunity for presidents to leave their mark on the nation, even as it subjects them to a volatile mass democracy that makes popular and enduring achievement unlikely.[92] As the discussion of the New Deal in the next chapter reveals, the legacy of progressivism appears to be a more active and better-equipped national state but one without adequate means of common deliberation and public judgment.

The New Deal Liberalism
and the Doctrine of Responsible
Party Government

The Progressive movement cast considerable discredit on the two-party system and advanced a new concept of democracy, in which candidates and public officials would form more direct ties with the public. But not all champions of direct democracy denigrated political parties. Some progressive leaders viewed the 1912 election and its aftermath as the signal for the transformation, rather than the dismantlement, of the two-party system. Prior to the election, Herbert Knox Smith, who helped organize the Progressive party's supporters in Connecticut, wrote an article in *Yale Review* which sought to place the current party battles in a broad historical perspective. The Progressive party was "a protest against the entire American political alignment, and for the forcing of a new and better one," he argued. Within eight years, Knox predicted boldly, the Progressives would be in power, with the Democrats as the party of opposition. Indeed, the new alignment was foreordained, and the platform of the Progressive party was calculated to define this realignment more clearly: "It raises specifically great vital modern issues that will themselves divide our people into Progressives and Conservatives."[1]

The Progressive party's strong showing in the election, combined with Taft's poor third-place finish, confirmed Knox's prediction for many reformers. Moreover, the Progressive party carried out organizational efforts in the aftermath of the election which abetted further bold predictions of party trans-formation. Frances Kellor, a leading New York reformer, was selected as the chair of the Progressive National Service, which was dedicated to establishing the Progressive party as the first truly nationalized and programmatic party in the United States. The work of the service would be done by four bureaus: Jane Addams became the director of the Bureau of Social and Industrial Jus-tice; Gifford Pinchot, the champion of enlightened management of natural resources, headed the Conservation Division; George Record, the militant New Jersey reformer, assumed command of the Department of Popular Gov-ernment; and Charles J. Bird, a Massachusetts industrialist, led the Bureau of Cost of Living and Corporation Control. The "First Quarterly Report of the Progressive National Service," issued in March 1913, stated its high purpose:

> It is political organization in the highest sense of the term. It is unbound
> by statutory forms and legal technicalities which combine men into
> mere political machines. It is unhampered by election law discrimina-
> tions which make it difficult and well nigh impossible for the indepen-
> dent voter to express his will. It places the burden not upon voting on
> election day but upon civic responsibility and duty year round, locally
> and nationally. Voting then becomes one expression of patriotism rather
> than the sum total of civic expressions.[2]

The Progressive National Service never fulfilled these high expectations. By the end of 1913, the party's national committee cut back the service's fund-ing, so as to devote more resources to the local and state elections that would occur the following year.[3] More problematic, the social workers and acade-mics connected with the service shunned the more practical tasks involved in organizing election campaigns. They dedicated themselves to the long-term objective of public education—to the cultivation of a "progressive con-science." But the more political organizers of the Progressive party, such as Theodore Roosevelt, former senator Albert Beveridge of Indiana, and George Perkins, the executive director of the Progressive National Committee, doubted that the new party could survive long enough to wait for social and political views to change. Either it would prove itself as a party in the near future by winning more offices, or it would cease to be a party.[4] "The great danger for us," TR wrote to Gifford Pinchot a week after the 1912 election, "is that with no clear purpose and no adequate organization our party may make so poor a showing in the local and state congressional elections during the next three years as to be put out of the ring."[5] Roosevelt and his more practical allies in the Progressive party agreed that the service played a valuable part in developing and publicizing progressive programs, but they believed that it did little to further the party's urgent need for grassroots organization and that those who ran it little understood the necessities involved in building and maintaining a party.

Indeed, as the previous chapter suggested, the very doctrine of the Progressive party, its celebration of "pure" democracy, was not congenial to party politics. Measures such as the direct primary subordinated parties as collective organizations with a past and a future to the ambitions of candidates and the issues of the moment. More significant, measures of direct government, such as the initiative, recall, and referendum, presupposed an ongoing dialogue between representatives and their constituents about issues which denied parties their traditional responsibility to secure harmony in the ranks of the people. "If the parties . . . are going to continue to do as they have done for the last fifty years, make the issues, then the Progressive party would probably little show," Progressive congressman Victor Murdock of Kansas wrote to Perkins in March 1914. "But the nature of the times and the pressing new problems are such that the issues are going to make parties."[6]

In this sense, we have argued, the Progressive party was a party to end party politics. Alice Carpenter, a member of the Progressive National Service's Department of Popular Government and the architect of the Working Man's Progressive Party League, dedicated to enlisting the support of labor, brought this to the attention of Perkins, who sought to control her organizational activities. "The principle upon which I have organized my League is the principle inherent in the direct primary, and is the principle above all upon which the progressive movement is based: namely that the people themselves should have the power to name their own candidates, and the PEOPLE not the political organizations should rule."[7]

Thus, there was an inherent tension between the Progressives' reform ambition and their need to maintain a political organization to sustain it. The poor showing of the Progressive party in the 1914 campaign and the return of TR to the Republican party led to the final dissolution of the Progressives; but the dissolution of the party was foreordained by the very principles it championed.

Among the progressives, the principal champion of *party* government was Woodrow Wilson, whose thoughts on political reform were greatly influenced by his studies of and affection for the British parliamentary system.

Conceiving the idea that it was possible to strengthen the party system by remodeling the presidency somewhat after the pattern of the British prime minister, Wilson advanced the doctrine of responsible party government. Localized democracy, he believed, had to be replaced by a party system composed of national policy-oriented organizations capable of carrying out platforms or proposals presented to the people during the course of an election. To be sure, as we have noted, Wilson embraced many aspects of direct democracy, such as the direct primary; and his acceptance of the Progressive proposal for an administrative regulatory commission to control the abuses of business, resulting in the creation of the FTC in 1915, tended to advance further the progressive obsession with direct popular government. But, unlike his counterparts in the Progressive party, Wilson believed that political debate and resolution required parties, that a more national programmatic party system, advanced by popular presidential leadership, was a critical ingredient of a democratic nation. In his first term as president, Wilson provided an example of unified, "responsible" party government, working closely with his fellow Democrats in Congress to enact much of the New Freedom program on which he had campaigned for office.

Wilson's presidency, in turn, had a strong influence on Franklin Roosevelt, whose extraordinary party leadership both anticipated and influenced the report of the American Political Science Association (APSA), *Toward a More Responsible Two Party System*, published in 1950, which gave prominence to the responsible party doctrine.[8] Indeed, E. E. Schattschneider, who chaired the APSA committee, notes in his seminal *Party Government* (1942), a volume that contains many of the ideas that would inform *Toward a More Responsible Two Party System*, that FDR's attempt to reform the Democratic party, particularly the so-called purge campaign of 1938, represented "one of the greatest experimental tests of the nature of the party system ever made."[9]

The New Deal test of the nature of the American party system is the central focus of this chapter. Roosevelt's party leadership and the New Deal marked a critical historical moment in the development of the American party system, namely the culmination of efforts, which began in the Progressive Era, to loosen the grip of partisan politics on the councils of power, with a view to shoring up national administrative power and extending the programmatic commitments of the federal government. No less than Progressive reformers, FDR and his New Deal allies viewed the traditional two-party system as an obstacle to the creation of a modern state. The New Deal commitment to building such a state meant that party politics had to be reconstituted or destroyed. Paradoxically, New Deal politics both transformed and weakened partisanship in the United States. On the one hand, Roosevelt's efforts to infuse the Democratic party with, as he put it, a commitment to "militant liberalism" established the foundation of a more national and programmatic party system.[10] On the other hand, the New Deal facilitated the development of a "modern presidency" and administrative apparatus that displaced party politics and collective responsibility with executive administration.

Roosevelt was, therefore, both very serious and somewhat unsure in his efforts to alter the basis of the American party system. Although FDR wanted to change the character of the Democratic party and thereby also effect a change in the two-party system, he concluded ultimately that the public good and practical politics demanded that partisan politics be deemphasized rather than restructured. In particular, once the presidency and the executive department were "modernized," some of the burden of party loyalty would be alleviated, freeing the chief executive, as leader of the whole people, to affect more directly the development of society and the economy. So shaped by this dual purpose, New Deal party politics, more than any other critical period of party development, reveals the possibilities and limits of party government in the United States.

Programmatic Liberalism and the American Party System

In the introduction to the 1938 volume on his presidential papers and addresses, written in 1941, Roosevelt explains that his efforts to modify the Democratic party were undertaken to strengthen party responsibility to the electorate and to commit his party more fully to progressive reform:

> I believe it to be my sworn duty, as President, to take all steps necessary to insure the continuance of liberalism in our government. I believe, at the same time, that it is my duty as head of the Democratic party to see to it that my party remains the truly liberal party in the political life of America.
>
> There have been many periods in American history, unfortunately, when one major political party was no different than the other major party—except only in name. In a system of party government such as ours, however, elections become meaningless when the two major parties have no differences other than their labels. For such elections do not give the people of the United States an opportunity to decide upon the

type of government which they prefer for the next two or the next four years as the case may be. . . .

Generally speaking, in a representative form of government, there are generally two schools of political belief—liberal and conservative. The system of party responsibility in American politics requires that one of its parties be the liberal party and the other the conservative party.[11]

Like his progressive forebears, then, Roosevelt's party politics were based on constitutional and policy considerations. He believed that democratic government required a more meaningful link between the councils of government and the electorate; furthermore, he reasoned that the clarification of political choice and centralization of authority would allow for more advantageous conditions to bring about meaningful policy action at the national level. He wanted to overcome the state and local orientation of the party system, which was suited to congressional primacy and poorly organized for progressive action by the national government, and to establish a national executive-dominated party that would be more suitably organized for the expression of national purposes.

At first glance, FDR's understanding of party government seemed to parallel that of Woodrow Wilson. According to Wilson, the major flaw of American political parties was their link with an interpretation of the Constitution which emphasized a decentralization of power. The decentralized structure of parties had served the country well enough during the nineteenth century, providing a useful context for facilitating consensus and coordinating the limited national purpose in government. But Wilson thought that further progress in American society required the development of party organizations that could be vessels of a stronger and more permanent expression of national purpose: "Party organization is no longer needed for the mere rudimentary task of holding the machinery together or giving it the sustenance of some common object, some single cooperative motive. The time is at hand when we can safely maximize the network of party without imperilling its strength. This thing that has served us so well might now master us if left irresponsible. We must see that it is made responsible."[12]

To make parties more responsible, Wilson initially proposed major institutional reforms that would establish closer ties between the executive and the legislature in an arrangement akin to the British cabinet system. Specifically, the young Wilson proposed that the Constitution be amended to "give the heads of the Executive departments—the members of the Cabinet—seats in

Congress, with the privilege of the initiative in legislation and some part in the unbounded privileges now commanded by the Standing Committees."[13] The president, who, in Wilson's view, had been rendered virtually useless in the aftermath of the Civil War, would become a figurehead like the monarch in England.

Wilson never abandoned the idea that the constitutional system of checks and balances should be replaced by an American version of the parliamentary system, but his preference did shift from Congress to the presidency as the institution through which to realize this end. Impressed by many aspects of the presidency of Theodore Roosevelt, Wilson concluded that the president, as leader of national opinion, could perform the task of "prime minister," concerning himself "as much with the guidance of legislation as with the orderly execution of the law."[14] For the president to perform such a role in fusing the executive and legislature, however, the party system would have to be modified so that it would serve the president. As noted in Chapter 3, Wilson disagreed strongly with TR about certain institutional and policy matters, but he credited him for charting a new path of presidential leadership. "Whatever else we may think or say of Theodore Roosevelt," Wilson said in 1909, "we must admit that he was an aggressive leader. He led Congress—he was not driven by Congress. We may not approve of his methods but we must concede that he made Congress follow him."[15]

Roosevelt's success persuaded Wilson that a new theory of party government was needed to justify and make routine the forceful display of presidential leadership. Roosevelt had shown that it was not necessary to amend the Constitution to bring about a closer relationship between its elected branches; rather, the task was to use the existing powers of the executive more fully. "His office," Wilson said of the president, "is anything he has the sagacity and force to make it."[16] Roosevelt had done much to fulfill the promise of the presidency, but Wilson believed that TR was too inclined to act in defiance and appeal over the heads of Congress. The radical potential of TR's leadership was confirmed by the 1912 election, in which he championed the right of the people to rule without suffering the interference of party organizations. For Wilson, constitutional democracy was representative democracy in which public officials were held accountable to the public. This form of responsible government was best accomplished not by direct popular rule, which risked demagogy, but by breaking down the barriers between the president and Congress. In this way, constitutional government's various parts would work in concert, but without violating the principles and institutions that protected the nation from an unhealthy aggrandizement of executive power.[17]

Wilson agreed with Roosevelt that the president must direct more attention to national problems, but he believed that executive leadership would be ineffective or dangerous unless it was accompanied by a fundamental change in the government's working arrangements. Such a change would combine the usually separated branches of the government. Most significant, the president's role as party leader would be strengthened. Instead of limiting executive power, as it had during much of the nineteenth century, the party system would be modified to enable the president to command Congress's support.

In practice, Wilson found it difficult to reconcile progressivism with the demands of party leadership. To be sure, he established himself as a leader of public opinion in a way that helped transform the presidency. Indeed, his ability to bring the pressure of public opinion upon Congress and assert dominance over the party caucuses in both legislative chambers made Wilson the principal spokesman for the Democratic party. At the same time, Wilson was persuaded by Postmaster General Albert Burleson, a veteran of Congress, to accept traditional partisan practices concerning legislative deliberations and appointments. This strategy, combined with his ability to mobilize public opinion, gave Wilson nearly absolute mastery of the Democratic party and its members in Congress, but it failed to strengthen the Democratic party organization or its commitment to progressive principles.[18]

Franklin Roosevelt was less committed than Wilson to working through existing partisan channels; more important, the New Deal was a more fundamental departure from traditional Democratic politics than Wilsonian progressivism. Until the 1930s, the patron saint of the Democrats had been Thomas Jefferson, and it was widely understood that this heritage implied a commitment to individual autonomy, states' rights, and a limited role for the national government. As discussed in Chapter 2, the Jeffersonian party system, designed to keep power close enough to the people for republican government to prevail, advanced a public philosophy that supported a strict interpretation of the national government's powers. With Jefferson, American political parties were organized as popular institutions, but they were formed when popular rule meant limiting the power of the national government. Before the New Deal, presidents who sought to exercise executive power expansively, or perceived a need to expand the national government's powers, were thwarted, as Stephen Skowronek notes, "by the tenacity of this highly mobilized, highly competitive, and locally oriented democracy."[19] Even Woodrow Wilson's program for extending the role of the national government remained in its essentials committed to the Jeffersonian principle of decentralized power. As the leader of the Democratic party, and thus as the progressive heir to Jefferson, Wilson promised tariff reform, an overhaul of the banking and currency system, and a vigorous antitrust program that would "disentangle" the "colossal community of interest" and restore fair competition to the economy.[20]

Indeed, Herbert Croly, whose progressivism sought to infuse the Hamiltonian tradition with democratic meaning and purpose, lamented Wilson's victory in 1912 as the triumph of "a higher conservatism over progressive democracy." As noted earlier, Croly supported Theodore Roosevelt and his Progressive party campaign, viewing TR as the only candidate in the campaign to advocate "the substitution of frank social policy for the individualism of the past."[21] After 1914, Wilson would come to support many elements of the Progressive program, such as direct leadership of public opinion, national administration of commercial activity, and civil service reform. But this conversion to advanced progressivism only exposed the yawning gap between, on the one hand, Wilson's pretenses to serving as a national progressive leader, and, on other hand, his allegiance to a decentralized and patronage-based party.[22]

The decisive break with the American tradition of limited government, anticipated by Theodore Roosevelt's Progressive party campaign of 1912, came with Franklin Roosevelt in the 1930s and his deft reinterpretation of the "liberal" tradition in the United States. Liberalism had always been associated with Jeffersonian principles and the natural rights tradition of limited government drawn from John Locke's *Second Treatise on Government* and the Declaration of Independence. Roosevelt pronounced a new liberalism in which constitutional government and the natural rights tradition were not abandoned but linked to programmatic expansion and an activist national government. As the public philosophy of the New Deal, this new liberalism, in its programmatic form, required a rethinking of the idea of natural rights in American politics.

Roosevelt first spoke of the need to modernize elements of the old faith in his Commonwealth Club address, delivered during the 1932 campaign and appropriately understood as the New Deal manifesto. The theme was that the time had come—indeed, had come three decades earlier—to recognize the "new terms of the old social contract." It was necessary to rewrite the social contract to take account of the national economy remade by industrial capitalism and the concentration of economic power. With the adoption of a new compact, the American people would establish a countervailing power—a stronger national state—lest the United States steer a "steady course toward economic oligarchy." Protection of the national welfare must shift from the private citizen to the government; the guarantee of equal opportunity required that individual initiative be restrained and directed by the national state:

> Clearly all this calls for a reappraisal of values. Our task now is not dis-
> covery or exploitation of natural resources or necessarily producing new
> goods. It is the soberer and less dramatic business of administering
> resources and plants already in hand, of seeking to reestablish foreign
> markets for our surplus production, of meeting the problem of under
> consumption, of adjusting production to consumption, of distributing
> wealth and products more equitably, of adapting existing economic
> organizations to the service of the people. The day of enlightened
> administration has come.[23]

The creation of a national state with expansive supervisory powers would be a "long, slow task." The Commonwealth Club address was sensitive to the uneasy fit between energetic central government and constitutional princi-ples in the United States. It was imperative, therefore, that the New Deal be informed by a public philosophy in which the new concept of state power would be carefully interwoven with earlier conceptions of American govern-ment. The task of modern government, FDR announced, was "to assist the development of an economic declaration of rights, an economic constitu-tional order." The traditional emphasis in American politics on individual self-reliance should therefore give way to a new understanding of individual-ism in which the government acted as a regulating and unifying agency, guar-anteeing individual men and women protection from the uncertainties of the marketplace. Thus, the most significant aspect of the departure from natural rights to programmatic liberalism was the association of constitutional rights with the extension, rather than the restriction, of the role of the national gov-ernment.

The need to construct an economic constitutional order, first articulated in the Commonwealth Club address, was a consistent theme of Roosevelt's long presidency. The 1936 platform was, at FDR's insistence, written as a pas-tiche of the Declaration and emphasized the need for a fundamental reexamination of rights; if the national government was to meet its obligations, the natural rights tradition had to be enlarged to include programmatic rights. With respect to the 1935 Social Security legislation, the platform claims:

> We hold this truth to be self-evident—that the test of representative government is its ability to promote the safety and happiness of the people. .
> . . We have built foundations for the security of those who are faced with the hazards of unemployment and old age; for the orphaned, the crippled, and the blind. On the foundation of the Social Security Act we are determined to erect a structure of economic security for all our people, making sure that this benefit shall keep step with the ever-increasing capacity of America to provide a high standard of living for all its citizens.[24]

As FDR would later detail in his 1944 State of the Union address, constructing a foundation for economic security meant that the inalienable rights protected by the Constitution—speech, press, worship, due process—had to be supplemented by a new bill of rights "under which a new basis of security and property can be established for all—regardless of station, race, or creed." Included in the second bill of rights were the right to a useful and remunerative job; the right to own enough to provide adequate food and clothing and recreation; the right to adequate medical care; the right to a decent home; the right to adequate protection from the economic fears of old age, sickness, accident, and unemployment; and the right to a good education.[25]

These new rights were never formally ratified as part of the Constitution, but they became the foundation of political dialogue, redefining the role of the national government. In the wake of the Roosevelt revolution, nearly every public policy was propounded as a right, attempting to confer constitutional status on programs like Social Security, Medicare, welfare, and food stamps. As such, the new social contract heralded by Roosevelt marks the beginning of the so-called rights revolution. With the advent of the New Deal political order, an understanding of rights dedicated to limiting government gradually gave way to a more expansive understanding of rights, a transformation in the governing philosophy of the United States which required major changes in American political institutions.

The defense of progressive reforms in terms of extending the rights of the Constitution was a critical development in the advent of a positive understanding of government responsibility. The distinction between progressives and conservatives, as boldly set forth by the New Nationalist campaign of 1912, all too visibly challenged the prevailing principles of constitutional government and the self-interested basis of American politics. Indeed, as noted in Chapter 3, the Progressives' dream of national community portended an unvarnished majoritarianism that threatened the Constitution's promise to protect individual freedom against the vagaries of public opinion. John Dewey's struggles during the 1920s to seek a reconciliation between localized democracy and progressive ideals suggested that progressivism could have an enduring effect on the American polity only insofar as it could be transformed into a new liberal tradition, one that viewed the state as the guarantor of social and economic welfare. Roosevelt's "economic constitutional order," in fact, bore striking resemblance to a six-part series Dewey contributed to the *New Republic* in 1929 and 1930 entitled "Individualism, Old and New," which anticipated many elements of the Commonwealth Club address. These essays drew on Croly's distinction between localized and progressive democracy; however, whereas Croly had called for the "*substitution* of frank social policy for the *individualism of the past*," Dewey advocated a reform program suited to a *new understanding of* individualism, one that was appropriate for the modern social and economic stresses of the late 1920s.[26] The great stock market crash of October 1929 seemed to vindicate Dewey's intense dissatisfaction with laissez-faire liberalism and to clarify the boundaries of the new liberalism he advocated. "Fear of loss of work, dread of the oncoming of old age, create an anxiety and eat into self-respect in a way that impairs personal dignity," he wrote. "Where fears abound, courageous and robust individuality is undermined."[27]

From Dewey, New Dealers discovered how to get around the American hostility to centralized administration and persuade Americans that expansive national power was consistent with their revered traditions. "The great tradition of America is liberal," the philosopher H. M. Kallen wrote in 1935, "and [Dewey] restates in the language and under the conditions of his time what Jefferson's Declaration of Independence affirmed in the language and under the conditions of his."[28]

Roosevelt's concept of an "economic constitutional order" borrowed from Dewey the idea that the personal dignity of the democratic individual now required a strengthening of national resolve. The New Deal understanding of reform, however, appealed more directly to the American constitutional tradition by asserting the connection between nationalism and rights, albeit rights that looked beyond the original social contract. Roosevelt gave legitimacy to progressive principles by embedding them in the language of constitutionalism and interpreting them as an *expansion* rather than a *subversion* of the natural rights tradition.

Roosevelt's reappraisal of values is important to understanding the New Deal, but it is also important in understanding his influence on the Democratic party. Under the leadership of Roosevelt, the Democrats became the instrument of greater national purpose. Ultimately, this purpose was directed to the creation of an administrative state that would displace partisan politics with "enlightened administration." The New Deal attempt to *transcend* rather than *reform* the American party system bespeaks the limited prospects for establishing party government in the United States.

For New Dealers, the idea of the welfare state was not a partisan issue. It was a "constitutional" matter that required eliminating partisanship about the national government's obligation to provide economic security for the American people. Nevertheless, such a displacement of partisan politics required in the short run a major partisan effort to generate popular support for the economic constitutional order. To a point, this made partisanship an integral part of New Deal politics, for it was necessary to remake the Democratic party as an instrument to free the councils of government, particularly the president and bureaucracy, from the restraints of traditional party politics and constitutional understandings.

Party Responsibility and the New Deal

Franklin Roosevelt was less diffident than Wilson about overcoming the limits of constitutional government, and he was more intent on transforming the principles and organization of the Democratic party. As president-elect, FDR prepared to modify the partisan practices of previous administrations and soon after his election began to evaluate the personnel policy of Wilson with a view to committing his own administration to more progressive appointments. Josephus Daniels, Wilson's secretary of the navy, wrote a letter to Roosevelt in December 1932 noting that President-elect Wilson had promised to "nominate progressives—and only progressives." The "pity," Daniels complained, was that, especially during his first term, Wilson adhered to traditional patronage practices and "appointed some who wouldn't recognize a Progressive principle if he met it in the road."[29] A few weeks later, FDR expressed to Attorney General Homer Cummings his desire to avoid Wilson's betrayal of the pledge to appoint reformers to the executive branch.

According to Cummings, Roosevelt was determined to proceed along different lines with a view "to building up a national organization rather than allowing patronage to be used merely to build Senatorial and Congressional machines."[30]

During his first term, FDR generally followed traditional partisan practices, allowing the Democratic national chairman, James Farley, to coordinate appointments in response to local organizations and Democratic senators, but the recommendations of organization people were not followed so closely after 1936. Beginning especially after 1938, Roosevelt's assault on the traditional party apparatus became more aggressive, and patronage practices began to circumvent the regular organization altogether. White House aides, notably Thomas Corcoran, became more influential in dispensing patronage. Ed Flynn, who became Democratic chairman in 1940, recalls the growing tension between Farley and Roosevelt:

> By reason of the coolness between the two, the President turned more and more frequently to the so-called New Dealers who were then surrounding him. Under the leadership of Corcoran, these people became more and more pressing in their urging of appointments. In a sense, this short-circuited the National Committee over which Farley presided. As a result, many of the appointments in Washington went to men who were supportive of the President and believed in what he was trying to do, but who were not Democrats in many instances, and in all instances were not organization Democrats.[31]

From a political point of view, Roosevelt's departure from conventional patronage practices resulted, as Paul Van Riper notes, "in the development of another kind of patronage, a sort of intellectual and ideological patronage rather than the more traditional partisan type."[32] In bypassing the state party leaders and the national committee in selecting personnel, the administration was in a sense politically nonpartisan, but careful attention was given to the political commitments and associations of appointees, thus resulting in a loosely knit, albeit well-defined, group of individuals whose loyalties were to the New Deal rather than the Democratic party.

FDR's attempt to make the Democrats into a more national party focused not only on the national committee, which was dominated by state and local party leaders, but also on Congress, which registered state and local policy interests at the national level. Whereas Wilson was careful to associate himself with legislative party leaders in the development of his policy program, Roosevelt relegated the party in Congress to a decidedly subordinate status. Though he used Farley and Vice President John Nance Garner, especially during the first term, to maintain close ties with Congress, party leaders complained that they were called into consultation only when their signatures were required at the bottom of the page to make the document legal. Moreover, FDR offended party leaders by his use of press conferences to announce important decisions before he communicated them to a coordinate branch of government.

Thus, by the end of Roosevelt's first term, Congress was "chafing at its subordinate position," and much more than after the first four years of Wilson's presidency it was looking for an opportunity to rebuke this popular president who threatened to relegate it to the position of a "rubber stamp."[33] Wilson's cultivation of party leaders in Congress reflected his interest in giving constitutional form to a parliamentary system, or at least an approximation of that system. In contrast, Roosevelt saw the party as a limited means to strengthen administration and reconstruct the nation's political economy. He supported a stronger role for parties, at least in the short run, to mobilize public support for his program. With respect to government, however, Roosevelt tended to view traditional party politics as an obstacle to be overcome more than an institution to be reformed.

Roosevelt, therefore, made little use of the congressional party caucus. He rejected as impractical, for example, the suggestion of Indiana representative Alfred Phillips Jr. "that those sharing the burden of responsibility of party government should regularly and often be called into caucus and that such caucuses should involve party policies and choice of party leaders." FDR politely suggested that Phillips' proposal to use the caucus as an instrument of party responsibility foundered on the rock of organization. "Frankly, it is a question of machinery—how to do it. . . . After all, there are four hundred and thirty-five Congressman and ninety six Senators, many of whom have very decided ideas on individual points which they are not at all hesitant to explain at any meeting which might be held."[34]

Roosevelt's refusal to confine his consultation to party leaders, relying instead on New Deal loyalists, many of whom had little connection to the regular Democratic organization, marked an unprecedented challenge to party responsibility as traditionally understood in American politics. "If Democrats on Capitol Hill have any pride in the New Deal," the former White House adviser Stanley High wrote in 1937, "it is certainly not the pride of authorship.

Its authorship goes back to the President himself, and to the assortment of political hybrids with which he was surrounded."[35]

In challenging traditional party practices, Roosevelt's primary concern was the South, a Democratic stronghold since the Civil War whose commitment to states' rights represented, as the journalist Thomas Stokes put it, "the ball and chain which hobbled the party's forward march."[36] An important victory in the campaign for a more national and programmatic party came in 1936 when the Roosevelt administration succeeded in abolishing the Democratic party's two-thirds rule. Adopted in 1832, this rule required backing from two-thirds of the delegates to Democratic national conventions for the nomination of president and vice president. The South had long regarded the rule as a vital protection against the nomination of candidates unsympathetic to its problems. Although assailed by certain quarters in the party as violating the democratic principle of majority rule, allowing as it did one-third plus one of the delegates to prevent a decision, it was defended and maintained by those Democrats who adhered to the parties' traditional support for local self-government, on the philosophical ground that American democracy owed protection to local interests. The two-thirds rule was also justified, its proponents argued, because it guarded the most reliable Democratic section since the Civil War, the South, against the less habitually loyal North, East, and West.[37]

Elimination of the rule weakened southern Democrats and removed an important obstacle to the transformation of a decentralized party responsible only to local concerns into an organization more responsible to the will of a national party leader—the president—and the interests of the national electorate. It was just this possibility that deeply troubled the conservative North Carolina senator Josiah Bailey. "The abolition of the two-thirds rule will enable the Northern and Western Democrats to control the Party, nominate its candidates and write its platform," he wrote soon after the 1936 convention. "All this will come out in 1940."[38]

To be sure, Roosevelt's command of the party, as the rise of the so-called conservative coalition in the Seventy-fifth Congress (1937–38) attests, did not overcome factionalism within Democratic ranks. But New Deal programs and party reforms did alter the structure of conflict within the party. Historically a decentralized party dominated by sectional interests, the Democrats after 1936 became a more national, bifactional party with durable ideological and policy divisions between liberals and conservatives.[39] Roosevelt's disregard for conventional partisan practices during his first term opened its ranks to an array of liberal groups and movements, thus making possible the reestablish-

ment of the party's majority for the first time since the Civil War. But the aspirations of the new liberal claimants—notably labor, blacks, Jews, and
women—clashed with those of most southern Democrats, who still maintained a strong presence in the party councils.[40] Southern Democrats played
the leading role in weakening the president's hours and wages bill and in
defeating the controversial institutional reforms that dominated Roosevelt's
second term, namely, the court reform bill and the executive reorganization
proposal. As Homer Cummings wrote in his diary on August 1, 1937, "It is generally felt that back of all these various fights, including the Supreme court
fight, there lies the question of the nomination of 1940, and incidental control
of party destinies."[41]

The most dramatic moment in this battle for the soul of the Democratic
party was the "purge" campaign of 1938. This involved FDR directly in one
gubernatorial and several congressional Democratic primary campaigns in a
bold effort to replace conservative Democrats with candidates who were "100
percent New Dealers." Roosevelt selected most of the individual targets of the
purge campaign from conservative southern and border states. If the Democratic party was eventually to become a national liberal party, southern
Democracy would have to be defeated.

The purge campaign was undertaken not only to overcome the obstacle
posed by conservative Democrats to completion of the New Deal but also to
alter the structure of the party system. Unlike Wilson, FDR always doubted
that political parties in the United States could be modeled after the British
system of party government. Nevertheless, he realized that if programmatic
liberals were to have a place in future Democratic administrations, chief executives had to be made less dependent on the convention system and the regular partisan apparatus, which was dominated by Congress and state party leaders.

Roosevelt's attempt to influence his party's nomination contests was not
unprecedented. William Howard Taft and Woodrow Wilson had made limited efforts to remove recalcitrants from their parties. But Roosevelt's campaign took place on an unprecedentedly large scale and, unlike previous
efforts, made no attempt to work through regular partisan channels. In all but
one case, Roosevelt chose to make a direct appeal to public opinion, rather
than attempt to cooperate with or reform the regular party apparatus. Indeed,
during the general election campaign, Roosevelt announced that he would
prefer liberal Republicans to conservatives of his own party and that he would
continue to campaign for the election of liberals in national and state politics,

regardless of their party affiliation.[42] The degree to which such action was viewed as a shocking departure from the norm is indicated by the press's labeling of it as the "purge," a term associated with Adolf Hitler's attempt to weed out dissension in Germany's National Socialist party and Joseph Stalin's elimination of "disloyal" party members from the Soviet Communist party. Although FDR's "purge" was hardly despotic, the "campaign for saving liberalism," as he called it, was a jarring departure from the traditions of party politics in the United States. As Democratic chairman James Farley observed, Roosevelt had violated "a cardinal political creed" of American politics: "that the President keep out of local matters."[43]

Roosevelt and his political allies believed, however, as one aide put it, that "The President, and not either party, was now the instrument of the people as a whole."[44] In truth, the conditions seemed right for a presidential challenge to partisan responsibility in 1938. Columnist Raymond Clapper, in fact, suggested that developments since Wilson's occupation of the White House had made the sort of campaign FDR waged against conservative Democrats inevitable. "It awaited only the appearance of a strong president in a highly controversial setting."[45]

First, the direct primary had become the principal method of nominating candidates, thus providing an opportunity for a direct appeal to the electorate. With the decline of progressive idealism, a vigorous movement emerged in the 1920s dedicated to restoring the convention system. Attempts to repeal direct primary laws were made in at least three-fourths of the states. For the most part, however, the repeal movement made little progress, its successes proving to be transitory. "The [party] organizations would repeal the [direct primary] laws if they had the power," the progressive reformer Charles Merriam wrote in 1926, "but the mass of voters apparently have no intention of returning to the old delegate system with which they were familiar twenty years ago and under which they suffered grievous misrepresentation."[46] By the 1930s, only three states—Connecticut, New Mexico, and Rhode Island— used the convention system of nomination exclusively. In the remaining forty-five states, candidates for most public offices were chosen in direct primaries.[47] This new primary system had begun to weaken greatly the grip of local party organizations on the electorate. For example, William H. Meier, a Democratic county chairman from Nebraska, wrote Farley in 1938 that his state's direct primary law had "created a situation which made candidates too independent of the party."[48]

The spread of the direct primary gave the president the opportunity to appeal directly to the people over the heads of congressional candidates and local party leaders. It thereby provided an attractive vehicle for an attack on traditional party politics, which Roosevelt saw as an obstacle to his policy objectives. Like TR and Wilson, Roosevelt supported the direct primary. In launching the 1938 purge, he noted: "Fifty years ago party nominations were generally made in conventions—a system typified in the public imagination by a little group in a smoke filled room who made out the party slates. The direct primary was invented to make the nominating process a more direct one—to give the party voters themselves a chance to pick their candidates."[49]

Furthermore, radio broadcasting had made the opportunity to appeal directly to large audiences even more enticing. Of course, the use of the mass media was bound to be especially tempting to an extremely popular president with as fine a radio presence as Roosevelt. Indeed, FDR's close associate Felix Frankfurter encouraged him to go to the country in the midst of his monumental struggles with the Seventy-fifth Congress, assuring him that "the contagiousness of [his] personality over the radio, the warmth of [his] voice and [his] being," would "renew [the public's] dependence on [him]." Frankfurter was "absolutely right," FDR responded a few days later. In anticipation of the purge campaign, he wrote, "I feel like saying to the country—'You will hear from me soon and often. This is not a threat but a promise.'"[50]

A few months later, the White House convened an "elimination committee," a small circle of New Dealers who were charged with the task of planning the assault on conservative Democrats which would take place during the 1938 primary campaigns. It was headed by two intimate White House advisors—Harry Hopkins, who assumed a general supervisory role, and Thomas Corcoran, who became the day-to-day head of operations. Roosevelt formally launched the purge campaign with a fireside chat to the nation on June 24, 1938. The speech was prepared by Corcoran and another member of the elimination committee, Ben Cohen; but Roosevelt himself dictated the most vital passage of the message, drawing a distinction between liberals and conservatives and proclaiming his intention to liberalize the Democratic party. Liberals, the President told the nation, insisted that "new remedies could be adopted and maintained successfully in this country under the present form of government if we use government as an instrument of cooperation to provide for these remedies." True liberals were opposed, therefore, "to the kind of moratorium on reform which, in effect, is reaction itself." In contrast to the liberal pursuit of circumspect but intrepid progress, conservatives rejected change willy-nilly. "The . . . conservative school of thought . . . does not recognize the need for government itself to step in and take action to meet these problems," FDR argued. "It believes individual initiative and private philanthropy will solve them—that we ought to repeal many of the things we have done and go back . . . to the kind of government we had in the twenties."[51]

The critical question in the coming primaries, Roosevelt concluded, was: To which of these schools of thought do the candidates belong? As head of the Democratic party, FDR argued, he was charged with the responsibility of carrying out liberal principles, to speak "in those few instances where there may be a clear issue between Democratic candidates for a Democratic nomination." Leaving little doubt as to where the most critical contests would take place, Roosevelt characterized his political opponents as "Copperheads," who, he reminded the nation, "in the days of the war between the States tried to their best to make Lincoln and his Congress give up the fight, let the nation remain split in two and return to peace—peace at any price."[52] That Copperheads were the antiwar faction of the northern Democratic party gave little comfort to southerners. Roosevelt's reference to the events of the Civil War and the fact that he most actively sought to unseat incumbent Democrats in the South conjured up images of a renewed northern assault on the region, one "that would precipitate another reconstruction era for us," as the conservative Virginia senator Carter Glass wrote a friend.[53]

A New Deal reconstruction of southern politics portended more than a cyclical realignment of parties. It suggested the possibility of a party transformation that progressive advocates of a responsible party system, beginning with Woodrow Wilson, had long advocated. "What he wanted," Farley feared, "was a European system of liberal and conservative."[54] Roosevelt's defense of his attack on conservative Democrats appeared to confirm such a view of the purge:

> My participation in these primary campaigns was slurringly referred to, by those who were opposed to liberalism, as a "purge." The word became a slogan for those who tried to misrepresent my conduct to make it appear to be an effort to defeat certain Senators and Representatives who had voted against one measure or another recommended by me. . . . Nothing could be further from the truth. I was not interested in personality. Nor was I interested in particular measures. . . . I was, however, primarily interested in seeing to it that the Democratic party and the Republican party should not be merely Tweedledum and Tweedledee to

each other. I was chiefly interested in continuing the Democratic party as a liberal, forward looking party in the United States.[55]

Administrative Reform and the Necessity of Party Decline

After the 1938 purge campaign, Raymond Clapper observed that "no president has ever gone as far as Mr. Roosevelt in striving to stamp his policies upon his party."[56] This extraordinary partisan effort began a process whereby the party system was eventually transformed from local to national and programmatic party organizations. At the same time, the New Deal made partisanship, at least as it affected the beliefs and habits of the electorate, less important. Roosevelt's partisan leadership, although it did effect important changes in the Democratic party, and eventually the Republican party as well, ultimately envisioned a personal link with the public which would better enable him to make use of his position as leader of the nation, not just the leader of the party governing the nation.[57]

The members of the "elimination committee," like most of the New Dealers, were executives and lawyers who were essentially without organizational and popular support in the party. "The New Dealers without Roosevelt were a sect, not a majority," the historian Joseph Lash wrote about the purge committee. "Roosevelt's majority in the absence of party control was impotent." In the face of this difficulty, the task as defined by FDR was not to overhaul the party organization systematically—the purge team, by temperament and background, was ill suited to such a project. Rather, Roosevelt sought to put his stamp on the Democratic party by transmuting collective into executive responsibility.

In the final analysis, the "benign dictatorship" Roosevelt sought to impose on the Democratic party was corrosive to the American party system. Wilson's prescription for party reform—extraordinary presidential leadership—posed a serious, if not intractable, dilemma. The decentralized character of American politics can be modified only by strong presidential leadership, but a president determined to alter fundamentally the connection between the executive and the party will eventually shatter party unity. Indeed, Herbert Croly criticized Wilson's concept of presidential party leadership precisely on these terms: "As the final test the responsibility is his rather than that of his party. The party that submits to such a dictatorship, however benevolent, cannot play its own proper part in a system of partisan government. It will either cease to have any independent life or its independence will eventually assume the form of a revolt."

Although he shared Wilson's view that executive power needed to be strengthened, Croly argued that the "necessity of such leadership [was] itself evidence of the decrepitude of the two-party system." A strong executive would not reform parties but instead would establish the conditions in which partisan responsibility would decline and a more direct and palpable link between the president and public opinion would be created. The emergence of a modern executive and the destruction of the two-party system, Croly wrote, was "an indispensable condition of the success of progressive democracy."[58]

The report of the APSA committee, published five years after the Roosevelt presidency, expressed a similar view but warned that the weakening of political parties in the United States was leading to an "overextension" of presidential power. In language strikingly similar to Croly's, the report asserted that such an aggrandizement of executive responsibility was a dangerous alternative to, rather than an instrument of, party responsibility: "When the President's program actually is the sole program, either his party becomes a flock of sheep or the party falls apart. This concept of the presidency disposes of the party system by making the President reach directly for support to the majority of the voters." Only the creation of a more responsible party system, the report argued, "which could furnish the President and Congress a political basis for cooperation within the Constitution," could restrain the popular power of the president. And yet the authors offered no solution to the dilemma posed by Wilson's prescription for strengthening party responsibility.[59]

Roosevelt was well aware of the limited extent to which his purposes could be achieved by party government in the American context. As a member of the Wilson administration, FDR knew all too well that Wilson had found it very difficult to reconcile his progressivism with the demands of party leadership. Unlike Theodore Roosevelt and Herbert Croly, Roosevelt was not willing to abandon the party system. He believed partisan leadership within the traditional two-party framework, at least for the time being, was necessary to organize public opinion into a governing coalition. FDR was persuaded, however, that strengthening the state required the decline, if not the demise, of partisan politics. He shared the view of New Nationalism that the traditional party apparatus was for the most part beyond repair, so wedded was it to the fragmented institutions of American politics. For example, when Ray

Stannard Baker wrote FDR in September 1936, complaining of the Democratic machine in Massachusetts, which was dominated by the notorious local boss, James Curley, Roosevelt's response was one of sympathetic resignation. "There is, I fear, much too much in what you say," the president answered, "but what is a poor fellow to do about it: I wish I knew."[60]

Even if the intransigent localism of the party could be eliminated and a more national party system formed, there would still be the Constitution's separation of powers to overcome. These institutional arrangements, even with nationalized parties, would still encourage the free play of rival interests and factions, thus making ongoing cooperation between the president and Congress unlikely. Roosevelt's skepticism about party government—about the possibility of parties providing a political basis for cooperation between the president and Congress within the Constitution—helps to explain why the purge campaign was limited to a few Senate and House contests, for the most part in the South, rather than undertaken as a comprehensive nationwide strategy to elect New Dealers.

Many members of the elimination committee wanted to make, with just a few exceptions, 100 percent "followship" of presidential measures the criterion, with support of the court and executive reorganization bills the acid test. Enthusiastic backers of the purge who participated in the committee's deliberations, including Harry Hopkins and Thomas Corcoran, were not discouraged that such a standard would mark one-half of the Democratic senators seeking renomination and fully a majority of the members of the House. This would be a "straightforward" way to go about the realignment of liberals and conservatives as recommended by FDR in his fireside chat, the more enthusiastic members of the purge committee believed.[61] But Roosevelt's finer political instincts dictated a less comprehensive list. "He sought to make a few examples," Clapper wrote, "hoping thereby to cow other Senators and Representatives into a more submissive behavior and to keep his fight and his program a live crusading, dynamic thing in the public mind."[62]

There has been a good deal of controversy among public officials and scholars regarding the effect of Roosevelt's purge campaign. To some, the 1938 campaign was a success, even though most of the efforts to defeat recalcitrant Democrats failed. Most immediately, FDR's participation in the midterm campaign helped the reelection efforts of pro–New Deal incumbents, such as Florida senator Claude Pepper and Senate Majority Leader Alben Barkley of Kentucky. The press tended to credit the president and the elimination committee for these victories, thus encouraging Congress to enact wages and hours legislation, along with other parts of Roosevelt's program. The purge also succeeded in a critical New York contest, in which the administration's candidate, James Fay, defeated the conservative House Rules Committee chairman John J. O'Connor. So pleased was the president to cleanse the party of O'Connor that he insisted that the victory in New York made the entire purge campaign worthwhile. "Harvard lost the schedule but won the Yale game," he happily told the press.[63] Like the successful endorsements of Pepper and Barkley, the purging of O'Connor was of major importance to Roosevelt in smoothing the path of his bills in Congress.[64]

In addition to these tangible results, it has been argued, Roosevelt's intervention in the 1938 primaries revitalized party politics and laid the groundwork for a significantly more liberal Democratic party. To a degree, even in those cases in which the purge drive failed, candidates had to make peace with the New Deal program. Those who survived the president's assault, such as Senate incumbents Walter George of Georgia, Millard Tydings of Maryland, and "Cotton" Ed Smith of South Carolina, were careful not to attack Roosevelt and the New Deal directly; instead, they sought to turn the attention of the primary voters from economic matters, which favored Roosevelt, to racial and sectional conflicts, which highlighted the impropriety of a president interfering in local contests. It may be, as defenders of the purge have argued, that had Roosevelt not taken on conservatives within his party in such dramatic fashion, the Democratic party would have reverted to its Jeffersonian traditions.[65]

Nonetheless, the purge failed to imprint the New Deal indelibly on the party majority, thus reinforcing FDR's disinclination to seek a fundamental restructuring of the party system. The purge campaign was successful in only two of the twelve states targeted, New York, Roosevelt's home state, and Oregon, where New Deal sympathizer Henry Hess defeated incumbent governor Charles H. Martin. But the triumph over Martin proved to be a Pyrrhic one; the purge left the Oregon Democrats in disarray, condemning them to defeat in the general election. Indeed, the purge galvanized opposition throughout the nation, apparently contributing to the heavy losses the Democrats sustained in the 1938 general elections. Former Wisconsin governor Philip La Follette, one of several progressives who went down to crushing defeat in 1938, wrote in the *Nation* soon thereafter: "The results of the so-called purge campaign by President Roosevelt showed that the fight to make the Democratic party liberal is a hopeless one." FDR's failure went beyond the incorrigible provincialism of the Democratic party, however. Another defeated progressive governor, Frank Murphy of Michigan, lamented the "combination of habit and tradition . . . that brought reactionary victories in many states." Roosevelt's defeats in 1938, he concluded, were "deep rooted" and could "be permanently overcome only by the slow process of education."[66]

E. E. Schattschneider, chairman of the APSA Committee on Political Parties, drew a different conclusion. In a 1948 lecture, he asserted that the failed purge campaign did not render the struggle for party government a moot point. "The outcome of the purge of 1938," he argued, "does not prove that a more serious attempt supported by the whole body of national leaders could not bring overwhelming pressure to bear on the local party leaders who control congressional nominations."[67] But neither FDR nor any president since has risked a similar effort, let alone a more expansive one, to hold his fellow partisans to a national party program. The purge campaign and its aftermath suggest that resistance to party government under presidential leadership is not merely built into the Constitution and laws but is deeply rooted in a political culture that gives preference to a different way of governing.[68]

The Roosevelt administration's rejection of party government thus developed for reasons both practical and principled—for constitutional reasons that are at once excruciatingly American and a severe challenge to the traditional concept of government responsibility. In the "economic constitutional order," New Deal programs like Social Security were regarded as rights. In principle, these programs were to be permanent entitlements, like speech and assembly, beyond the vagaries of public opinion, elections, and party politics. Once they were established, programmatic rights would become an enduring feature of American government. As one New Dealer put it: "We may assume the nature of the problems of American life are such as not to permit any political party for any length of time to abandon most of the collectivist functions which are now being exercised. This is true even though the details of policy programs may differ and even though the old slogans of opposition to governmental activity will survive long after their meaning has been sucked out."[69]

Thus, the most significant institutional reform of the New Deal did not promote party government but fostered instead a program that would enable the president to govern in the *absence* of party government. The president would be manager of the people's rights. This program, as embodied in the 1937 executive reorganization bill, was based on the Brownlow Committee report.[70] It proposed measures that would significantly expand the staff support of the executive office and greatly extend presidential authority over the executive branch, including the independent regulatory commissions. As

Luther Gulick, a member of the committee, anticipated, the strengthened executive that would emerge from this reform would be delegated authority to govern. Laws would be little more than "a declaration of war, so that the essence of the program [would be] in the gradual unfolding of the plan in actual administration."[71]

Localized democracy shaped by party politics, therefore, would be replaced by the activities of a dominant and dominating presidency. Wilson had proposed and slouched toward a reconstituted party system in the hope of establishing stronger linkages between the executive and the legislature. In contrast, the administrative program of the New Deal would combine executive action and public policy, so that the president and administrative agencies would be delegated authority to govern, thus making unnecessary the constant cooperation of party members in Congress and the states. Louis Brownlow, in a 1943 memo, reflected on this objective of executive reorganization: "We must reconsider critically the scholarly assumption, that the way to produce unity between legislature and executive is to take steps toward merging the two." Thus, commenting specifically on a book proposal that the United States abandon its presidential system in favor of a parliamentary system, Brownlow added:

> In view of the extreme improbability that such a measure would receive organized support, it is worth mentioning only because it carries to a logical conclusion the common proposals (1) to have the Congress establish by statute a cabinet or administrative council for the president; (2) to give department heads or "Cabinet" members seats in the Congress, the right to take part in Congressional discussions, or the duty to defend their administration before Congress; (3) to set up a joint legislative-executive committee, or committees, to plan policy and supervise administration; and (4) to create a committee of congressional leaders to advise the President. . . . *In direct opposition to this assumption and these proposals, it may be suggested that the objective to be sought is not to unify the executive and legislature, but to unify governmental policy and administration.*[72]

Roosevelt and his administrative management committee believed responsible party government was contrary to American traditions. They looked instead to presidential government as a means to achieve an activist regime in the United States. To be sure, party politics were not irrelevant to the task of strengthening national administration. In fact, the Democratic party was to be used as a means to provide the president with greater control over the New Deal state, so that the executive office could become a more independent policymaker than was hitherto possible in American politics. The executive reorganization act became, at FDR's urging, a party program. Ironically, a policy aimed at making party politics less important became a major focus of party responsibility. So strongly did Roosevelt favor this legislation that House Majority Leader Sam Rayburn appealed for party unity before the critical vote on the executive reorganization bill, arguing that its defeat would amount to a "vote of no confidence" in the president.[73]

FDR lost this vote of confidence on administrative reform in April 1938 as the House of Representatives, with massive Democratic defections, voted down the legislation. It was a devastating defeat for Roosevelt, which, together with that of the court-"packing" bill, also closely linked to administrative power, led FDR to undertake the purge campaign a few months later. Significantly, the two Supreme Court decisions that enraged FDR the most were *Humphrey's Executor v. United States* and *Schechter Poultry Corp. v. United States*, both of which imposed constraints on the president's personal authority.[74] The *Humphrey* case denied the president the right to remove appointees from the independent regulatory commissions, a legal power that Roosevelt and his advisors thought had been settled by the 1926 case of *Myers v. United States*.[75] The *Schechter* ruling was a direct challenge to the modern state. It declared that the discretionary authority that Congress had granted, at Roosevelt's request, to the National Recovery Administration, the leading economic agency of the early New Deal, was an unconstitutional delegation of legislative power to the executive.

Thus, Roosevelt's "purge" campaign—his attempt to liberalize the Democratic party—marked an extraordinary effort to uphold a legislative program dedicated to establishing the presidency, rather than the Congress or the party organizations, as the principal agent of popular rule, "the steward of the public welfare." The purge failed at the polls, but it frightened some recalcitrant Democrats, who became more conciliatory toward their president on a few matters after the 1938 elections. Administrative reform was one of these, and in 1939 a reorganization bill passed Congress. Although considerably weaker than the original proposal, the 1939 Executive Reorganization Act provided authority for the creation of the Executive Office of the President, which included the newly formed White House Office and a strengthened and refurbished Bureau of the Budget; and it enhanced the chief executive's control of administrative agencies. As such, this legislation was, in effect, the organic statute of the "modern" presidency, which was better equipped to govern independently of the separation of powers. It set off a new dynamic whereby executive administration, coupled with the greater personal responsibility of the president enhanced by FDR's political leadership and the emergence of the mass media, displaced in important ways the collective responsibility of the president and Congress.

The battle for the destiny of the Democratic party during Roosevelt's second term, therefore, was directly tied to strengthening the presidency and the executive branch as the vital center of government action. FDR's success transformed the Democrats into a party of administration, dedicated to enacting an institutional program that would make parties less important. Like the Progressive party, the Democratic party became a party to end party politics. Theodore Roosevelt, Herbert Croly, and many of their allies had conceived of the Progressive party campaign as an assault on party politics. "FDR . . . ran against one opponent in his life—Teddy Roosevelt, his relative," one of his aides observed. "He admired Teddy's maverick tactics and his bold attacks on his own party. He did the same thing."[76]

Significantly, FDR accepted the nomination of his party in person at the 1932 Democratic convention. As noted in Chapter 3, the only previous major presidential candidate to accept the nomination of his party at a convention was Theodore Roosevelt, who, having bolted from the Republican party, appeared before the gathering in Chicago which launched the Progressive party campaign in 1912. It fell to FDR to institutionalize the challenge to regular party practices represented by the 1912 Progressive campaign. Unlike his cousin, Franklin Roosevelt presided over a full-scale partisan realignment, the first in American history to place executive leadership at the heart of its approach to politics and government. The traditional party system had provided presidents with a stable basis of popular support and, episodically, during critical partisan alignments, with the opportunity to achieve national reform. What was once episodic, New Deal reformers insisted, must now become routine. As the Brownlow Committee report put it, "Our national will must be expressed not merely in a brief, exultant moment of electoral decision, but in persistent, determined, competent day-by-day administration of what the nation has decided to do."[77]

Thus, the New Deal realignment prepared the ground for the decline of party, a development that FDR explicitly appreciated and supported. Interestingly, he chose the 1940 Jefferson-Jackson Day dinner, a party event, to herald a less partisan future. To establish the right mood, FDR went so far as to invite the Republican leaders to the Democratic celebration, an invitation they declined. In his address, Roosevelt observed that the independent vote was on the increase, that party loyalties were becoming less significant, and that "the future [lay] with those wise political leaders who realize[d] the great public [was] interested more in government than in politics." The future of the American political system, then, was predicated on the emergence of a policymaking state; its development meant that party politics and debate were subordinated to a "second bill of rights" and the delivery of services associated with those rights.

For a time, the modern presidency was at the center of this new political universe. With the strengthening of executive administration, the presidency became disassociated from party politics, undermining the latter's importance. As the presidency evolved into a ubiquitous institution, it preempted party leaders in many of their limited but significant tasks: linking the president to interest groups, staffing the executive department, policy development, and, most important, campaign support. Presidents no longer were elected and governed as head of a party but rather as the head of a personal organization created in their own image.

But the purpose of New Deal reform was not to strengthen presidential government per se. Rather, the presidency was strengthened on the assumption that as the national office it would be an ally of progressive reform. Consequently, executive power was refurbished in a way that was compatible with the objectives of programmatic liberalism, and administrative reform was intended to insulate reformers and reforms from the presidential election cycle. By executive orders issued with authority granted by the 1939 Executive Reorganization Act, most of the emergency programs of the New Deal were established as permanent institutions. Moreover, the Roosevelt administration obtained legislative authority in the 1940 Ramspeck Act to extend civil service protection for New Deal loyalists who were brought to Washington to staff the newly created welfare state.[78] New Deal civil service reform, therefore, did not replace politics with administration, nor did it replace patronage practices with civil service procedures dedicated to "neutral competence." Rather, it transformed the political character of administration. Previously, partisans and reformers offered a choice between politics and spoils on the one hand and nonpartisan, nonpolitical administration on the other. The New Deal celebrated an administrative politics that denied nourishment to the regular party apparatus but fed instead an executive department oriented toward expanding liberal programs.

Conclusion: The New Deal Legacy and the Doctrine Of Responsible Party Government

The reform vision of Woodrow Wilson, his hope of establishing a "responsible" two-party system, was preempted by the New Deal institutional program, which chartered an alternative path to a more national and programmatic government. This path, the New Dealers believed, was more compatible with the principles and history of American constitutional government. One of the architects of this program, Charles Merriam, observed in 1931 that he did not expect to see the development of a British-style party government in the United States. "There is little probability of a modification of the Constitution either by amendment or custom in such a fashion as to permit the adoption of a parliamentary system," he surmised, "in view of the fact that the trend is strongly in the direction of Presidential government, with constant strengthening of presidential power."[79] Merriam's commentary was not simply prescient; as a member of the Brownlow Committee, he would play an important part in consolidating the trends he observed. The consolidation of the modern presidency, however, was made possible by a dramatic though short-lived commitment to party responsibility.

Roosevelt imposed the task defined by the Brownlow Committee on the Democratic party and in doing so strengthened partisanship in the short term and carried out a great experiment on the character of the party system. But the test of responsible government transformed the Democratic party into a way station on the road to administrative government, to a centralized and bureaucratic form of democracy which focused on the president and executive agencies for the formulation and administration of public policy. Concomitantly, this development diminished the role of traditional party politics, Congress, and state legislatures.

To be sure, Roosevelt did not overcome the antibureaucratic tradition in the United States, which continued to play an important role in our political life. Indeed, Roosevelt's championing of a "second bill of rights" showed him to be ambivalent about this tradition. Roosevelt did not abolish the obstacles to the creation of a strong national state in the United States; in giving rise to economic rights, to what came to be called "entitlements," he unintentionally created new ones that would continue to deny the "national will." Now viewed as entitlements, New Deal programs became autonomous islands of power which would constrain presidents no less than localized parties. As Martha Derthick has written about the Social Security program, its architects "sought to foreclose the options of future generations by committing them irrevocably to a program that promises benefits by rights as well as those particular benefits that have been incorporated in an ever expanding law. In that sense they designed social security to be uncontrollable."[80]

In the final analysis, the New Deal gave rise to an administrative Constitution that established an uncertain foundation of strong presidential leadership. On the one hand, the rise of political administration as the center of government activity during the 1930s established the conditions for presidential government. FDR's extraordinary party leadership was institutionalized with the 1939 Executive Reorganization Act, for this statute ratified a process whereby public expectations and institutional arrangements established the president as the center of government activity. On the other hand, the administrative presidency was conceived with the expectation that it would be an ally of programmatic liberalism. It is not surprising, therefore, that when this expectation was violated with the rise of a conservative administrative presidency beginning in the 1970s, serious conflict developed between the presidency and the bureaucracy. Nor is it surprising that this conflict led to still another reform of administrative law with the objective of more effectively insulating reform programs from presidential influence.

Remaking American Politics

*Participatory Democracy
and the Triumph of
Administrative Politics*

Franklin Roosevelt's leadership and the institutional reforms he championed prepared the executive branch to be a government unto itself and established the presidency rather than the party as the locus of party responsibility. But the modern presidency was created to chart the course for, and direct the voyage to, a more liberal America. Roosevelt's pronouncement of "a second bill of rights" proclaimed and began this task, but it fell to Lyndon Johnson, as one journalist noted, "to codify the New Deal vision of the good society."[1] This program entailed expanding the economic constitutional order with such policy innovations as Medicare and, even more significant, extending more of its benefits to African Americans.

But Johnson was not content to complete the New Deal political order. He was not satisfied to go down in the history books as a successful president in the Roosevelt tradition. In a 1965 interview with LBJ, the historian William Leuchtenburg was startled by the president's strident criticism of Roosevelt, for whom Johnson had long expressed great reverence. FDR, Johnson declared, had won a great electoral victory in 1936, only to squander his political capital in the pursuit of executive dominion. Just as Roosevelt had aroused fears of executive aggrandizement in the court-"packing" and administrative reform bills, Johnson asserted, so his administration had to overcome "the fear of [presidential imperialism] that destroyed Franklin Roosevelt."[2]

In truth, Johnson's feelings for FDR were as competitive as they were pious; "he wanted to be the greatest of them all, the whole bunch of them."[3] LBJ's opportunity to surpass the reform accomplishments of his illustrious predecessor came with the landslide victory he won over conservative Republican Barry Goldwater in the 1964 election, which also swelled the Democratic margins in Congress. Johnson interpreted this victory as a mandate not only to expand but also to radicalize the reform aspirations of the 1930s: to build a Great Society. From the beginning of his presidency, in fact, Johnson had an ambitious program that advanced not only the New Deal goal of economic security but also the "quality of American life." In seeking to out-Roosevelt Roosevelt Johnson played a principal part in advancing a new version of programmatic liberalism which would remake American politics during the late 1960s and 1970s.

Interpreting the legacy of the Great Society for politics and government in the United States is a difficult business. Scholars tend to agree that the reforms of the 1960s and 1970s marked a transformation of political life no less important than the Progressive Era and the New Deal. Unlike these earlier reform periods, however, the 1960s and 1970s did not embrace national administrative power as an agent of social and economic justice. Instead, reformers of the 1960s and 1970s championed "participatory democracy" and viewed the very concept of national governmental authority with deep suspicion. Indeed, Hugh Heclo characterizes the reform legacy of the 1960s and 1970s as one of intractable fractiousness, as a "post-modern" assault on the modern state. "In the end, it appears that a great deal of post-modern policy making is not really concerned with 'making policy' in the sense of finding a settled course of public action that people can live with," he writes. "It is aimed at crusading for a cause by confronting power with power."[4]

Still, the institutional reforms of the 1960s and 1970s are miscast as an antinomian attack on government authority. To be sure, there was a large element of hostility to centralized administrative power evident in the politics of the New Left reformers who played an important part in the civil rights and antiwar movements of the 1960s. Moreover, the reform politics of these movements, championing community action and grassroots participation, inspired the self-styled "public interest" advocates of the 1970s who advanced policies that increased the national government's responsibilities to ameliorate racial and sexual discrimination and to enhance consumer rights and environmental protection. Notwithstanding their antiestablishment rhetoric and profound suspicion of centralized power, however, reform activists of the 1970s

were intrepid liberals who sought to remake rather than to dismantle government institutions. As Jeffrey Berry has written, "leaders of the new [public
interest groups] wanted to transcend 'movement politics' with organizations
that could survive beyond periods of intense emotion."[5] In truth, the public
interest movement sought to harness the revolutionary fervor of the civil rights
and antiwar movements as an agent for change within the system.

In seeking a departure from the progressive reforms of the past, public
interest advocates targeted the modern presidency. Committed to strengthening national administrative power in the service of economic security,
Franklin Roosevelt and his New Deal allies had advanced political reforms
that established the president, rather than Congress or the party organizations,
as the principal agent of popular rule. But the Great Society launched a new
phase of liberalism, emphasizing "quality of life" concerns and rejecting the
New Deal practice of delegating power to the executive branch. The president and executive agencies could perhaps distribute monthly checks to indi-
gents and sponsor public-work programs, thus contributing to income maintenance and job security. Many of the expressed concerns of the 1960s and
1970s, however, had little to do with money or public management. As Harry
McPherson, who served as a special counsel to Lyndon Johnson, put it, the
Great Society was born of the notion that "people were suffering from a sense
of alienation from one another, of anomie, of powerlessness. This affected the
well to do as much as it did the poor."[6] Consequently, reformers of the 1960s
and 1970s championed statutes and judicial rulings that would reduce the discretionary power of presidents and administrative agencies. Just as significant,
institutional arrangements were designed to foster "participatory democracy"—that is, to give power to those people most affected by government policy. Thus, the reform politics of the Great Society rediscovered the deeply
ingrained American distrust of national administrative power. As Anthony
King notes, "In the 1960s it came to be thought good for both the participating
individuals and the polity that ordinary men and women should have a direct
say not merely in the choice of public office holders but in the making of public policy."[7]

Rejecting the Jeffersonian tradition that championed political parties
centered in the states and localities as critical agents of political participation,
reformers of the 1960s and 1970s celebrated an idea of community *without*
party. We have noted that John Dewey held that progressive reforms would
reach their fulfillment in the creation of a "Great Community" that would
"order the relations and enrich the experience of local associations." So new

liberals hoped that the Great Society would free political participation from partisanship and thus cultivate a more enlightened form of community.[8]

Despite his desire to surpass Roosevelt's accomplishments, Johnson had no wish to depart from the style of politics in which he was steeped. Like FDR, Johnson was a presidentialist: the thrust of his institutional approach was to strengthen the managerial tools of the presidency with a view to enhancing the programmatic vision and energy in the executive branch. But the vision of the Great Society presupposed a "hunger for community" which suggested the limits of presidential government. It is not surprising, therefore, that one of the outside task forces established by Johnson to identify and seek solutions to social problems recommended that community action be made an integral part of the War on Poverty. In pursuance of this proposal, the Community Action Programs (CAPs), governed by federal guidelines requiring "maximum feasible participation of residents of the areas and groups served," were established to administer antipoverty policy.[9] Such programs actually played a limited part in the Johnson administration, which in an unprecedented fashion relied on presidential politics. But the Community Action Programs were an important and revealing prelude to the emergence of participatory democracy as a leading principle of the reformers of the late 1960s and 1970s who gained influence with the weakening of the modern presidency.

In part, the effort of reformers to circumscribe executive administration can be attributed to the emergence of "divided government" as a regular feature of political life in the United States. Richard Nixon's election in 1968 marked the beginning of an increased tendency for voters to place the presidency in Republican hands and Congress under the control of Democrats; this pattern of ticket splitting would endure for more than two decades. (As we will see in the next chapter, the election of 1994 reversed this pattern, at least for the moment.) New Deal reforms were conceived with the view that the modern presidency would be an ally of programmatic reform; in contrast, the liberalism of the late 1960s and 1970s was born of institutional confrontation between a conservative Republican president and a reform-minded Democratic Congress. Greatly suspicious of, if not avowedly hostile to, presidential power, reformers and their allies on the Hill were determined to protect liberal programs from unfriendly executive administration.

The battles that Democrats and Republicans waged for control of departments and agencies transcended narrow partisanship, however. As the unhappy term of Jimmy Carter revealed, one-party control of the White House and Congress did not assure institutional harmony. In fact, the restraints imposed on presidential power during the 1970s, reflecting a strong suspicion of centralized power, marked an impressive effort to ameliorate what Alexis de Tocqueville called the "puerilities of administrative tyranny."[10] As such, the reforms of the 1970s attempted to make national administrative power more legitimate by appealing to the primordial antistatism of the American people.

Paradoxically, however, these reforms fixed the business of government more on administration. In their efforts to enhance the representative character of government action, reformers did not seek to retrain administrative power but rather attempted to recast it as an agent of democracy. This required that Congress, the courts, and public interest groups become more involved in the details of administration. Thus, the reforms of this era circumscribed the administrative power of the president but at the cost of making other government and political institutions more bureaucratic in their organization and activities. In the final analysis, the reform of government during the 1970s provided participatory opportunities for only a small circle of public lobbyists, while corroding the link between citizens and their government.

The Twilight of the Modern Presidency

Soon after Lyndon Johnson left the White House, one of his presidential assistants, George Reedy, wrote, "We may be witnessing the first lengthening shadows that will become the twilight of the modern presidency."[11] This pessimistic view reflected the beleaguered state of the executive office at the end of the 1960s. The evolution of the modern presidency had given rise to an exalted office, but the occupant of that office faced increasingly less tractable conditions: growing opposition to unilateral use of presidential power; increased public cynicism about the merits of presidential policy proposals; and greater inclinations on the part of the press to challenge presidential assertions and proposals.

Johnson and his aides tended to see themselves as victims of these circumstances. The unhappy denouement of LBJ's presidency, his withdrawal from the 1968 election amid the collapse of the liberal political order, followed tragically from circumstances that were beyond his control. As Johnson aide Harry McPherson lamented:

> Johnson was a manipulator of men when there was a rejection of power
> politics; he was a believer in institutions at a time when spontaneity was

being celebrated; he was a paternalist when parental authority was being rejected; and he came to political authority during the 1930s when democracy was threatened by fascism and communism, making him an unbending anti-communist. To the young, this experience of the 1930s might as well have happened during the Renaissance.[12]

Nevertheless, Johnson's presidency also helped to initiate the assault on prevailing institutions during the 1960s and 1970s. For in seeking to surpass the accomplishments of Franklin Roosevelt and the New Deal, LBJ unwittingly encouraged the rise of a new version of liberalism which would denigrate the office of the presidency. He summoned the American people to build "a Great Society of the highest order," a calling that required fundamental changes in the institutional fabric of American politics.

LBJ "tested" the term "Great Society" at an April 1964 Democratic dinner in Chicago and in other venues that spring. Encouraged by the enthusiastic response to his declaration of a new reform era, Johnson gave the signature speech of his administration on May 22 at the University of Michigan.[13] The new phase of liberalism "demanded an end of poverty and racial injustice," the president told his audience, "but this is just the beginning." Challenging them to embrace more ambitious goals for America, LBJ described his vision of a good society as one "where the city of man serves not only the needs of the body and the demands of commerce but the desire for beauty and hunger for community."[14]

Johnson remained strongly committed to this more radical form of liberalism, even as he took America into a war in Southeast Asia. His 1966 State of the Union address declared that the Great Society led the nation along three roads—economic growth, "justice" for all races, and finally "liberation," which would use the economic success of the nation, so robust at this stage of the country's history, for the "fulfillment of our lives": "A great people flower not from wealth and power, but from a society which spurs them to the fullness of their genius. That alone is the Great Society. . . . Slowly, painfully, on the edge of victory, has come the knowledge that shared prosperity is not enough. In the midst of abundance modern man walks oppressed by forces which menace and confine the quality of his life, and which individual abundance alone will not overcome."

There followed a list of noneconomic goals: an expansion of health and education programs; the rebuilding of entire sections of neighborhoods in urban areas to establish "a flourishing community where our people can come to live the good life"; a stronger effort to put an end to the "continued poisoning of our rivers and air"; a highway safety act to end "the destruction of life and property on our highways"; and action to prevent the exploitation of the American consumer by deceptive business practices.[15]

This shift from concern with the "quantity" to the "quality" of life in America was the vehicle by which Johnson hoped to become "a national interest leader," as his aide Horace Busby put it, to surpass FDR's rights-based politics.[16] LBJ's actions were rooted in his assessment that American political life was threatened by the indignities, loneliness, and indifference of mass industrial society. The social movements of the 1960s, LBJ and his aides believed, revealed that America was ready for another, bolder episode of reform. "The civil rights revolution demonstrated not only the power and possibility of organized protest, but the unsuspected fragility of resistance to liberating changes," notes Richard Goodwin, who drafted the Great Society speech. Indeed, the civil rights movement established the model for other social movements that grew out of the 1960s—the feminist movement, consumerism, environmentalism, and others. Another social movement for which civil rights politics was paradigmatic, the antiwar movement, would help drive LBJ from office. But in the relatively halcyon early days of LBJ's leadership, Goodwin, and the president himself, envisioned such social forces as potential agents of a new generation of reform. "Johnson intended to align himself with the cause of blacks and women and consumers," Goodwin claims. "And I saw [their cause] as evidence that the country was ready for leadership committed to social change."[17]

In discussing the preparation of Johnson's landmark Great Society speech, Goodwin credits some of the ideas of the New Left. He reflected on the Port Huron Statement for example, which was issued in 1962 by the newly formed Students for a Democratic Society (SDS). One aspect of that address, in particular, impressed the presidential aide as expressing a yearning that went well beyond the utopian vision of radical fringe groups and was shared by a great many Americans:

> Some would have us believe that Americans feel contentment amidst prosperity—but might it not better be called a glaze above deeply felt anxieties about their role in the new world? And if these anxieties produce a developed indifference to human affairs, do they not as well produce a yearning to believe there is an alternative to the present, that something can be done to change circumstances in the schools, the

workplaces, the bureaucracies, the government? It is to this latter yearning, at once the spark and agent of change, that we direct our present
appeal.[18]

Hard as it may be to imagine Lyndon Johnson embracing New Left doctrine, Goodwin avers, not without reason, that such ideas corresponded to the
president's "own impulses, [and] could help to define and fuel the large purposes he wished to pursue."[19] In truth, the ideas that animated social movements of the 1960s were not so far afield from certain aspects of the New Deal,
parts of the reform impulse of the 1930s which Johnson understood well.
Johnson's first government job was to serve as Texas director of the National
Youth Administration (NYA)—one of the few New Deal agencies singled out
by the 1943 National Resources Planning Board report for successfully avoiding bureaucratic torpor and for effectively linking itself to the grassroots aspirations of the people it served. "Those NYA experiences were valuable to me,"
LBJ wrote in his memoirs, "suggesting some of the solutions we were searching for in the present."[20]

John Dewey, who influenced the thinking of many New Dealers, had
urged liberal reformers "to become radical in the sense that, instead of using
social power to ameliorate the evil consequences of the existing system, [they]
shall use power to change the system." Realizing the radical potential of liberalism, Dewey insisted, required efforts to provide individuals with effective
opportunities to share in the "cultural resources of civilization." "No economic state of affairs is merely economic," he insisted. "Any liberalism that
does not make full cultural freedom supreme and that does not see the relation between it and genuine industrial freedom as a way of life is a degenerate
and delusive liberalism."[21]

It was in this sense, in the service of Dewey's claim that the state had the
responsibility for creating institutions in which individuals could effectively
realize "the potentialities that are theirs," that the Great Society marked a
departure from the New Deal and in doing so radicalized the programmatic
liberal tradition.[22]

Still, Johnson's bold leadership was tempered by reticence. In the final
analysis, the New Deal represented an abiding commitment to "enlightened
administration." Firmly rooted in FDR's tradition, Johnson would seek to
uphold, indeed expand upon, the modern presidency. An improved quality of
life, he proposed in his 1966 State of the Union message, required that he
"take steps to modernize and streamline the executive branch," as well as the

"relations between city and state and nation."[23] In fact, the program development of the Great Society gave new meaning to the idea of a *president's* program. More and more policies began to be invented by politically appointed policy advocates of the White House Office, who were dedicated to devising and moving quickly on the president's agenda. Concomitantly, career staff in the regular agencies and the longtime institutional policy analysis professionals in the Bureau of the Budget became less influential in legislative program development.

To a point, Johnson's dominance of the political process was an extension of developments that began under John F. Kennedy. Kennedy's promise to "get the country moving again" reflected a desire for policy innovation that was inconsistent with the practice prior to the 1960s of letting domestic proposals emerge methodically through the executive branch agencies, undergoing screening and clarification in the Bureau of the Budget. As a consequence, policymaking initiatives began to shift during JFK's administration from the routines and institutional channels established during the Truman and Eisenhower years to the more freewheeling process of the White House Office. This change originated with Kennedy but reached fruition under Johnson. Indeed, the personalization of the executive office was not only extended during the Johnson years but institutionalized. In terms of policy development, one of the most significant innovations of the Johnson administration was the creation of several task forces under the supervision of White House aide Joseph Califano. Califano's work had an enduring effect on the modern presidency—the group of task forces he assembled was the precursor of the Domestic Policy Council, established by Johnson's successor, Richard Nixon, and the domestic policy staffs that have continued to be a feature of later administrations.[24]

The Great Society task forces included leading academics throughout the country who prepared reports during the Johnson presidency in many areas of public policy, including government organization, education, environmental quality, and urban planning. Several specific proposals that came out of these meetings, such as the Education Task Force's elementary-education proposal, became public policy, forming the heart of the Great Society. The Johnson administration took great care to protect the work of these organizations from political pressures, even keeping the task force procedure secret. Moreover, members were told to pay no attention to any political considerations; they were not to worry about whether their recommendations would be acceptable to Congress or to party leaders.[25]

This separation of presidential from party politics would eventually isolate Johnson, depriving his administration of a stable basis of popular support. Indeed, the claim has often been made that the Johnson administration's indifference to the party system accentuated the decline in authority and influence of the presidency during the 1960s and 1970s. This party decline was confirmed by the McGovern-Fraser reforms carried out after the 1968 Democratic convention in Chicago. In pursuance of these changes, party leaders were virtually stripped of their authority to nominate presidential candidates, displaced by a selection process dominated by primary elections and participatory caucuses. One consequence, as Donald Horowitz has written, is that "a President can no longer depend on a large core of committed supporters who will stay with him through thick and thin. Likewise, with the tenuous bonds of common party across the branches loosened further by changes in the presidential nominating process, there is less restraint in Congress on benefitting from a protracted [presidential] crisis."[26]

Yet, throughout the twentieth century, presidents with reform ambition had found party politics to be more an obstacle to leadership than an asset. Since the Progressive Era, in fact, reformers had condemned parties as the cornerstone of an old order that celebrated democratic individualism and presumed the absence of centralized administrative authority. New Deal reforms, as noted in Chapter 4, began to develop a policy process outside traditional bureaucratic and partisan channels. Created during the Roosevelt presidency were the White House Office and the Executive Office of the Presidency, which reduced the influence of party leaders and cabinet members on the development of public policy. Similarly, the shift of the Bureau of the Budget from the Treasury Department to the Executive Office of the President tended to strengthen the president's power and the nonpartisan administration of the affairs of state. The more the emergent "presidential branch of government" preempted the party organization in its tasks, the less vital and vigilant that organization became. This trend was greatly accelerated during the Great Society and ultimately led to the creation of a fully developed political and policy network outside the regular political process.

Eventually, the efforts being made to circumvent traditional political channels by the Johnson administration also became prominent in staffing and campaigns, laying the foundation for the disintegration of parties which became so visible after the 1968 Democratic convention. As the *Wall Street Journal* reported in late 1967, these actions greatly "accelerated the breakdown of state and local machinery," placing organizations "in acute distress in nearly every large state."[27]

Ironically, by contributing so much to this development, Lyndon Johnson helped construct the road that eventually enabled insurgents to challenge his presidency successfully. To be sure, the events that took place at the 1968 Democratic convention and the party reforms that followed were the result of longstanding efforts to free the presidency from traditional partisan influences. As such, the expansion of presidential primaries and other changes in nomination politics initiated by the McGovern-Fraser Commission were the logical extension of the modern presidency. The fact that the "revolution" in party rules which took place during the early 1970s was accomplished so quietly is evidence in itself that the party system had begun to falter by the end of the Johnson era. As David Truman has written, the McGovern-Fraser reforms could certainly not have been carried out over the opposition of an alert and vigorous party leadership.[28]

What Johnson did not recognize, of course, was that by failing to reverse, and even advancing, the decline of party, he was contributing to the rise of a new politics that would eventually turn on him. The Roosevelt revolution dedicated itself to tangible government entitlements, thus forging a coalition of blacks, liberal intellectuals and professionals, labor union members, and white ethnic groups which looked to the modern presidency for leadership. The Great Society helped bring to power issue-oriented independents, representing broad causes and movements, who resisted presidential "management" and who were less willing to delegate policy responsibility to administrative agencies. The reformers who took control of the Democratic party after the Chicago convention followed the progressive tradition of scorning partisanship—of desiring a direct relationship between presidential candidates and the people. But they rejected the concept of presidential leadership which prevailed during the Progressive and New Deal eras. As James Ceaser has noted about the system of reform associated with the McGovern-Fraser Commission: "One finds no notion of leadership similar to that of Woodrow Wilson in which the leader possesses a formative influence over public opinion. There is, in fact, no attention given to the question of the type of leadership or the type of executive that is desired. The reformers' views on groups and leadership were no doubt influenced by the general ideas current in the late 1960s that group politics was now directed by mass movements."[29]

Johnson's uneasy relationship with the War on Poverty provides perhaps the best example of the strengths and limitations of the modern presidency in relationship to the Great Society. In part, the Johnson White House's delegation of administrative responsibility to Community Action Programs was merely an extension of the modern presidency. Viewing the state and local party organizations as obstacles to good government, to the "enlightened" management of social policy, the Johnson White House viewed CAPs as a local arm of the Office of Economic Opportunity, which was established in the executive office as the principal federal poverty agency, thus enabling the administration to bypass the entrenched, usually Democratic machines. Federal guidelines, in fact, stipulated that Community Action Programs had to be conducted by a public or private nonprofit agency (or some combination thereof) other than a political party.

From this perspective, the CAPs were evidence of the further displacement of party politics by executive administration. In truth, the concern for "community" involvement during the Johnson presidency revealed how an emphasis on the quality of life in American society was potentially in tension with the centralization of authority required by an extensive welfare state. Furthermore, these programs revealed the uneasy alliance of expertise and romanticism which characterized reformers' efforts to transform political and government institutions during the late 1960s and 1970s. It is important to remember, as Samuel Beer points out, that the "antipoverty program was not shaped by the demands of pressure groups of the poor—there were none—but by deliberations of government task forces acting largely on the research-based theories of two sociologists, Professors Lloyd Olin and Richard A. Cloward of the Columbia school of social work."[30] At least in part, then, the communal concerns of the Johnson presidency were closely connected to administrative invention.

Still, the administrative invention that gave rise to the War on Poverty was an attempt to respond to real problems that could not be readily addressed by executive administration. Daniel Patrick Moynihan has argued that the Johnson administration blundered into the Community Action Programs and that the phrase mandating "maximum feasible participation" was a shallow rhetorical bow to the Jeffersonian tradition.[31] Yet, as James Morone has pointed out, Johnson and his aides were not so simple minded; rather, they were attempting to secure support for a controversial program "by invoking the powerful myths of the democratic wish."[32] That idea of democracy—abhorring centralized administration—had been severely challenged but not overturned by the New Deal. Johnson, in an admittedly halting way, was seeking to reconcile the New Deal state with the historical American antipathy to bureaucracy. As he wrote in his memoirs with respect to his attraction to the idea of community action: "This plan had the sound of something brand new and even faintly radical. Actually it was based on one of the oldest ideas of our democracy, as old as the New England town meeting—self-determination at the local level."[33]

Indeed, in those few cases in which citizen involvement in federal programs was accomplished, it contributed to the success of the projects involved. For example, Head Start, which was created as part of the Community Action Programs, employed considerable and effective efforts to involve parents of participating children in the day-to-day activities of the centers, thereby, according to Peter Skerry, helping it to establish a "tangible presence to ordinary citizens," a quality lacking in many federal programs.[34] Thus although the efforts to involve those affected by federal programs in shaping them were rarely a response to public demands and did not involve a large number of citizens in the actual running of federal programs, a genuine commitment emerged by the late 1960s to a norm of participation which was allied with, and to a point transcended, concerns to check abuses of presidential power. As a result, the assault on the prerogative of the modern presidency was associated with a new liberal philosophy and attendant institutional changes dedicated to reconciling the New Deal commitment to "enlightened administration" and the New Left's celebration of "participatory democracy."

Johnson, with the encouragement of aides like Richard Goodwin, had championed the pursuit of a new liberal order. But he was too much of a New Dealer, too dedicated to the presidency, to accept the consequences of "movement" politics. By 1968, he had become the hated symbol of the status quo, forced into retirement lest he contribute further to the destruction of the liberal consensus. "I could not be the rallying force to unite the country and meet the problems" confronted by the nation abroad and at home, he told Hubert Humphrey in their private meeting of April 3, "in the face of a contentious campaign and the negative attitudes towards [me] of the youth, Negroes, and academics."[35]

LBJ thus saw the mantle of liberal leadership pass to the likes of Eugene McCarthy, whose insurgent candidacy drove the president from office, and George McGovern, whom the Democratic party nominated for president in 1972. In 1972, clearly, the Democratic party was still the party of programmatic rights. But these rights had been extended to broad, less tangible causes that could not easily be accommodated to the New Deal institutional framework.

Richard Goodwin, who left the White House to work for the McCarthy crusade, then for Robert Kennedy, gave expression to this character of liberalism soon after the 1968 election. Speaking of McCarthy's ability to touch many members of the American middle class, he wrote, "They were not asking to be promised better schools or lower taxes, although they want them. They were looking for some way in which they could regain control and play a real part in the enterprises of society. It was this same nerve that Robert Kennedy touched in two other groups—the blacks and poor whites—when he talked of the need for community control and local power."[36] This search for new answers could be satisfied neither by political parties nor the modern presidency. Indeed, it involved a full-scale assault on the modern presidency, even as it expanded the national government's administrative power.

Nixon and the New Congress

In a generally sympathetic biography, Stephen Ambrose attributes the fall of Richard Nixon to his lack of virtue. "In a free, open, and democratic society, politics is above all an education process," Ambrose observes. "The leader leads through persuasion and consent. Nixon tried to lead through surprise and manipulation."[37] The ugly events of Watergate were not simply the result of Nixon's character flaws, however; in part, they grew out of his determination to uphold the modern presidency in the face of growing doubts about it.

In the first instance, the administrative actions of the Nixon presidency were a logical extension of the practices of the Roosevelt and Johnson presidencies. The centralization of authority in the White House and the reduction of the regular Republican organization to perfunctory status during the Nixon years were hardly new. The complete autonomy of the Committee to Re-Elect the President (CREEP) from the Republican organization in the 1972 campaign was but the final stage of a long process of White House preemption of the national committee's political responsibilities. And the administrative reform program that was pursued after Nixon's reelection, in which executive authority was concentrated in the hands of White House operatives and four cabinet "supersecretaries," was the culmination of a longstanding tendency in the modern presidency to reconstitute the executive branch as a formidable and independent instrument of government.

Indeed, the strategy of pursuing policy goals through the administrative capacities that had been created for the most part by Democratic presidents was considered especially suitable by a minority Republican president who faced a hostile Congress and bureaucracy intent on preserving those presidents' programs. Nixon actually surpassed previous modern presidents in viewing the party system as an obstacle to effective governance. Yet, mainly because of the Watergate scandal, Nixon's presidency had the effect of strengthening opposition to the unilateral use of presidential power, even as it further attenuated the bonds that linked presidents to the party system.

In the final analysis, Nixon's downfall grew out of his bitter relations with Congress. To be sure, the Watergate scandal—CREEP's attempt to bug offices in the Democratic National Committee and the subsequent efforts by the president and his aides to cover up the break-in—was the principal cause of Nixon's having the unhappy distinction to be the only president in American history to resign. Nixon's impeachment was assured by the Supreme Court action in *United States v. Nixon*, which rejected the president's sweeping claims of executive privilege and forced the release of tapes that showed the president had participated in the cover-up.[38] But the willingness of Congress to take the extraordinary step of removing a president was in part a response to Nixon's repeated attempts to circumvent the legislature.[39] Certainly, Congress's resolve was strengthened by the ideological and partisan struggles that marked the relations between the president and Congress. Just as important, Congress had undergone important changes during the 1960s which prepared it to undertake an assault not only on Nixon but also on the authority of the executive office.

The reconstruction of Congress began in 1958 with the significant gains Democrats made outside the South in congressional elections. Liberals, in fact, now made up a majority of the House Democratic party. Frustrated by the advantage that the seniority rule continued to accord conservatives from the noncompetitive South in obtaining powerful committee chairs, liberal Democrats created the House Democratic Study Group (DSG) in 1958. This group of liberals within the House Democratic caucus focused their efforts on lessening the power of the conservative committee chairs and spreading that power more widely among all Democrats, particularly the liberal majority.[40]

Nevertheless, the "conservative coalition"—the tacit alliance forged between southern Democrats and northern Republicans during Roosevelt's second term—continued to thwart liberal legislation through the Kennedy presidency. Johnson's mastery of legislative matters enabled him to overcome the opposition of southern Democrats in the enactment of the 1964 Civil

Rights Act, and the landslide victory achieved soon thereafter brought enough northern liberal Democrats into Congress to wrest power in the House and Senate from the conservative coalition. With the passage of the 1965 Voting Rights Act, moreover, Johnson ensured the transformation of southern Democracy which eluded FDR. The weakening of the conservative coalition and the concomitant rise of the DSG combined to cause the transformation of the legislative branch, culminating in the procedural changes of the early 1970s which dramatically altered the congressional power structure.

The reconstructed Congress was not content to protect programmatic liberalism from an indifferent or hostile presidency. Rather, it pursued an ambitious liberal agenda that sought dramatically to extend the boundaries of FDR's economic constitutional order. Widespread hunger, for example, was "discovered" in America just as LBJ was cutting back on the War on Poverty to make room in his budget for the military buildup in Vietnam. This was no accident—it was the result of efforts by a few senators, notably Robert Kennedy, George McGovern, and Joseph Clark, and their allies in the labor movement (especially Walter Reuther), foundations (such as the Ford and Field foundations), newly formed "citizens" groups, and media to make the problem of hunger apparent to the American people and thus to revitalize the flagging War on Poverty. As a result, the politics of food stamps changed suddenly and dramatically toward the end of the Johnson era.

The coterie of food stamp reformers, dedicated to the creation of a right to a "nutritionally adequate diet," had previously seen the president and the Department of Agriculture as their primary allies in the fight against the conservative coalition in Congress. They now turned on Lyndon Johnson and his secretary of agriculture, Orville Freeman—a member in good standing of the Minnesota Democratic Farmer Labor Party—whom they accused of being callously cautious. The liberal reform strategy focusing on executive administration became what R. Shep Melnick calls "a boisterous 'outside' strategy." Liberal Democrats in Congress, using the Senate Select Committee on Human Needs as a forum, worked with the press and a small but skilled group of "hunger lobbyists" to force Johnson's hand and to write legislation requiring program expansion. Food stamps—both their programs and politics— would henceforth become the province of a new form of liberal politics, centered in a new set of institutional arrangements.[41]

The hunger issue was part of a broader endeavor that reshaped liberalism during the 1970s. When the right to a "nutritionally adequate diet" first emerged in 1967, it was tied to an attack on LBJ, who was falling out of favor with liberals active in the civil rights and antiwar movements. McGovern, Kennedy, and Reuther were not only important actors in the "dump Johnson" movement but also part of the "new politics" Democratic faction that was intent upon moving liberalism well beyond the New Deal. As noted earlier, the expansion of the liberal agenda included commitments not just to programmatic advances in the War against Poverty but also to new issues such as community control and "participatory democracy" which led liberal activists to challenge New Deal institutions. Once Nixon sat in the White House, partisan politics sharpened the reformers' attacks on the executive branch. Although Nixon's attack on the liberal state was modest by contemporary standards—indeed, his administration proposed and implemented the largest expansion of the food stamp program in history—he was constantly scorned by food stamp advocates. Before long, however, the enemy had become not just the Nixon administration in particular, but the modern presidency in general.

In his battles with the liberal establishment, Nixon relied on what Benjamin Ginsberg and Martin Shefter call "institutional combat," a form of political warfare befitting an era of partisan decline and electoral stalemate. With the advent of divided government, they write, "the Democrats and Republicans continue to contest elections. But rather than pin all its hopes on defeating its foes in the electoral arena, each party has begun to strengthen the institutions it commands and to use them to weaken its foes' governmental and political base."[42] Thus, the "new" politics of the 1960s and 1970s was gradually developing into a form of party politics centered on government rather than the electorate. Furthermore, this partisan and institutional combat revolved around the task of controlling the administrative levers of power, thus further eroding and making unlikely the renewal of partisan attachments in the electorate.

Indeed, the liberal response to Watergate emphasized the need to tame rather than win back the modern presidency. Above all, this domestication of the president's administrative power required circumscribing executive prerogative in foreign affairs. The Nixon administration's primary defense of its aggressive expansion of executive powers was that these actions were motivated by concern for the country's future during wartime. Nixon even justified the firing of the special prosecutor, Archibald Cox, who issued a subpoena that would force the president to release tapes of White House conversations related to the Watergate investigation, on the ground that acquiescence to Cox's aggressive investigation would make the president appear weak in the eyes of Soviet leader Leonid Brezhnev and other foreign leaders.[43]

Thus, the protection of—and hope of extending further—the programmatic achievements of liberalism depended on imposing strong restraints on the executive's initiative in foreign policy. The legislation passed during the 1970s designed to accomplish this task, such as the War Powers Resolution, should be viewed only in part as an attempt to revive Congress's constitutional prerogative; just as surely, such measures were intended to facilitate an ambitious expansion of welfare and regulatory programs. Similarly, the passage of the Budget and Impoundment Control Act of 1974, which was designed to give Congress control of the executive budget, was intended to protect social reform from the sort of fiscal assault on social welfare programs which Nixon sought to carry out after his 1972 reelection.

These laws in and of themselves would only have a marginal effect on presidential power. But their enactment was associated with a determination of the "new" Congress to reestablish itself as an equal partner, indeed, the dominant force in the government and nation. It was this determination that gave rise to the procedural reforms of the early 1970s which remade the legislative power structure. The result was a decentralized yet aggressive legislature that was well equipped to participate in the details of administration. The most important reforms were those that increased the number, power, autonomy, and staff of congressional subcommittees. A decentralized institution since the rebellion against Speaker Joseph Cannon during the Progressive Era, Congress became even more so; in effect, the power of standing committees devolved into subcommittees. But this time the legislative rebellion was carried out by insurgents whose target was as much the president as their more stolid and conservative adversaries in Congress. Thus, the rise of subcommittee government resulted in a severe challenge to the modern president's preeminence in legislative and administrative matters. As Melnick has written about this administrative reform:

> Using subcommittee resources, members initiated new programs and revised old ones, challenging the president for the title of "chief legislator." No longer would Congress respond to calls for action by passing vague legislation telling the executive to do something. Now Congress was writing detailed statutes which not infrequently deviated from the

president's program. Subcommittees were also using oversight hearings to make sure that administrators paid heed not just to the letter of legislation, but to its spirit as well.[44]

It is important to realize that the reform assault on the modern presidency was not simply a pragmatic adjustment of institutional arrangements to ensure a more strident and consistent commitment to liberal programs. In fact, the restraints imposed on the presidential power during the 1970s reflected a strong suspicion of any administrative power that was not open to public participation. In important respects, such a suspicion was a logical outgrowth of the reform vision of the Great Society. Just as the Community Action Programs represented more than a substitute for substantive benefits during the Johnson era, so the procedural niceties in statutes enacted during the 1970s were not simply intended by Congress to be an ersatz government benefit. Nor were congressionally created procedural rights merely a method for avoiding issues on which legislators received conflicting pressures. There was a strong antibureaucratic, anti-institutional ethos in the "new" Congress; in fact, those legislators who had revolted against the seniority system claimed to support "participatory democracy" within Congress. Republican control of the presidency made liberal Democratic legislators even more enthusiastic about guaranteeing public interest groups and "average" citizens, most of whom were adversaries of the Nixon administration, an active role in the administration of government programs. Consequently, by one count, there were approximately 226 citizen participation programs mandated by federal statutes by 1977, and the courts were vigilant in making sure that state and federal agencies adhered to the letter and spirit of these participation requirements.[45] The assault on the prerogatives of the modern presidency, then, was associated with institutional changes that expanded the national government's administrative power but tied the use of such power to procedural safeguards designed to reconcile centralized administration and participatory democracy.

Public Participation and the Reform of Administrative Politics

The effort to enhance the representative character of the administrative state was most closely associated with the expansion of regulatory programs during the late 1960s and 1970s. Most significant, ambitious new undertakings were launched in the area of "social" regulation, leading to the creation of new administrative agencies and the redirection of certain existing ones to address issues such as employment discrimination against minorities and women, environmentalism, consumer protection, and health and safety. The rise of social regulation began with the 1964 Civil Rights Act, which created the first of the new social regulatory agencies: the Equal Employment Opportunity Commission, charged with administering Title VII (concerned primarily with employment discrimination) of the landmark civil rights statute. During the late 1960s and 1970s, a vast array of new federal laws were enacted and new federal agencies were created which looked well beyond civil rights, thus giving concrete expression to the "quality of life" concerns that most clearly distinguished the New Deal and Great Society.[46]

In part, this new social regulation constituted a change in the political economy which required unprecedented centralization of the national government's administrative power. Business found the new social regulation especially disturbing, because it empowered executive agencies to intrude into broad problem areas with detailed prescriptions for the manufacture and sale of products. As Bernard Falk of the National Electrical Manufacturers' Association noted about the expansion of the government's regulatory role in the 1970s, "In the past going back ten or fifteen years, you didn't have a consumer movement. The manufacturer controlled the make-up of his own product, and Washington could be ignored. Now we all have a new partner, the federal government."[47]

Yet, paradoxically, this centralization of power went hand in hand with changes in administrative law which reflected strong suspicion of administrative power. As such, the institutional initiatives that were linked with the social reforms of the 1970s were motivated by concerns to recast the concept of citizenship in American politics to conform with the expansion of national administrative power. These changes reflected the view, first articulated by the champions of the new politics during the 1960s, that the New Deal, while bringing valued reforms, had devolved into an impersonal, bureaucratic, centralized form of governance which was dehumanizing American society. Moreover, reformers during the late 1960s and 1970s believed that the procedures by which decisions were made in the administrative state were controlled by large business interests that were inattentive to the prominent social problems dominating the political agenda of the 1970s, such as the despoliation of the environment and the manipulation of consumers, which were depicted by reformers as a by-product of the capture of the public sector by corporate interests.

The apparent tension between national administrative power and democratic citizenship created a real dilemma within the American political system. On the one hand, local government and community control remained at the heart of the American idea of democracy. On the other hand, since the New Deal, Americans had come to accept as just and inevitable the development of a strong national government, deemed necessary to provide for economic security, protect freedom from foreign threats, limit the power of corporations, and guarantee equal protection of the law.

The public interest advocates who had such a strong influence on public policy during the 1970s were committed to expanding the programmatic responsibilities of the national government, and, therefore, were not predisposed to reduce the prerogatives of the executive departments and agencies. The task in large part was to establish new agencies, such as the Environmental Protection Agency, and refurbish existing ones, such as the Federal Trade Commission, thereby creating new and renewed centers of administrative power which would not become as inefficient and unresponsive as regulatory agencies typically had been in the past. Consequently, as Ralph Nader urged, regulatory bodies were not to be delegated responsibility to act for the public but to be governed instead by administrative mechanisms providing liberal provision for public participation, "so that agency lethargy or inefficiency could be checked by interested citizen activity."[48] The achievement of civil rights, consumer, and environmental regulations was deemed worthless so long as the administrative process was not opened up to direct citizen action.

The commitment to public participation required an ongoing presence of public interest groups in administrative decision making. Hence the culmination of liberalism was associated not with the renewal of party politics but with the rise of public interest groups tailored to facilitate the direct participation of citizen activists in the administrative process. To be sure, many regulatory reform groups that arose in the 1970s resembled the organizations that became part of the New Deal coalition. For example, labor and civil rights groups, which were major constituencies of the New Deal coalition, often worked with but did not formally become part of the Democratic party. The emergence of these auxiliary party organizations signaled a new form of presidential coalition which both converted independents to Democratic allegiance and made conventional, partisan participation less important.[49] But public interest activists, lacking the well-defined popular support that labor unions and civil rights groups could draw upon, largely abstained from partisan strategies of grassroots mobilization and electoral alliance as a means of developing effective political influence. Although conceding that the goal of expanding popular electoral participation may be valuable in itself, public interest liberals found such a strategy largely irrelevant in the face of the New Deal institutional legacy—unrelated to the task of making either the bureaucratic state or corporate elites accountable to the public.[50] As Richard Ayres, the senior attorney for the National Resources Defense Council (NRDC), noted with respect to the creation of this environmental group:

> The motivating or animating idea of the NRDC was the realization that in the twentieth century and especially since the New Deal the executive branch is the most powerful of the three and the interests of the public get lost for lack of expertise and knowledge of the administrative process. In the past environmental or other citizen groups won victories in the legislative branch only to lose in the executive branch. It is clear that the administrative process is where the action is. . . . It is interesting that Labor, which clearly challenged the political-economic establishment, never learned how important the administrative arena was. . . . They haven't got for all their legal expertise, an organization like the NRDC. They are involved in Congress and party politics which matter less and less.[51]

In little more than a decade, as Walter Rosenbaum noted toward the end of the 1970s, the attempt to marry administration and democracy had led to a "radical redefinition of public rights in the federal administrative process." Beginning with a few precarious innovations in the 1960s, the "new" public involvement "now threatened to become a cliche as a multitude of statutory mandates and agency regulations . . . prescribed citizen involvement in agency affairs vastly exceeding the standard once considered appropriate."[52] One of the earliest of these new programs could be found in the Federal Water Pollution Control Act Amendments of 1972. As Section 101(e) of the statute read: "Public Participation in the development, revision and enforcement of any regulation, standard, effluent limitation, plan or program established by the Administrator, or any State under this Act shall be provided for, encouraged and assisted by the Administrator and the states."[53] Beginning in 1975, Congress intensified its efforts to foster public participation and began to legislate provisions explicitly authorizing direct aid to finance the participation of citizen groups in specific regulatory actions of certain agencies, most notably the Federal Trade Commission, the Consumer Products Safety Commission, and the Environmental Protection Agency.[54]

The first, pathbreaking enactment of legislative authorization for financial assistance came in the Federal Trade Commission Improvement Act of 1975 (the Magnuson-Moss Act). This legislation created an "intervenor funding program," which authorized the FTC to pay attorney fees and expert witness costs and other expenses of participation by parties otherwise unable to represent their interests in rule-making proceedings.[55] These funds overwhelmingly went to public interest groups supportive of the ambitious proconsumer policies that were increasingly pursued by the FTC after 1975. Indeed, the list of grants made under the intervenor funding program looked very much like an honor roll of staunch consumer advocates, including Americans for Democratic Action ($177,000 in grants to participate in five separate rule-making proceedings), Action for Children's Television ($84,614 to participate in a children's advertising proceeding), and the Consumers Union ($132,257 to participate in four separate rule-making proceedings).[56] It is ironic that these "public" participation funds were concentrated among a relatively few organizations and law firms that came to constitute a specialized "proconsumer FTC bar." Yet consumer activists claimed that the failure to foster genuine "grassroots" participation was symptomatic of the great difficulty involved in striking a balance between the technical competence demanded by the administrative state and "participatory" democracy. Those groups that were part of the privileged "public" asserted that without the continuity of representation achieved by a few organizations receiving federal support to participate in several regulatory proceedings, the consumer activists could not achieve equality with business and trade groups.[57]

The attempt to reconcile centralized administration and participatory democracy through funding a rather limited universe of "public" interest groups was troublesome. No less problematic was the development of the judiciary during the 1960s and 1970s as a critical channel for public participation in administrative rule-making procedures. The judiciary did not intervene in the details of FTC proceedings because this agency was created during the Progressive Era as an independent regulatory commission and is thus entitled to act as a court of equity in defining and enforcing values. Yet many other agencies, particularly those created at the height of the "participatory revolution," were subjected to extensive judicial oversight that played a significant part in expanding regulatory activities in the areas of civil rights, environmentalism, public health, and safety. This expansion went hand in hand with the courts' recognition of elaborate procedural rights for groups directly affected by government programs, as well as for organizations claiming to speak for the "public."

The alliance forged between citizen action and the judiciary was a strange one, because the courts are organized within the American constitutional framework to be extensively independent of public views. But the statutes passed during the 1960s and 1970s were often couched in terms of entitlements—as statutory rights rather than bureaucratic obligations—thereby inviting the federal judiciary to become a forceful and consistent presence in administrative politics.[58] Until the 1960s, the executive was guided by the Administrative Procedures Act, which, reflecting the New Deal commitment to guaranteeing economic security and its faith in "enlightened administration," left departments and agencies considerable autonomy from judicial and legislative interference. With the formulation of a new version of liberalism during the Great Society, there was a great expansion of programmatic rights: the right to be free of discrimination; the so-called collective rights associated with consumer and environmental protection; and, significantly, the right of those affected by government programs (and those representing the "public") to participate in the administration of these programs. As public participation evolved into a procedural right during the 1970s, the courts became vigilant in making sure that federal agencies adhered to the newly recognized procedural requirements. These developments resulted in a de facto, if not de jure, amendment of the Administrative Procedures Act. As Martin Shapiro has written, during the late 1960s and 1970s, the courts "invented a host of procedural requirements that turned rulemaking into a multi-party paper trial. They also imposed a rulemaking record requirement that allowed courts to review minutely every aspect of that trial. . . . The courts . . . did these things to reduce the independence and discretionary scope of a mistrusted bureaucracy and to subordinate it to more control by the regulated, the beneficiaries of regulation, and the public at large."[59]

The statutory provisions relating to procedural rights reinforced the courts' extensive efforts beginning in the late 1960s to expand participation of those claiming to speak for the poor, racial minorities, consumers, and environmentalists. In particular, lawsuits in the 1960s and 1970s helped to establish the standing of citizen groups to sue federal agencies for law enforcement.

Moreover, many statutes, especially environmental laws, lent Congress's support to this development by granting automatic standing to sue and establishing liberal provisions for class actions. Consequently, the lawsuit, once considered the province of the privileged, became the principal tool during the 1970s to open up the administrative process. As Richard Stewart wrote in the wake of this transformation of administrative law, "Courts have changed the focus of judicial review (in the course of expanding and transforming traditional procedural rights), so that its dominant purpose is no longer the prevention of unauthorized intrusion on private autonomy, but the assurance of fair representation for affected interests in the exercise of legislative power delegated to agencies."[60] As with intervenor funding, however, it was "public" interest groups, rather than the public, which benefited directly from this development.

Public Participation and the Crisis of the Liberal Order

Although the public interest movement gained substantial influence on the policy process by building elaborate organizational networks and making effective use of the media, this influence was never really solidified into an enduring political coalition. The emphasis of public interest groups on single-issue advocacy and use of the media was characteristic of what James Q. Wilson refers to as "entrepreneurial politics"; social regulatory policy was dominated by a small number of Washington-based activists, who served as "vicarious representatives" of diffuse and poorly organized interests.[61] To a point, such advocacy was necessary, for environmental, consumer, and health laws and regulations conferred general benefits on the public at the expense of small, albeit well-organized, segments of society. Since the incentive to organize is relatively weak for beneficiaries but strong for opponents of such policies, it is perhaps necessary for public interest advocates to position themselves as representatives of the public. Nevertheless, the defense of "collective" rights puts public lobbyists in a precarious position. As defenders of general rather than specific concerns, they are often without strong political allies.

The public interest movement, then, while capable of eliciting popular support by dramatizing corporate abuse and defending unassailable values such as clean air and consumer rights, was, in fact, built on a fragile institutional foundation. The institutional structure was well suited to harnessing symbolic political campaigns into regulatory programs yet incapable of establishing deeply rooted political affiliation among the public. As consumer advocate and former chairman of the FTC Michael Pertschuck admitted:

> It might be said that we represented the late New Deal liberal tradition. . . . We were disproportionately Ivy Leaguers, do-gooders, knee-jerk liberals, occupied with alleviating the hardships of others, fueled by faith in the capacity of government to represent the people against "private greed," so long as the government was peopled or stimulated by us. We defended ourselves against charges of elitism with the strong evidence that the principles we stood for and the causes we enlisted in enjoyed popular, if sometimes passive, support. But if we were "for the people," for the most part we were not comfortably "of the people."[62]

The "elitist" character of the public interest movement was reinforced by its emphasis on administrative politics. In the final analysis, the reformers of the 1970s embraced administrative politics, even as they sought to make it more accessible to direct political action. Indeed, the role of the courts and the Congress in the "new" American political system involved less a challenge to administrative government—and the revival of legislation and adjudication per se—than an incorporation of the legislative and judicial branches into the "details of administration." The institutional reforms in Congress during the 1970s which devolved policy responsibility to subcommittees and increased the number of congressional support staff members were compatible with the attention being paid by legislators to policy specialization, which increased congressional oversight of the executive while making Congress more administrative in its structure and activities. By the same token, the judiciary's decreasing reliance on constitutional decisions in its rulings affecting the political economy and its emphasis on interpreting statutes to determine the programmatic responsibilities of executive agencies were symptomatic of its new role as the "managing partner of the administrative state."[63]

Thus, whereas the reformers of the 1960s and 1970s rejected the New Deal instrument of progressive government—the modern presidency—as undemocratic, they devolved public authority to a less visible coalition of bureaucratic agencies, courts, congressional subcommittees, and public interest groups. Public interest groups did generate large rosters of supporters through direct mail solicitations. But these appeals to the public asked not so much for citizens' votes, time, energy, and ideas as for small contributions to fund campaigns waged by legal experts. Consequently, as Hugh Heclo has pointed out, with the recasting of liberalism in the 1970s, American society further "politicized itself" and at the same time "depoliticized government leadership."[64]

The root of this problem is the moral basis of contemporary liberalism. The pursuit of "quality of life" issues resulted in an indifference to, if not a rejection of, the self-interested basis of American politics. Whereas the New Deal emphasis on economic security essentially accepted commercial values as an inherent part of American life, the expressed aims of the Great Society explicitly rejected a view of the individual as essentially defined by acquisitive desires. The Johnson administration's indictment of material self-interest was for the most part restrained; for all his commitment to reform, Lyndon Johnson was a cautious leader. But such restraint was less evident in the rhetoric and political action of citizen activists, who expressed a far less compromising commitment to addressing problems of the "spirit rather than the flesh." As Ralph Nader wrote in 1971: "This year the gross national product of the United States will exceed one trillion dollars, while the economy will fail to meet a great many urgent needs. . . . Indeed, the quality of life is deteriorating in so many ways that the traditional statistical requirements of the 'standard of living' according to personal income, housing, ownership of cars and appliances, etc. have come to sound increasingly phony."[65]

It is easy to dismiss such a concern to deflect attention from material progress as mere rhetoric. But the moral principles that animated programmatic liberalism during the 1960s and 1970s resulted in a dramatic transformation of constitutional government in the United States. The American constitutional framework established conditions whereby "ambition would counteract ambition," thus fostering a system of mutual constraints among a diversity of interests. The New Deal altered this free play of self-interest in significant ways, particularly by shifting the locus of decision making to the executive, but the institutional reforms of the 1970s extensively displaced the pluralistic character of American politics. The institutional arrangements that emerged by the 1970s subordinated particularistic political ambitions to the programmatic ambitions of reformers, though these programs were usually constructed within discrete issue areas.

The moral basis of the public interest movement required it to maintain an uneasy, paradoxical relationship to the American public. Although advocating a participatory democracy, public lobby groups articulated an ethos that indirectly expressed grave reservations about the core principles and standard procedures of American political life. As Michael McCann has argued, whereas traditional, narrowly focused interest groups had often been celebrated for moderating deep social and economic divisions in the United States, public interest advocates "sought to promote a fundamental ideological debate over the very purposes and standards of public authority . . . by pitting quality against quantity, people against profits, and health against wealth."[66]

If the frenetic materialism and conspicuous consumption of American society could merely be attributed to the machinations of corporate capitalism, then direct and widespread citizen action might be consistent with the strident criticism of public interest advocates. To the degree that relentless materialism was deeply embedded in the American way of life, however, "citizen" advocacy was in tension with a commitment to democratic politics. Widespread support could readily be obtained for many of the specific goals of social regulation, yet the principles underlying these specific programs were largely unacceptable in the context of American politics and, when unchecked, capable of arousing a strong political backlash against the public interest movement. To be sure, these movements were not anticapitalist— there was no vision that conveyed an urgency to eliminate private property or to redistribute wealth. In fact, reformers of the late 1960s and 1970s defended values, such as clean air and product safety, which cut across traditional class conflicts, explaining in large part their success in achieving broad, if not deeply rooted, support among the American people. Yet the emphasis on "quality of life" issues, the warning against resource limitations, and the criticism of consumer preference which characterized much public interest advocacy indirectly rejected the foundation of a society dedicated to the pursuit of material satisfaction.

Thus, in seeking to depart from the New Deal's emphasis on economic security, contemporary social reformers were alienated from the values and institutions that earlier progressives accepted as an inherent part of American life. Undoubtedly, reformers of the 1960s and 1970s were not simply antimaterialistic. Nor is American political culture simply materialistic; the concerns for democratic citizenship and the criticisms of big business which characterized the reform activists during this period have a long tradition in the United States. But the public plainly was not willing to reject the degree of materialism which many citizen advocates found unacceptable. It is not surprising, then, that the contemporary liberal reformers focused on administrative and legal channels that were far removed from the more democratic institutions in American politics. Administrative tribunals and the courts were certainly more appropriate forums than Congress and the parties for efforts to remake so substantially the character of the American political system. It is ironic and tragic that the resulting triumph of administrative politics, designed to strengthen citizen action, signified a distressing deterioration of representative democracy.

The Legacy of Liberal Reform for Politics and Government

Throughout American history, critical partisan realignments, character-ized by pervasive shifts in party support and major departures in public policy, have refreshed democratic politics and restored the vigor of public authority. The strengthening of public authority, so that the nation's resolve could be expressed less episodically, was the great contribution of the New Deal realignment. This realignment reinforced the fragile sense of national com-munity in the United States, and did so, seemingly, without undermining the personal independence of democratic individualism. Yet the link between administrative power and entitlements forged by the New Deal began a process whereby democratic and decentralized institutions that facilitated public debate and choice were displaced by executive administration.

Although the reformers of the 1960s and 1970s set out to temper the administrative state, and to revitalize self-government in the United States, they continued, even increased, the dominance of political administration in the councils of government. The "institutional partnership" that liberals forged during the 1970s limited the administrative power of the president but involved Congress, the courts, and public interest groups in the details of administration. In the final analysis, the institutional developments of this era not only fixed the business of government more on administration but also accelerated the decline of political parties.

In the wake of this development, the modern president was relegated to the role of modulating the liberal state; the executive was no longer in com-mand of it. Nixon, Ford, and even the Democrat Jimmy Carter sought to put a lid on "uncontrollable" spending and to moderate the activities of the many regulatory agencies that were refurbished and created by the newly resurgent Congress. Most dramatic were the battles between Republican presidents and the Democratic Congress over spending and deficit levels. But conflict between the president and Congress, especially with respect to budgetary matters, became institutionalized after 1974. Carter, although he was slightly less conservative than his Republican predecessors, tried to hold budget costs down, especially as inflationary pressure mounted during the latter part of his term. He was no more successful than Nixon and Ford, however, in getting the liberal Democratic Congress to respond to his call for fiscal restraint.[67]

The most important development of the administrative presidency during the 1970s was Nixon's reorganization of the budget bureau. Just as the subcommittee became the soul of Congress during the 1970s, so the Office of Management and Budget (OMB) became the nerve center of the administrative presidency.[68] Not only did the enlarged OMB review spending requests and legislative proposals, as it had prior to the 1970s, but proposed agency rules as well. The reshaping of liberalism during the 1970s, establishing a loose coalition of bureaucratic agencies, congressional subcommittees and staff, courts, and public advocacy groups, eroded considerably the discretion of presidents and executive officers to shape public policy. These channels posed a direct threat to presidential governance. Moreover, the explosion of regulation and the recasting of administrative institutions coincided with, and to a degree contributed to, increasing public doubt about the expansion of government. Beginning in the early 1970s, therefore, presidents were compelled to undertake the unenviable task of controlling the expanding and increasingly disparate activities of the bureaucracy.[69]

But after the fall of Nixon, Ford and Carter were unable to regain control of the president's domain. The OMB became an important competitor in the administrative process during their presidencies, but it did not dominate it. Consequently, federal administrators found themselves whipsawed between the competing demands of subcommittees and the lieutenants of the president in the executive office. The end of the Carter years seemed to mark the triumph of the new institutional partnership that had been built to house liberalism while creating considerable doubt about the viability of the Democratic party as an instrument of government.

Carter's ostensible purpose was to move his party to the center and thus prepare it to compete more effectively at a time when the New Deal and Great Society appeared to be losing support in the country. He said often and earnestly that he intended to cut waste, run things efficiently, and balance the budget. But Carter's presidency marked the culmination of institutional separation between the presidency and the party. His 1976 campaign demonstrated how the new rules that governed the nominating process made it possible for an outsider to win his party's nomination; moreover, Carter's election demonstrated the striking decline of the regular party organization that reformers since the Progressive Era had decried as a stain on the American political process. Indeed, like Lyndon Johnson, Carter represented the emergence of antipartisan southern progressives as an important political force in the country. Because of the one-party dominance below the Mason-Dixon line, southern liberals like Johnson or Carter were especially likely to discount party.

Ronald Reagan's ferocious challenge to President Ford in the Republican primaries in that same election strongly suggested the decline of party organizations. Carter's election confirmed it. As such, Carter's presidency represented a celebration of what Woodrow Wilson called the "extraordinary isolation" of the presidency. To Carter and his supporters, any consideration of electoral or party politics in the administration's councils was unseemly. Whereas Roosevelt and, to a lesser extent, Johnson took these political concerns into account and then calculated how to circumvent them, Carter was an antiparty outsider whose devotion to "enlightened administration" was profound. By the late 1970s, transcending parties was no longer part of a calculated agenda — it was now an assumed, indeed, almost a sacred, truth. Carter's "trusteeship politics," as Charles Jones calls it, presupposing the absence of party considerations, underscores the extent to which the New Deal and Great Society had marginalized the party system.[70]

At the same time, Carter's unsteady command of the nation revealed that the splendid isolation of the presidency spawned by the New Deal and Great Society was at best a mixed blessing. Presidents and legislators had become independent entrepreneurs, establishing their own constituencies. As a result, they were less likely to view each other as partners in a shared endeavor, dedicated to promoting a party program. "I learned the hard way," Carter noted in his memoirs, "that there was no party loyalty or discipline when a complicated or controversial issue was at stake — none. Each legislator had to be wooed and won independently. It was every member for himself, and the devil take the hindmost!"[71]

Carter never did anything to ameliorate this disarray; in fact, he greatly contributed to it. His relationship to his party was usually aloof, occasionally accommodating, but never purposeful. In matters of public policy, the White House staff reflected the president's desire to be fiercely independent and a scourge to traditional Democratic approaches. But his appointees to the cabinet were liberal Washington insiders such as Joseph Califano (Health, Education, and Welfare) and Patricia Roberts Harris (Housing and Urban Development), thus setting the stage for enervating conflict between the White House and the executive departments. Furthermore, acting oftentimes on the recommendations of Ralph Nader, Carter appointed aggressive public interest advocates to many regulatory agencies, such as Pertschuck and Joan Claybrook (National Highway and Transportation Administration), who proceeded to convert strong commitments to social regulation into government policy. The impression that Carter gave was one of an irresolute leader who was eager to accommodate all sides.

Carter never seemed to be in control of events, but his weakness was not merely attributable to his personal inadequacies; rather, they were symptomatic of the crisis of the liberal order. As Erwin Hargrove has suggested, Carter was president at a time of transition, after a Democratic period of reform and achievement and before a Republican resurgence. "The Ford and Carter presidencies belong together in this respect," Hargrove concluded, "both providing few possibilities for heroic leadership."[72] Liberals in Congress, prodded by their institutional partners in public interest groups, the courts, administrative agencies, and the media, had imposed severe constraints on the executive since the end of Nixon's reign, reflecting a profound suspicion of the modern presidency. Not surprisingly, they provided an unreceptive audience for decisive leadership that challenged the prevailing pattern of liberal policy demands.

In the notorious, best-remembered address of his presidency—his "malaise" speech of July 15, 1979—Carter described the fractiousness of the 1970s as a "fundamental threat to American democracy." In fact, Carter never used the term "malaise"; the press, taking their cues from White House pollster Patrick Caddell, dubbed it so. Caddell convinced Carter that a speech that probed the deep roots of America's crisis of confidence would elevate his presidency.[73] But the press, unaccustomed to the extraordinary spectacle of a president "scolding his fellow citizens . . . like a . . . pastor with a profligate flock," found parts of the address "awkward and uncomfortable."[74] "This is not a message of happiness or reassurance," Carter announced gravely, "but it is the truth. And it is a warning." Carter's unhappy truth told of a "crisis of confidence":

> We have always believed in something called progress. We have always
> had a faith that the days of our children would be better than our own.
> Our people are losing that faith. Not only in government itself, but in

their ability as citizens to serve as the ultimate rulers and shapers of our democracy. . . . In a nation that was proud of hard work, strong families, close-knit communities and our faith in God, too many of us now tend to worship self-indulgence and consumption. Human identity is no longer defined by what one does but by what one owns. But we have discovered that owning things and consuming things does not satisfy our longing for meaning.

Like Lyndon Johnson's sermons a decade earlier, Carter sought to summon the American people to a higher calling. But his speech lacked the hopefulness that animated the Great Society; in contrast to LBJ's celebration of government reform, Carter's words bespoke a profound distrust, indeed a "growing disrespect," for government and its leaders. "Looking for a way out of this crisis, our people have turned to the Federal Government and found it isolated from the mainstream of the nation's life," he lamented.[75]

By speaking truth to the fractious politics and public estrangement of America, Carter hoped that he could rally its people to the moral equivalent of war against the energy crisis. But the president's words seemed only to reinforce the country's growing doubts about the liberal order. Tellingly, Carter's "crisis of confidence" anticipated the Reagan "revolution" that would force him from office. Carter spoke of the federal government as an adversary, even as he sought to uphold a substantial federal presence in the economy and society. But his liberal centrism was overwhelmed by a Republican president who promised to act boldly to tame the leviathan state.[76] Carter's unhappy isolation did not give him the presence of a modern-day Isaiah, righteous in his scorn for a profligate nation; instead, the American people tended to view him as the rear guard of a decrepit liberalism that had rendered effective presidential leadership an elusive, if not unattainable, prospect.

More penetratingly, Carter's tortured moralism sheds light on the love-hate relationship that Americans had formed with the state—the defining characteristic of contemporary liberalism's legacy for political life in the United States. Even as liberalism became a discredited doctrine, the Reagan "revolution" would fail to roll back many of its programmatic achievements. As we will see in the next chapter, Republicans would win dramatic electoral victories, most notably in 1980 and 1994, by promising to get government off the backs of the people. Yet the public's persistent commitment to middle-class entitlements, such as Social Security and Medicare, environmental and consumer protection, and health and safety measures, made the renewal of local self-government impractical. In part, the public's ambivalence about the role of government reveals the profound difficulty of combining a positive state with the American natural rights tradition. Just as surely, it sheds light on a chronic political disease that threatens to suck the meaning out of representative government in the United States. Since the 1930s, liberalism has promoted government responsibility for economic and social life; at the same time, it has defended a panoply of rights and entitlements, especially for favored constituencies, which created immunities from politics, thus reducing government authority. These cross-purposes, as Wilson Carey McWilliams concludes, "amount to a long-term prescription for frustration and failure."[77]

The uneasy foundation of the liberal state helps us understand why the continual efforts during the twentieth century to advance democratic administration have been self-defeating; why the culmination of these efforts during the 1960s and 1970s provided participatory opportunities for only a small circle of program advocates. The decline in turnout in elections, the emergence of the "plebiscitary presidency," and the vitiation of the legislative process during these years testify that the noble experiment to combine centralized administration and democratic citizenship had gone badly awry. This was the conundrum, and this was the challenge, that programmatic liberalism had left the country with by the end of the 1970s.

Divided Government
and Beltway Partisanship

Can There Be
Another Realignment in
American Democracy?

The resurgence of Congress and other developments during the 1970s seemed not only to curb the worst abuses of the modern presidency but to undermine its authority. By the end of Jimmy Carter's term in office, the view that presidential power had become excessive began to be displaced by the notion that presidential power had become distressingly anemic. This view was expressed by former president Gerald Ford, who understandably felt the reaction against presidential "imperialism" had gotten out of hand. "Some people use to complain about what they called the imperial presidency," he wrote in 1980, "but now the pendulum has swung too far in the opposite direction. We have not had an imperial but an imperiled presidency."[1]

Like Ford, Carter faced serious competition for his party's nomination at the end of his presidency. Although he did manage to fend off a strong challenge from Massachusetts senator Edward Kennedy for the Democratic nomination, he entered the 1980 campaign as damaged goods. His defeat at the hands of Ronald Reagan in the general election marked the first time an elected president had been defeated since Herbert Hoover. The unhappy bond that linked Carter and Hoover, and the impressive manner in which Reagan assumed command of the country, ignited considerable speculation that the 1980 election, like that of 1932, marked a realignment in American politics. Indeed, in many respects, Reagan seemed to represent the forceful challenge to the New Deal which ardent conservatives had long awaited. Much more than Nixon, he presented himself in word and policy as the founder and first magistrate of a conservative political dynasty—as the Republican FDR.

In fact, the results of the 1980 election were somewhat ambiguous. In a three-man race between Reagan, Carter, and independent candidate John Anderson, Reagan won an overwhelming landslide in the electoral college, claiming forty-four states and 489 electoral votes. Yet he won only 51 percent of the popular vote, a mere 2 percent increase over Gerald Ford's total in 1976. Nor were the results of the congressional races decisive. To be sure, for the first time since 1955, the Republicans held the majority of Senate seats, and several liberal senators—including George McGovern—were defeated. Still, although the GOP picked up thirty-three seats in the House, the Democrats retained control of the lower chamber. Thus, Reagan faced political conditions that were considerably more favorable than those Nixon and Ford were forced to deal with, but there was no unambiguous realignment. The Reagan presidency advanced significant changes in the nation's political alignments, especially in the South. But when the Democrats reassumed control of the Senate in 1986, the opportunity for a full-scale partisan realignment seemed to have been lost.

Indeed, the tumultuous events of the 1960s and 1970s raised doubts about whether the New Deal and Great Society had left room for major realignments in American politics. The most significant New Deal institutional development—the modern presidency—had been founded to secure a less partisan future. The logic of the New Deal had thus yielded a candidate-centered political process and an executive-centered government that left voters little reason to express themselves in a partisan manner. This was especially so because programs or benefits were presented as "rights." The tendency to view programs such as Social Security as "entitlements" created a veritable "administrative constitution," in which government programs were viewed as tantamount to rights and thus worthy of protection from the vagaries of party politics and elections. The reformers of the 1960s and 1970s reinforced this development, deepening the commitment to programmatic rights even as they limited the administrative power of the president. As noted in the previous chapter, this expansion of the administrative constitution not only fixed the business of government more on administration but also accelerated the decline of parties.

Consequently, the declining influence of traditional party organizations was reflected not only in administrative politics and the presidential selection process but also in the political loyalties of the American people. Institutional changes that deemphasized partisan politics and governance, combining with television's emergence as the most important platform of political action, were "freeing more and more millions of Americans," as Theodore White wrote in 1973, "from unquestioning obedience to past tradition, their union begetting what has been called the age of ticket-splitting."[2] Indeed, for all but four years between 1968 and 1992 (Jimmy Carter's one term in the White House), the voters delivered a split verdict in national elections, handing control of the presidency to the Republicans and Congress, as well as most state and local elections, to the Democrats.

No clear consensus has emerged on what effect divided government has on public authority and policy, but many commentators view partisan cohabitation of the councils of government with alarm. Benjamin Ginsberg and Martin Shefter argue that the routine existence of separate partisan realms between 1968 and 1992 encouraged "institutional combat" that made it very difficult for presidents to govern. Even Reagan, the only president during this period to complete two full terms in office, saw his second term disrupted by the Iran-contra affair and battles to control social regulation which were marked not just by differences between the president and Congress about policy but also by each branch's efforts to weaken the other. Despite his promise to pursue a "kinder, gentler" version of conservatism which would encourage a spirit of bipartisanship in executive-legislative relations, these institutional battles continued during the presidency of George Bush.[3]

In the aftermath of this pitched warfare between the two branches, the authors of a leading textbook of American constitutional history called "divided government under the separation of powers the central constitutional problem of the 1980s."[4] By the 1992 elections, this view was widely accepted, apparently contributing to the Democratic party's first successful presidential campaign since 1976. With Arkansas governor Bill Clinton as their candidate, Democrats not only captured the presidency but also retained control of both congressional chambers, ending twelve years of divided rule in American politics. Since 1968, the public's striking ambiguity about the parties usually had left the government in a crossfire between a Republican president and a Democratic Congress. In 1992, however, an exit poll revealed that 62 percent of the voters now preferred to have the presidency and Congress controlled by the same party, in the hope that the ideological polarization and institutional combat encouraged by separate partisan realms would be brought to an end.[5]

This hope would soon be disappointed. As the presidency of Jimmy Carter had demonstrated, one-party control of the White House and Congress does not ensure harmony between the branches of government. To be sure, Clinton cultivated his party leaders in Congress more than Carter had, and his efforts were rewarded with rather strong partisan unity during the first two years of his presidency.[6] But congressional support for his programs was sometimes undercut by recalcitrant moderate Democrats, many of whom shunned the president's ambitious health care initiative. More damaging to Clinton was the steadfast opposition of the Republican minority in both the House and Senate. The bitter partisan disputes that ensued over budgetary politics and health care during Clinton's first two years testified to his failure to lead the country beyond the polarizing conflict that had dominated the federal government since the late 1960s. Republicans exploited this failure with great success in 1994, winning dramatic victories in congressional and gubernatorial contests.

With the 1994 elections, which saw the Republicans assume command of both houses of Congress for the first time in forty years, divided government was restored, this time in a form that had not occurred since Harry Truman confronted the Republican-controlled 80th Congress. Not surprisingly, once the Republicans assumed control of Congress in 1995, Clinton resorted to the very same tactics that Reagan and Bush had used to withstand Democratic majorities in Congress. His bitter partisan showdown with the Republicans during the 104th Congress set the stage for the 1996 election, which sustained separate and combative partisan realms.

The bitter partisan disputes between Clinton and the Republican Congress were not resolved by the election. Instead, the Democrats and Republicans on Capitol Hill would wage a historic struggle, which saw the House bring two articles of impeachment against Clinton. Amid surveys that showed the American people scornful of the militantly partisan impeachment process, the Senate conducted only the second impeachment trial of a president in the 209-year history of the Republic. The determination of Republicans to carry on the political prosecution of the president against the tide of public opinion testified to the importance of partisanship in the capital; at the same time, the American people's scorn of the politics that precipitated this constitutional crisis raised troubling questions about the very legitimacy of the two-party system.

The rigidity of partisan lines during the impeachment process points to profound changes in the parties and their struggle for power during the past quarter century. At the end of the day, it was clear that the age of divided government had brought not the decline but rather the transformation of the American party system. The new party system could muster a significant polarizing of politics within the Washington beltway, but recent developments have raised serious doubts about the capacity of these emergent national parties to build popular support for political principles and programs. Indeed, as fierce partisan battles were waged within the beltway, the influence of the Democrats and the Republicans on the perceptions and habits of the American people continued to decline. The weak partisan attachments of the electorate were exposed by the 1992 presidential campaign of H. Ross Perot, whose 19 percent of the popular vote was the most significant challenge to the two-party system since Theodore Roosevelt's Progressive party campaign of 1912. The constitutional episode that engulfed the Clinton presidency could only have intensified the public's estrangement from partisan politics.

As one astute observer of executive-legislative relations has written, "there is a basic disconnection between the [parties'] lack of a role in the government's relationship with the public and its increasingly important role in the government's relationship with itself."[7] Just as parties were becoming less important to the American people, partisan commitments were playing an increasingly significant role in the institutional clashes and policy disputes of constitutional government. If we are to make sense of the causes and consequences of divided government, then, we have to explain the seeming contradictory patterns of party decline and renewal.

The Reagan Revolution and the Revival of Parties

Ronald Reagan represented a different breed of Republican than Richard Nixon. Nixon never articulated a philosophy of government which galvanized the Republicans as a vital opposition to programmatic liberalism. Under his command, the GOP was treated as an obstacle to presidential politics and administration, as an organization that threatened the objective of making the government responsive to him personally. Reagan, in contrast, embodied a historical link with the effort made in 1964 to refashion the Republican party as an anti–New Deal party, as a party against administration. In fact, Reagan's words were but a variation on the theme he had been enunciating since he gave a nationwide television address on behalf of Barry Goldwater on October

27, 1964. "The Speech," as his speech writers referred to it, consisted of a single, abstract idea, universal in application: the idea that centrally administered government tended to weaken a free people's character. By acting "outside its legitimate function," a central state perverted the concept of rights—"natural unalienable rights" were presumed to be a "dispensation of government," thus stripping people of their self-reliance and their capacity for self-government. "The real destroyer of the liberties of the people," Reagan warned, "is he who spreads among them bounties, donations, and benefits."[8]

After the confusing array of solutions offered to treat the social and economic maladies of the nation during the Carter years, Reagan's message, rooted in fundamental principles of government, focused the nation's attention on the need to steer a different course. His inaugural address was the first in almost fifty years to make an appeal for limited government, thus defining clearly his intention to preside over a redirection of public policy for the country: "In this present crisis, government is not the solution to our problem, government is the problem. From time to time we've been tempted to believe that society has become too complex to be managed by self-rule, that government by an elite group is superior to government for, by, and of the people. Well, if no one among us is incapable of governing himself, then who among us has the capacity to govern someone else?"[9]

Thus, Reagan's rhetoric presumed that the era of "enlightened administration" had come to a close. Yet, paradoxically, this challenge to the Roosevelt legacy was issued in terms that paid homage to Franklin Roosevelt. Whereas Democrats since the 1960s had been searching for a message and programs that looked beyond the New Deal, Reagan made an extraordinary effort to associate himself with FDR. In 1980, for example, he made frequent references to Roosevelt in his speech accepting the Republican nomination. So strong was Reagan's claim of kinship with FDR at the Detroit convention that the day after his acceptance speech, the New York Times lead editorial had an eye-catching title: "Franklin Delano Reagan."[10]

In truth, Reagan's invocation of FDR did not signify that he had "moved to the center," as the Times editorial had claimed. Rather, as William Leuchtenburg discerned, "Reagan had not modified his views but exploited Roosevelt for conservative ends."[11] Reagan was a post–New Deal president who skillfully grafted the New Deal concept of leadership onto the anti–New Deal posture of traditional Republicans. His identification with Roosevelt reflected his desire to lead as FDR had led, to exploit fully the powers of the executive office in getting the United States to move toward a new "rendezvous with destiny." Richard Nixon had seen the possibilities of the modern presidency being used to take the country away from the New Deal, but not to the same degree that Reagan saw it. Indeed, Reagan's principles were less reminiscent of Nixon than an earlier, less pragmatic defender of limited government— Calvin Coolidge. Coolidge's leadership had "a major effect on Reagan as a teenager and his ideas greatly influenced those that governed the Reagan presidency," a speech writer in the Reagan White House noted. "Coolidge, of course, was a champion of individualism, free enterprise and traditional values."[12]

Reagan lacked Coolidge's circumspect view of executive power, however, especially when it came to dealing with Congress. As the Iran-contra scandal would reveal, post–New Deal conservatives tended to reject such constitutional sobriety. Still, Reagan's public addresses, like Coolidge's, conveyed the president's commitment to limited government in moral terms, as a righteous cause that served humanity at home and abroad. This rhetorical purpose was most clearly reflected in Reagan's speech on March 8, 1983, to the National Association of Evangelicals in Orlando, Florida. This speech became known as the "evil empire" speech, but it was not simply an effort to liken the Soviet Union to the dark forces depicted in a popular movie. Rather, it represented an effort to state the principles of the Reagan "revolution" in moral and religious terms:

> I believe . . . the source of our strength in the quest for human freedom is not material, but spiritual. And because it knows no limitation, it must terrify and ultimately triumph over those who would enslave their fellow man. For in the words of Isaiah: "He giveth power to the faint; and to them that have no might He increased strength. . . . But they that wait upon the Lord shall renew their strength; they shall mount up with wings as eagles; they shall run and not be weary. . . ."
>
> Yes, change your world. One of our Founding Fathers, Thomas Paine, said, "We have it within our power to begin the world again." We can do it, doing together what no one church could do by itself.[13]

Reagan's use of this passage from Paine's *Common Sense* suggested the depth of his commitment to *individual* rights. Paine went on to say the opportunity to "begin the world again" had not happened "since the days of Noah."[14] In 1776, this was a radically heterodox statement, rejecting an older tradition of political science which subordinated individual freedom to religious and political obligation. Paine implied that the Founding of America signaled humanity's emancipation from the limits of nature and the duties of the community—in America, individuals served their fellow citizens by pursuing gain and increasing the general prosperity.[15]

Paine's view of natural right presupposed a sharp distinction between government and society—and an unyielding defense of limited government. "Society is produced by our wants, and government by our wickedness; the former promotes our happiness *positively* by uniting our affections, the latter *negatively* by restraining our vices," he wrote. "Society in every state is a blessing," Paine continued, "but government even in its best state is but a necessary evil."[16]

Reagan's conservatism thus sought to resuscitate natural right as a radical idea, as a fundamental challenge to centralized government. Americans recoiled when Jimmy Carter preached about sacrifice and limitations; they responded enthusiastically to Reagan's more optimistic sermons that appealed to the nation's primordial faith, which exalted the American experiment in self-rule as the "business of the world."[17]

In this quest to restore the country's devotion to natural rights and limited government, Reagan benefited from and in turn helped to galvanize the renewal of party politics. His bolder conservative posture coincided with the construction of a formidable national Republican organization with strength at the federal level which was unprecedented in American politics. The refurbishing of the GOP organization was largely the work of William Brock, who during his tenure as chair of the Republican National Committee (RNC) from 1976 to 1980 set out to rejuvenate and ultimately to transform the national party. After 1976 the RNC and the two other national Republican campaign bodies, the National Republican Senatorial Committee and the National Republican Congressional (House) Committee, greatly expanded their efforts to raise funds and provide services at the national level for state and local GOP candidates. Moreover, these efforts carried the national party into activities, such as the publication of public policy journals and the distribution of comprehensive briefing books for candidates, which demonstrated its interest in generating programmatic proposals that might be politically useful. The Democrats lagged behind in party-building efforts, but the losses they suffered in the 1980 elections encouraged them to modernize the national political machinery, openly imitating some of the devices employed by the Republicans. As a result, the traditional party apparatus, based on patronage and state and local organizations, gave way to a more programmatic party politics, based on the national organization. Arguably, a party system had finally evolved which was compatible with the national polity formed during the Progressive and New Deal eras.[18]

The revival of the Republican party as a force against government by administration seemed to complete the development of a new American party system. The nomination and election of Ronald Reagan galvanized the Republican commitment to programs, such as "regulatory relief" and "new federalism," which severely challenged the institutional legacy of the New Deal. Had such a trend continued, the circumvention of the regular political process by administrative action may well have been displaced by the sort of full-scale debate about important political questions usually associated with critical realignments.

Significantly, it was Reagan who broke with the tradition of the modern presidency and identified closely with his party. With the important exception of the 1984 election, discussed below, the president worked hard to strengthen the Republicans' organizational and popular base. Indeed, Reagan surprised his own political director with his "total readiness" to shoulder partisan responsibilities such as making numerous fund-raising appearances for the party and its candidates.[19] Apparently, after having spent the first fifty years of his life as a Democrat, Reagan brought the enthusiasm of a convert to Republican activities.

The experience of the Reagan administration suggests how the relationship between the president and the party can be mutually beneficial. Republican party strength provided Reagan with the aid of a formidable institution, solidifying his personal popularity and facilitating the support of his program in Congress. As a result, the Reagan presidency was able to suspend the paralysis that seemed to afflict the executive office in the 1970s, even though the Republicans did not attain control of the House of Representatives. In turn, Reagan's popularity served the party by strengthening its fund-raising efforts and promoting a shift in voters' party loyalties, placing the Republicans by 1985 in a position of virtual parity with the Democrats for the first time since the 1940s.[20] Thus, the 1980s seemed to promise a new political era and a renewed link between presidents and the party system.

The New Party System and Divided Government

The Reagan presidency demonstrated that ardent leadership of the reconstructed party could be an effective instrument for working with, rather than circumventing, Congress and persuading, rather than manipulating, public opinion. But the revival of partisanship continued to be retarded by progressive reforms that had marginalized party organization in politics and government. The McGovern-Fraser reforms carried out during the 1970s marked the completion of a candidate-centered system of presidential selection which discouraged close cooperation between presidential candidates and their fellow partisans during the course of a general election. To be sure, during the 1980s, there were significant efforts to "reform the reforms," and the decline of party due to its loss of control over the nomination process was ameliorated by the strengthening of the financial and organizational capacity of the national and congressional committees. Yet the process of selecting presidential candidates by a series of state primaries and caucuses is so fractious as to discourage substantial efforts to cultivate party unity. Early victories by a candidate ostensibly allow for unity to develop behind a front-runner before the convention. Nonetheless, the media-driven primaries and caucuses require candidates to form personal organizations, dedicated to direct mass appeal. Nominated on their own, presidential candidates have little incentive to identify with the collective mission of their party.

The campaign finance laws passed during the 1970s, which provide public funds directly to candidates, made the problem of partisan harmony more acute. According to Frank Fahrenkopf, who chaired the RNC during Reagan's presidency, the system of public funding, which distributes matching funds to any candidate who can raise $5,000 in each of twenty states in contributions of $250 or less, makes it all too easy for candidates who are not legitimate contenders for the nomination to run, thus reducing the serious business of presidential selection to a virtual free-for-all.[21]

During the 1980s, the modern nominating process created especially difficult problems for Democrats, who were more divided than Republicans on most issues and were therefore less able to develop a strategically unified national party organization. The fragility of the Democratic party-building efforts was revealed all too clearly during the 1988 campaign. The 1988 Convention Rules Committee was controlled by Massachusetts governor Michael Dukakis, who was eager to placate his chief rival for the nomination, Jesse Jackson. The committee agreed to changes in the nomination rules for 1992 which subordinated the interests of the party to short-term tactical considerations of the leading candidates. These changes—one tied the selection of the Democratic delegates more closely to each candidate's share of the primary or caucus vote, and another reduced sharply the number of "superdelegates" (party and elected officials with guaranteed seats as uncommitted delegates) at the 1992 convention—were a retreat from efforts made by Democratic officials to strengthen the role of party leaders in the nominating process. Representative David Price (D-N.C.), a leader in the efforts to reform the reforms, observed with dismay: "It's a familiar path we see. Candidates meet their short-term needs but sell out the long-term interests of the party."[22]

The problem of nurturing partisan community was also aggravated by the tendency of national parties to rely on Washington activism and "high-tech" campaigning, which failed to reach beyond the capital. Indeed, the celebrated Republican machine initially had far more success in presidential campaigns than it had at the state and local level. Acknowledging the limits of the Republican national organization, Loren Smith, who served as chief counsel for the 1980 Reagan campaign, expressed skepticism that the parties were back in business:

> For all the talk about the revival of parties there has been very little consideration of what this means. Are parties more effective in screening the nomination of candidates, providing services to them, acting as a link between candidates and voters? While it is true that the national party organization, especially in the case of the Republican party, has become a source of services to candidates, the party remains weak at state and local level, no longer serving, as it once did, as a link between candidates and the people. There may be a revival of parties in some respects, but it is not clear this means very much to the American people.[23]

In the final analysis, the limits of national parties reflected a problem that went deeper than their limited appeal on the hustings—the failure of party transformation to remedy sufficiently what militant programmatic reformers have long considered the deficiencies of constitutional government in the United States. The constitutional separation of political institutions provides a precarious setting for comprehensive party programs. The emergence of strong national party organizations did not fundamentally alter the limited possibilities for party government under the American Constitution, a fact that would continue to encourage modern presidents, particularly those intent on ambitious policy reform, to emphasize popular appeal and administrative action rather than "collective responsibility." It is not surprising, therefore, that the Reagan presidency frequently pursued its program with acts of administrative discretion which short-circuited the legislative process and weakened efforts to carry out broad-based party policies.

Reinforcing this bow to practicality was conviction, revealing modern conservatives to be products of the New Deal revolution. Republican administrative aggrandizement was supported by a modern conservative movement, with which the Reagan administration frequently expressed common cause, whose advocates preferred not to limit the national state but rather to put it to new uses. Consequently, the Reagan administration, while promising to bring about "new federalism" and "regulatory relief," was stalled in these tasks by the conviction that a strong national state was necessary to foster economic growth, oppose communism, and "nurture" family values. The Iran-contra scandal, for example, was not simply a matter of the president's being asleep on his watch. Rather, it revealed the Reagan administration's determination to assume a more forceful anticommunist posture in Central America in the face of a recalcitrant Congress and bureaucracy.

Senator Richard Lugar, who as chair of the Foreign Relations Committee from 1985 to 1987 acted as Reagan's Senate floor leader in matters of foreign policy, considers the Iran-contra affair to have been a "glaring exception" to Reagan's general willingness to consult with Congress and to work closely with the Republican leadership. The irony, according to Lugar, is that this uncharacteristic inattention to partisan responsibility made possible the president's "most signal policy failure."[24]

In truth, many, if not most, members of the president's party supported the administration's efforts to aid the contras. Although expressing doubts about the wisdom and legality of the diversion of funds from Iran to the contras, the Republican senators and representatives who signed the minority report of the select committees charged with investigating the Iran-contra scandal endorsed the thrust of Reagan's policies with respect to Central America. "Our only regret," read the report, "is that the administration was not open enough with Congress about what it was doing." The long-term prospects for building political support for its policies, the report argued, would have been enhanced by taking on congressional opposition directly. The president should have vetoed the Boland amendment, they insisted, even though it was a specific rider within an omnibus appropriations bill. To take on the issue openly in this way would have given the president the opportunity to challenge Congress on the merits before the nation.[25]

Yet a close examination of policymaking during the Reagan years provides other examples of the administration's resorting to unilateral executive action. As a matter of course, when the president and his advisors confronted legislative resistance on an issue, they charted administrative avenues to advance their goals. Indeed, often they did not even try to modify the statutory basis of a liberal program, relying instead on administrative discretion as a first resort. Even in the area of regulatory relief, a project ostensibly designed to "get government off the backs of the people," the Reagan administration's efforts came not through legislative change but through administrative action, delay, and repeal. Reagan's executive orders 12291 and 12498 mandated a comprehensive review of proposed agency regulations by the Office of Management and Budget. Reagan also appointed a Task Force on Regulatory Relief, headed by Vice President Bush, to apply cost-benefit analysis to existing rules. This pursuit of conservative policy options through the administrative presidency continued with the accession of George Bush to the White House. The burden of curbing environmental, consumer, and civil rights regulations fell on the Competitiveness Council, chaired by Vice President Dan Quayle, which, like its predecessor, the Task Force of Regulatory Relief, required administrative agencies to justify the costs of existing and proposed regulations.[26]

The importance of presidential politics and executive administration in the Reagan presidency may actually have weakened the prospects for a Republican realignment. The journalist Sidney Blumenthal argued that Reagan "did not reinvent the Republican party so much as transcend it. His primary political instrument was the conservative movement, which inhabited the party out of convenience."[27] Blumenthal's observation was only partly correct—Reagan's commitment to strengthening his party was sincere and, in many respects, effective. Nevertheless, his administration's devotion to certain tenets of conservative ideology led it to rely on unilateral executive action and on the mobilization of conservative citizen groups in a way that ultimately compromised the president's support for the Republican party. "Too many of those around [the president] seem to have a sense of party that begins and ends in the oval office," William Brock, then secretary of labor, lamented in 1987. "Too many really don't understand what it means to link the White House to a party in a way that creates an alliance between the presidency, the House, and the Senate, or between the national party and officials at the state and local level."[28] This criticism was echoed by many GOP officials during the final five years of the Reagan presidency.

To some extent, at least, Republican leaders were justified in blaming

Reagan's emphasis on the administrative presidency for his failure to convert his personal popularity into Republican control of government. From a broader historical perspective, however, Reagan's emphasis on presidential politics and government was a logical response to the New Deal and its consolidation of the modern presidency. Although Roosevelt's leadership had been the principal ingredient in a full-scale Democratic realignment, it had aimed to establish the president rather than the party as the steward of the public welfare. The New Deal, like its successor the Great Society in the 1960s, was less a partisan program than an exercise in expanding both the president's power and the liberal administration of the affairs of state. It is not surprising, then, that the challenge to liberal policies which culminated in the elevation of Ronald Reagan to the White House in 1980 produced a conservative administrative presidency, which further retarded the revival of partisan politics. The question raised by the Reagan "revolution" is whether the administrative constitution had advanced so far that a political realignment could occur without a full-scale partisan transformation.

Such a realignment would mark a remarkable triumph of the administrative presidency. But even without the devastating influence of the Iran-contra affair, such a triumph would have been unlikely, for although forceful and centralized executive administration might appear to be a logical and necessary response to the legacy of liberal reform, it is unlikely to nurture the substantial change in public values and institutions required to bring about a fundamental departure in the prevailing patterns of governance.

Even Reagan's most impressive legislative achievement was marred by the absence of serious public debate and choice. The budgetary and tax reforms achievement in 1981 brought dramatic departures in fiscal policy: more than $35 billion in domestic cuts; a multiyear package that projected nearly $750 billion in tax cuts; and a three-year 27 percent increase in defense spending. But this legislative breakthrough was achieved by employing some of the same tactics that were used during the Great Society to subordinate public debate and resolution to executive responsibility. In doing so, ironically, the Reagan administration was able to use the Budget and Impoundment Control Act, which had been enacted to strengthen Congress's role in fiscal policy, to impose his will on the legislature.

The driving force for programmatic change was the political support aroused by Reagan during the 1980 campaign and the early days of his presidency. But the reconciliation process represented a critical action-forcing mechanism that overcame the fractious character of Congress. "The constitu-

tional prerogatives of the legislative branch would have to be, in effect, sus-
pended," Reagan's OMB director, David Stockman, boasted. "Enacting the
Reagan administration's economic program meant rubber stamp approval,
nothing less. The world's so-called greatest deliberative body would have to be
reduced to the status of the ministerial arm in the White House."[29] As Jeffrey
Tulis has written, "Like Lyndon Johnson's, this public policy was prepared
hastily in the executive branch, and like the War on Poverty, the nation's legislature played no substantive role in planning the program. In short, there
was no public deliberation."[30] As a result, Reagan's budgetary program was
enacted in the face of repeated claims by most economists, including many
members of his administration, that it was based on unsubstantiated theory
and false projections.

The justification for such large tax cuts, which far exceeded the reduction of domestic spending and came at the same time that defense spending
was being increased, was the supply-side economic theory that high levels of
taxation were stifling economic productivity. Economists such as Arthur Laf-
fer and Paul Craig Roberts argued that a large tax cut would provide such a
stimulus that tax revenues would actually increase and allow the budget to be
balanced in 1984, despite unprecedented levels of defense spending and
growth in major entitlement programs, such as Social Security, which were
not affected by the 1981 reconciliation act. But, as Stockman admitted at the
time, "None of us really understand what's going on with these numbers."[31] At
the end of the day, the administration's unrealistic economic forecasts, combined with Democratic resistance to its modest proposals for entitlement
reform, produced a Republican version of Keynesianism. The country
became saddled, contrary to supply-side projections, with the largest national
debt in United States history.[32]

Equally important, the Reagan administration failed to justify its program
in partisan terms, to give the voters a compelling reason to endorse a Republican realignment or a fundamental reshaping of institutional arrangements
that sheltered liberal programs. Little wonder that Reagan's landslide victory
in 1984, relying as it did on soft-focus issues—"It's Morning in America"—
rather than sharp issue stands that clarified the choice between Democratic
and Republican views of the nation's future, had little effect on the partisan
alignment of Congress. The Republicans gained just 14 seats in the House,
failing to compensate for the losses in the 1982 midterm election, and they suffered a net loss of 2 seats in the Senate, reducing their majority in that body to
53–47. The Democratic party's recapture of the Senate in the 1986 elections,

followed soon thereafter by the damaging Iran-contra scandal, appeared to derail the resurgence of the Republican party, to short-circuit a full-scale partisan realignment.

The restoration of divided government was widely viewed by Republican partisans as a disaster that need not have happened. It was not unusual, of course, for the party in control of the White House to lose ground in midterm elections—Eisenhower, Johnson, and Nixon, for example, saw their parties sustain serious congressional defeats at similar junctures of their administrations. But the popularity that Reagan enjoyed in 1986 and the economic prosperity the country was experiencing might have worked against the tide of history. As Alan Ehrenhalt wrote soon after the election, "All the other midterm Senate debacles of modern times occurred against the backdrop of serious problems in the country—a national recession in 1958, the Vietnam War in 1966, the Watergate scandal in 1974. No such problem existed for the Republicans this year."[33]

To be sure, Reagan displayed his characteristic support for his party during the campaign, taking part in fund-raisers for the GOP and campaigning for Republican candidates; moreover, the political office in the White House worked closely with the Republican National Committee, as well as with the House and Senate campaign committees. But a conscious decision was made within the White House to avoid a highly charged campaign in 1986, a determination that was imposed on the vaunted Republican machine.[34] The deliberate choice to work closely with the GOP campaign organization and candidates while avoiding a thematic partisan campaign was an unwitting betrayal of the party the president hoped to elevate to majority status, Minnesota representative Vin Weber argued. Weber, a member of the militantly partisan Conservative Opportunity Society, lamented that "the campaign was not run as a national partisan campaign, highlighting the philosophical differences between the Republicans and Democrats. Instead the focus was on state and local issues and the same feel good, empty rhetoric that dominated the 1984 race."[35]

Reagan's speech for Senator James Broyhill in North Carolina, whose campaign for reelection failed, offers a fairly typical example. It did not present any broad themes that might have projected the GOP as a governing party but instead presented the president and Broyhill as part of a team that modulated the excesses of the liberal establishment. "Will you choose the Democratic leaders who in 1980 weakened our nation and nearly brought our economy to its knees," the president asked, "who raised your taxes and have announced their plans to do so again, and who opposed efforts to build a defense to protect us from attack by nuclear ballistic missiles? Or will you choose to give the cleanup crew of 1980 a chance to finish the job?" In characterizing himself as part of a "cleanup crew," Reagan failed to give the voters a sustaining reason to support this party.[36] More to the point, this strategy displayed the risks involved in centering political responsibility within the White House, divorced from the fate of a collective organization that might restrain, even as it enlarged, the president's pride and ambition.

The failure of the Reagan administration to bring forth a party realignment both circumscribed and left unresolved the achievements of the Reagan era. The president himself granted as much in one of his last important public speeches, delivered on December 13, 1988, before administration officials. In these farewell remarks, Reagan blamed the disappointments of his tenure, the greatest of which he counted as the failure to balance the federal budget, on an "iron triangle," composed of "parts of Congress, the media, and special interest groups." This unholy trinity had not only made it impossible for him to carry out a comprehensive program of domestic reform but had also weakened the presidency in order to retain control over the federal government:

> When I came to office, I found in the Presidency a weakened institution. I found a Congress that was trying to transform our government into a quasi-parliamentary system. And I found in Washington a colony—that through the iron triangle—was attempting to rule the Nation according to its interests and desires more than the Nation's. I've used the President's ability to frame the broadest outlines of debate to compensate for some of the weakening of the office. . . . But we have not restored the constitutional balance, at least not fully, and I believe it must be restored.[37]

Thus, Reagan acknowledged that the modern presidency of the 1980s did not, as it had during the early days of the Johnson administration, command the political system. Instead, as noted in the previous chapter, it was challenged forcefully by a "modern" Congress that had developed considerable tools of its own during the 1970s to exert influence on domestic and foreign policy. For example, members of Congress, acting in partnership with the courts, bureaucratic agencies, interest groups, and the press, were able to fend off the Reagan administration's challenge to New Deal entitlements and circumscribe its program of regulatory relief for corporations and other private institutions. Executive agencies were important in this institutional partnership, but they were sustained, and sometimes harassed, by the political support mobilized by programmatic advocates in public interest groups, Congress, and the courts.

In effect, the opposition to programmatic liberalism did not result in a challenge to national administrative power but in a battle for its services. The political toll of this battle appeared to be a badly frayed connection between American government and its citizenry, a frightening deterioration of American civil society. Political parties, which once provided a connection between the governing institutions and the public, were certainly not absent from the administrative politics spawned by the New Deal and the opposition it aroused. But, in the wake of the New Deal, parties had been weakened as electoral institutions. Both parties had shifted much of their attention from the building of a vital link with the public to an "inside the beltway" administrative politics. Moreover, this administrative politics had been associated with the expansion of new rights that had further shifted partisan disputes away from parties as associations that organized public sentiments as an electoral majority. Even conservatives in the abortion debate talked of the rights of the unborn in a way that required centralized administration—consider the so-called gag rule of the Reagan and Bush administrations.[38] When rights dominate policy discourse, majority sentiments are commonly viewed as a problem and not the solution.

The struggle over the proper definition of new rights camouflaged and added moral outrage to the administrative conflict that characterized presidential-congressional relations during the Reagan and Bush years. It is not surprising that this struggle for the Constitution led to an unprecedented battle to control the judiciary, which had become a critical agent in overseeing the competition between the president and Congress for mastery over the administrative state. The culmination of Reagan's efforts to remake the judiciary came with the nomination of Federal Appeals Court judge Robert Bork to the highest court in 1987. In a resounding defeat for the Reagan administration, Bork became the twenty-sixth Supreme Court nominee in history—but only the fourth in the twentieth century—to fail to be confirmed by the Senate. No previous nominee had been worked over the way Bork was in his nearly thirty hours of testimony, and the rejection of his nomination (58–42) was by the widest margin in history. In spite of Bork's defeat, the eight years of Reagan judicial appointments and other Reagan nominees to lower federal tribunals left uncertain the future direction of the courts. Still, nothing as decisive as the 1937 constitutional revolution that validated the New Deal took place during the 1980s.[39] In truth, the Reagan administration's close attention to judicial appointments in its pursuit of an enduring legacy testified to its failure to bring about the sort of realignment that occurred in the 1930s. As one conservative scholar wrote soon after the Bork debacle:

> The Reagan administration has not tried to hide the fact that it hoped to leave its longest-lasting legacy through the process of judicial appointments. This is little more than a tacit admission that it has been unable to change the political landscape through the political process. Its failure to do so—and its failure in a sense even to attempt to do so, which has given the impression that the Republican party is grown accustomed to, if not fond of, its minority status—has in turn proved extremely costly in the waning years of the Reagan presidency. The President's inability to get confirmation of his leading nominees to the Supreme Court is but one case in point.[40]

Bork's rejection and other nomination battles during the Reagan and Bush presidencies signaled a heightened level of conflict over judicial rulings in an era of divided government. This conflict was not limited to appointments. Congress was not hesitant to reverse rulings it did not like, even as the White House sought to uphold the judiciary's retreat on certain social policies. For example, Congress overturned the Supreme Court's 1984 decision in *Grove City College v. Bell,* which narrowed the reach of Title IX of the 1972 Education Act Amendments. Reagan vetoed this civil rights restoration bill; however, Congress overrode his veto, with no Democratic senator and only ten Democratic representatives voting to sustain the president's action.[41] Similarly, the Civil Rights Act of 1991 nullified nine Supreme Court rulings, thus restoring legal standards that placed the burden of proof in antidiscrimination lawsuits on employers. Bush had vetoed a similar bill in 1990, arguing that it would lead to quotas for minorities and women in hiring practices. But in the wake of the explosive Clarence Thomas hearings, he decided to sign a modified version of the bill, albeit not without offering a more narrow interpretation of the legislation than Democratic members of Congress were willing to accept.[42] The ongoing dispute between Democratic legislators and the Republican White House about judicial rulings and appointments exposed the limits of the Reagan legacy with respect to the courts. Just as significant, the federal courts now rivaled elections as the primary institutional focus of partisan politics.

Thus, during the Reagan-Bush era, divided government was dominated by a politics of entitlements which tended to belittle efforts by Democrats and Republicans alike to define a collective purpose with a past and a future and yielded instead a partisanship joined to a form of administrative politics which relegated electoral conflict to the intractable demands of policy advocates. Indeed, a partisanship that emphasizes national administration in support of programmatic rights has little chance to reach beyond the Washington beltway and influence the perceptions and habits of the American people. This development did not mean, certainly, that the Democrats and Republicans considered elections unimportant and despaired of extending their influence through them. It does suggest that, as parties of administration, the Democrats and Republicans were hobbled in their efforts to form vital links with the public. The emergence of parties of administration strengthened the national party organization and created more discipline among party members in Congress, but at the cost of weakening party loyalties among the electorate. The tendency for growing numbers of voters to split their tickets, or to stay at home on election day, represents their estrangement from these parties of administration—a plague on both your houses.[43]

The indecision at the polls and the concomitant perpetuation of divided government also reflect the fact that more is at stake in American politics than at any other time in history, with the notable exception of the Civil War. The commitment to limited government which prevailed until the New Deal tended to reduce the stakes of political conflict in the United States, to confine political battles to "safe issues." Yet the emergence of activist government after the 1930s attenuated the constitutional boundaries that once contained political conflict, and the Reagan "revolution" further eroded the wall that separated politics and society. The checks that divided government has imposed on the parties have not led to "policy gridlock"; during the Nixon, Reagan, and Bush presidencies, a number of important laws were passed, in spite of, and in some cases because of, the persistence of separate partisan realms.[44] Indeed, to a point, divided government has restrained the extreme tendencies of the Democrats and Republicans, thus providing some protection against the abuses of centralized administration. But this security did not come without its costs. As the extraordinary budgetary evasions and the jarring nomination fights of the previous two decades had revealed, the dark side of divided government is that it tends to obscure political responsibility and to mire government in petty, virulent clashes that undermine respect for American political institutions.

Bill Clinton and the "New" Politics of Divided Democracy

Bill Clinton dedicated his 1992 campaign to principles and policies that "transcended," he claimed, the exhausted left-right debate that had afflicted the nation for two decades. In 1990, Clinton became the chairman of the Democratic Leadership Council (DLC), a moderate group in the Democratic party which developed many of the ideas that became the central themes of his run for the presidency. As Clinton declared frequently during the campaign, these ideas represented a new philosophy of government which would "honor middle class values, restore public trust, create a new sense of community and make America work again." He heralded "a new social contract," a "new covenant," one that would seek to constrain, in the name of responsibility and community, the demands for rights summoned by the Roosevelt revolution. Invoking Roosevelt's Commonwealth Club address, in which FDR first outlined the "economic constitutional order," Clinton declared that the liberal commitment to guaranteeing economic security through entitlement programs such as Social Security, Medicare, Medicaid, and Aid to Families With Dependent Children had gone too far. The objective of the New Covenant was to correct the tendency of Americans to celebrate individual rights and government entitlement programs without any sense of the mutual obligations they had to each other and their country.[45]

Clinton's commitment to educational opportunity best exemplified the objective of restoring a balance between rights and responsibilities; its central feature, a national service corps, was emblematic of the core New Covenant principle—national community. According to Clinton, a trust fund would be created, out of which any and all Americans could borrow money for a college education, so long as they paid it back either as a small percentage of their life's income or with two years as service as teachers, police officers, child care workers, or by participating in other activities that "our country desperately needs."[46]

Clinton's campaign thereby promised to correct and renew the progressive tradition as shaped by the New Deal. Vital parties require some compromise between a deep and abiding commitment to rights and a due attention to common deliberation and choice—some decisions must be left to a party majority. Roosevelt's party politics, however, rested on a new understanding of rights, one associated with the expansion of national administrative power, which is not congenial to such partisan responsibility. In challenging the explosion of rights and hidebound bureaucracy that arose from the New Deal and the opposition it spawned, Clinton pledged to dedicate his party to a new public philosophy that could redress many of the troubling aspects of the New Deal legacy—the decline of parties as civic associations, the rise of virulent administrative politics, and the deterioration of public trust in American political institutions.

In truth, Clinton and his allies in the Democratic Leadership Council were ambivalent about party politics. Clinton—the first president of the baby boom generation—cut his political teeth during the late 1960s and 1970s when parties were under siege. He rose to national prominence as a luminary of the "new" politics that matured during the 1970s, in which those ambitious for higher office saw no reason to seek the support of old machines and regular organizations. Instead, as a 1984 article celebrating Clinton and other practitioners of the new politics observed, they were "tough, outspoken champions of the movements they [stood] for." Eschewing party politics, they viewed politics as an "exercise in narrowcasting," seeking out people who "shared their vision."[47]

Clinton's disinclination to rely on party organization was reinforced by the tension between the Democratic Leadership Council and the regular party apparatus. The DLC was founded for the most part by elected Democratic officials who believed that the national committee and congressional caucus had become too responsive to liberal constituency groups. In fact, the DLC was divided between those who wanted to reform the party and those who preferred to build a progressive coalition that would transcend parties entirely.[48] Clinton himself appeared to be torn between these two objectives. Even as he styled himself a "new" Democrat who would challenge the liberal orthodoxy of his party, he formed a campaign organization that included many traditional liberals and promised congressional Democrats that he would work in "harness" with them to pursue policies of mutual interest.[49] Clinton's artful fence-mending allowed the Democrats to run a unified, effective campaign in 1992; at the same time, his campaign rhetoric was at odds with the majority of liberal activist groups and Democratic members of Congress. The difficulty of reconciling "new" Democratic principles and the traditional commitments of the party would be a constant source of trouble for Clinton, threatening to undermine his authority as a moral leader.

Indeed, Clinton's words and actions during the early days of his presidency seemed to betray his campaign pledge to dedicate the Democratic party to the new concept of justice he espoused. No sooner had he been inaugurated than Clinton announced his intention to lift the longstanding ban on homosexuals in the military. The president soon learned, however, that there was no prospect that such a divisive issue could be resolved through the "stroke of a pen." The development of the administrative presidency gave presidents more power to exercise domestic policy autonomously. Yet with the expansion of national administration to issues that shaped the direction and character of American public life, this power proved to be illusory. Intense opposition from the respected head of the Joint Chiefs of Staff, Colin Powell, and the influential Democratic chair of the Senate Armed Services Committee, Sam Nunn of Georgia, forced Clinton to defer the executive order for six months while he sought a compromise solution. But the delay and the compromise aroused the ire of gay and lesbian activists who had given strong financial and organizational support to Clinton during the election. Most damaging for the new president was that the issue became a glaring benchmark of his inability to revitalize progressive politics as an instrument to redress the economic insecurity and political alienation of the middle class.

The bitter partisan fight in the spring and summer of 1993 over the administration's budgetary program served only to reinforce doubts about Clinton's ability to lead the nation in a new, more harmonious direction. Even though Clinton's budget plan promised to reduce the deficit, it involved new taxes and an array of social programs that Republicans and moderate Democrats perceived as traditional tax-and-spend liberalism. The Republicans marched in lockstep opposition to Clinton's economic program, especially to his $16 billion stimulus package, which he offered as a partial antidote to the economic contraction that he feared deficit reduction would cause. In April 1993, Senate Republicans unanimously supported a filibuster that killed the stimulus package. Congress did enact a modified version of the president's budgetary plan a few months later, albeit by razor-thin margins and without any support from Republicans, who voted unanimously against it in the House and Senate. Clinton won this narrow, bruising victory only after promising moderate Democrats that he would put together another package of spending cuts in the fall. But this uneasy compromise failed to dispel the charge of his political opponents that Clinton was a wolf in sheep's clothing — a conventional liberal whose commitment to reform had expired at the end of the presidential campaign.[50]

The failure of the Clinton administration and congressional leaders to fulfill their promise of a second round of spending cuts further belied Clinton's claim to be a new Democrat. In a major blow to the administration, the Congressional Budget Office dramatically downgraded claimed savings from the administration's plans to "reinvent government," the principal part of the White House's program to achieve the promised savings. Unable to come up with an alternative package that satisfied deficit hawks in his party, Clinton nearly suffered a devastating defeat to his economic program. Despite intense administration opposition, a tough bipartisan deficit reduction bill, sponsored by Minnesota Democrat Tim Penny and Ohio Republican John Kasich, lost by only four votes in the House.[51] Sounding an ominous note, Representative Penny complained that the reinventing government initiative was symptomatic of one of Clinton's most serious faults, the tendency to "oversell and underdeliver his programs."[52]

In fact, Clinton said and did little about a New Covenant during the first two years of his presidency. He appointed Donna Shalala to head the Department of Health and Human Services, even though she had not expressed support for reshaping welfare policy. And in a February 1993 address to Congress, in which he laid out his administration's goals, Clinton, instead of trumpeting reciprocal obligations between citizens and their government, proposed instead a new set of entitlements in the form of job training, a college education, and health care. Clinton's proposal to make college loans available to all Americans did include the campaign-touted plan to form a national service corps. But news of the enactment of a scaled-down version of this educational reform program in August was lost amid Clinton's promises to expand the welfare state. In fact, the reciprocal obligation Clinton expected of the beneficiaries of college loans seemed almost apologetic. They will be able to pay the country back with a small percentage of their income, thereby avoiding national service—this option to public service, it seems, greatly dilutes the concept of national community.[53]

The apologetic stance that Clinton displayed in the face of traditional liberal causes was, to a point, understandable; it was a logical response to the modern institutional separation between the presidency and the party. The moderate wing of the Democratic party which he represented—including the members of the Democratic Leadership Council—was a minority wing. The majority of liberal interest group activists and Democratic members of Congress still preferred entitlements to obligations and regulations to responsibilities. Only the unpopularity of liberal groups and the emphasis on candidate-centered campaigns in presidential politics made Clinton's nomination and election possible. The media-driven caucuses and primaries that dominate the presidential nomination process gave him an opportunity to seize the Democratic label as an outsider candidate but offered no means to effect a transformation of his party when he took office.

Clinton's Democratic predecessor, Jimmy Carter, who intended to be fiercely independent and a scourge to traditional liberal approaches, faced a situation of nearly complete political isolation during his unhappy term in office. To bring about the new mission of progressivism which he advocated during the election, Clinton would have to risk a brutal confrontation with the major powers in the Democratic party, a battle that might have left him even more vulnerable politically than Carter had been.[54] In truth, no president had risked such a confrontation with his party since Roosevelt's failed purge campaign. It is not surprising, therefore, that Clinton's allies in the Democratic Leadership Council urged him to renew his "credentials as an outsider" by going over the heads of the party leadership in Congress and taking his message directly to the people. Most important, the president needed to take his New Covenant message directly to the large number of independents in the electorate who voted for Perot, the DLC leaders argued, so as to forge "new and sometimes bipartisan coalitions around an agenda that moves beyond the polarized left-right debate."[55]

In the fall of 1993, Clinton took a page from his former political associates in his successful campaign to secure congressional approval of the North American Free Trade Agreement (NAFTA). The fight for NAFTA caused Clinton to defend free enterprise ardently and to oppose the protectionism of labor unions, which still represented one of the most important constituencies in the national Democratic party. Clinton's victory owed partly to the active support of the Republican congressional leadership; in fact, a majority of Republicans in the House and Senate supported the free trade agreement, while a majority of Democrats, including the House majority leader and majority whip, opposed it. No less important, however, was the Clinton administration's mobilization of popular support. Indeed, the turning point in the struggle came when the administration challenged Perot, the leading opponent of NAFTA, to debate Vice President Gore on "Larry King Live." Gore's optimistic defense of open markets was well received by the large television audience, rousing enough support to persuade a bare majority of legislators in both houses of Congress to approve the trade agreement.[56]

With the successful fight over NAFTA, moderate Democrats began to hope that Clinton had finally begun the task of dedicating his party to principles and policies he had espoused during the campaign. But the next major legislative battle was for the administration's health care program, which promised to "guarantee all Americans a comprehensive package of benefits over the course of an entire lifetime." The formulation of this program appeared to mark the apotheosis of New Deal administrative politics; it was designed "behind closed doors" by the Health Care Task Force, which was headed by the first lady, Hillary Rodham Clinton, and the president's long-time friend Ira Magaziner. Moreover, the health care proposal would create a new government entitlement program and an administrative apparatus that would signal the revitalization rather than the reform of traditional social welfare state policy.[57]

Significantly, in his September 1993 speech to Congress on health care reform, Clinton brandished a red, white, and blue "health security card," a symbol of his ambition to carry out the most important extension of social policy since the enactment of Social Security in 1935. In fact, the Clinton administration's proposal offered an alternative to more liberal and conservative plans. But the president's "third way," which purported both to guarantee universal coverage and to contain costs, resulted in a Rube Goldberg contraption that appeared to require an intolerable expansion of the federal bureaucracy. With its complexity (the bill was 1,342 pages long) and obtrusive bureaucracy, the Clinton proposal was an easy target for Republicans.[58]

Although the administration sounded conciliatory overtures to the plan's opponents, hoping to forge bipartisan cooperation on the Hill and a broad consensus among the general public, the possibilities for comprehensive reform hinged on settling differences over the appropriate role of government which had divided the parties and country for the past two decades. In the end, this proved impractical—the health care bill died in the 103d Congress when a compromise measure, negotiated between Senate Democratic leader George Mitchell of Maine and Republican senator John Chafee of Rhode Island, could not win enough Republican support to break a threatened filibuster.[59] By proposing such an ambitious health care reform bill, Clinton enraged conservatives. By failing to deliver on his promise to provide a major overhaul of the health care system, he dismayed the ardent liberals of his party. Most significant, the defeat of the president's health care program created the overwhelming impression that he had not lived up to his campaign promise to transcend the bitter philosophical and partisan battles of the Reagan and Bush years.

Indeed, the willingness of Senate Republicans to resort to the filibuster to block many of Clinton's initiatives was a mark of the fundamental conflicts that divided the parties in Congress and prevented harmonious relations between the executive and legislature. Such a course was virtually unprecedented; historically, the filibuster had been employed by mavericks or regional minorities to obstruct party leaders. That its use was orchestrated by the Senate minority leader, Robert Dole, to ensnare President Clinton testified to the bitter partisanship that lingered from the Reagan-Bush era, as well as to Clinton's inability to move the country beyond the institutional conflicts spawned by partisan estrangement.[60]

The president and his party paid dearly for these failures in the 1994 election. In taking control of the Congress, the Republicans gained fifty-two seats in the House and eight in the Senate. Moreover, they won dramatic victories at the state and local level: Republicans increased their share of governorships from nineteen to thirty, their first majority since 1970; they also reached near parity in state legislatures, a status they had not enjoyed since 1968. The Republicans achieved this victory in an off year campaign that was unusually ideological and partisan. The charged atmosphere of the campaign owed largely to House minority leader Newt Gingrich (R-Ga.), the founder of the Conservative Opportunity Society. Gingrich, his party's choice to be the new Speaker of the 104th Congress, persuaded more than three hundred House candidates to sign a "Republican Contract With America," a "Covenant" with the nation which promised to restore limited government by eliminating programs, ameliorating regulatory burdens, and cutting taxes. Clinton's attack on the Republican program during the campaign seemed to backfire, serving only to abet Republicans in their effort to highlight the president's failure to fulfill his promise to "reinvent government." Examining exit polls that suggested that a "massive anti-Clinton coalition came together" to produce the "revolution" of 1994, political analyst William Schneider wrote of the voters' desire for change, "If the Democrats can't make government work, maybe the Republicans can solve problems with less government."[61]

The Republican triumph was especially notable in the South. For the first time in this century, southern Republicans emerged from an election in control of a majority of the governorships, a majority of the seats in the Senate, and a majority of seats in the House. Republicans also gained 119 southern state legislative seats and captured control of three state legislative chambers, the Florida Senate, North Carolina House, and South Carolina House.[62] For the first time since Reconstruction, Republicans elected the Speakers of two southern legislatures.

The Republican triumph below the Mason-Dixon line in 1994 marked a dramatic new chapter in a story that had been unfolding for a generation. The playing out of the New Deal and Great Society, and the Republican response, had sharply reduced the presence of traditional southern Democracy in Congress, thus emancipating the party from the ball and chain that hobbled its liberal march. In the 75th Congress that balked at FDR's court-"packing" plan, there were 120 House seats in the thirteen southern states (the old Confederacy, plus Kentucky and Oklahoma). A full 117 of those 120 were in Democratic hands. On their own, southern Democrats possessed more than half the votes needed to carry a majority of the House on any question. By the end of the Reagan era, those same states had 124 seats. But only 85 of them were Democratic; more than a quarter had migrated to the GOP side of the aisle. Moreover, the 1965 Voting Rights Act had substantially increased the number of black voters in the South, tending to transform the voting behavior of those southern representatives who remained on the Democratic side of the aisle. As Alan Ehrenhalt wrote in 1987:

> In the vast majority of districts across the South, a Democratic incumbent knows two things. Blacks will provide the basis of his support against any Republican, and they can cause him trouble in a Democratic primary if they turn against him. For both reasons, the black community and its wishes have to be listened to. It was a sign of the times in 1983 when Southern Democrats voted 78–12 in favor of the holiday in honoring Reverend Martin Luther King.[63]

The 1994 elections revealed how these changes in southern politics prepared the ground for a dramatic Republican victory. Although white southerners had been rebelling against national Democratic politics since the 1950s, Democratic candidates in the South assumed they could insulate themselves from what southern voters regarded as the most unappealing aspects of the national party. But Clinton's first two years as president stripped them of this illusion. "Clinton had earned praise as one of the brightest, most agile governors in his region," Dan Balz and Ronald Brownstein wrote after the 1994 elections; "but, as President his policies, from his advocacy of ending discrimination against homosexuals in the military to his economic and health care programs that stressed big-government activism, often seemed like a stick in the eye of his native South."[64] Southerners had expressed a sense of betrayal in their reaction to the progressive policies of Lyndon Johnson and

Jimmy Carter; with Clinton, however, their anger spilled over to Democrats in Congress and state government. White southerners' long memories of the Civil War and Reconstruction had helped the Democrats to control the Congress for most of the post–New Deal era, even as the South became estranged from the national Democratic party. Now they identified with the Republican party in roughly the same percentages as northern Protestants, the most loyal Republican constituency since the party was founded. As William Galston observed in the wake of this dramatic partisan transformation, "the Civil War is finally over."[65]

The dramatic Republican triumph in the 1994 midterm elections again led scholars and pundits to suggest that the nation might be on the threshold of a critical partisan realignment.[66] It remained to be seen, however, whether the New Deal and its aftermath had left room for still another rendezvous with America's political destiny. The emphasis on rights and administrative politics which characterizes contemporary political struggles seems to belie the sort of collective partisan affiliations that have made full-scale party realignments possible in the past. To be sure, the Reagan years showed that party conflict had not withered away, that the New Deal and the opposition it spawned brought a new blending of partisanship and administration, in which administration had become a vehicle for both Democratic and Republican objectives. But the American people had become alienated from these parties of administration by the 1990s, so much so that the renewal of partisan loyalties in the electorate, let alone a full-scale partisan transformation, seemed unlikely. Indeed, the 1994 elections attenuated the moderate wings of both parties, thus threatening to deepen this alienation. Just as the defeat of southern Democrats strengthened the influence of liberals within the party councils, so the expansion of Republican power in the South deepened the conservative tendencies of the GOP, particularly its commitment to social issues such as school prayer and abortion.

The new Republican majority in Congress and the states was not unmindful of these obstacles to realignment. They promised to pursue a program dedicated to rebuilding the wall of separation between government and society, and to cultivate a vital debate about the role of the state in "promoting the General Welfare." Significantly, the "Republican Contract With America" was silent on the abortion issue. The failure to mention the "rights of the unborn" in this "covenant" with the electorate suggested that some Republican leaders were willing to approach controversial social issues such as abortion more pragmatically. More to the point, this political strategy appeared to signify the determination of some conservatives to moderate programmatic ambitions that presupposed new uses of, rather than a fundamental challenge to, the centralized administrative power created in the aftermath of the New Deal realignment.

The determination of the new conservative majority to challenge the administrative state was also apparent in the sweeping changes that the new Speaker and his allies made in the House rules. House Republicans reduced the number of standing committees and their staffs, limited the tenure of committee chairs, and prohibited closed-door hearings and unrecorded votes. These reforms promised to restrain the institutions that had encouraged the House to focus excessively on management of the executive, at the expense of serious public debate about major issues of national policy. Indeed, Speaker Gingrich pledged to Democrats and moderate Republicans a renewed emphasis on legislative debate that would "promote competition between differing political philosophies."[67]

Although the new Republican majority promised to rededicate the government to principles of limited government and states' rights, they were hardly unreconstructed Jeffersonians. The Republican contract proposed to strengthen national defense in a form that would require the expansion rather than the rolling back of the central government's responsibilities; and the GOP's proposals to reduce entitlements for the poor and to get government off the back of business demanded the creation of alternative national welfare and regulatory standards. Finally, the Republican party was reluctant to challenge middle-class entitlements such as Social Security and Medicare, which dwarfed the spending of programs that guaranteed a minimum standard of living to the destitute, thus making unlikely a serious reexamination of the core assumptions of the New Deal.[68]

In the absence of a meaningful debate between conservative and liberal principles, the first session of the 104th Congress threatened to degenerate into the same sort of administrative politics that had corroded the legitimacy of political institutions since the presidency of Nixon. This time, however, the struggle between the branches assumed a novel form: institutional confrontation between a Democratic White House and a Republican Congress. Amid this struggle, Republicans in the House began to regret, indeed, to reconsider, the institutional reforms they enacted at the beginning of the 104th Congress which reduced the capacity of the legislature to oversee the activities of the executive. Just as Clinton resorted to a more aggressive use of the administrative presidency to defy Republican majorities in Congress, so Republicans began to make extensive use of the levers of administrative power accumulated on Capitol Hill since the 1960s in an effort to torment a Democratic president with the same sort of investigations and "micromanagement" of domestic and foreign policy with which Democratic Congresses assaulted Reagan and Bush.[69] Significantly, Republicans had opposed the reauthorization of the 1978 Ethics in Government Act, which provided for fixed terms and judicial appointments of independent counsels who investigated possible abuses in the executive branch. But their resistance to Democratic efforts to reauthorize the statute came to an end in the winter of 1993, when the Whitewater real estate scandal implicating the Clintons gained prominence. Suddenly, as the political scientist Kathy Harriger observed wryly, "the advantages of independent investigation became more apparent to erstwhile opponents of the office."[70]

The battle between Clinton and Congress became especially fierce in a contest over legislation to balance the budget. More than any other idea celebrated in the GOP's Contract With America, Republicans believed that a balanced budget bill would give them their best opportunity to control Congress for years to come. But their proposal for a constitutional amendment to require a balanced budget died in the Senate, where, facing stiff resistance from the president and his Democratic allies, it failed by one vote to get the necessary two-thirds support.

With the defeat of this constitutional amendment, Republicans in the House and Senate put their faith in a bold legislative plan to balance the budget by 2002. The most controversial part of this program was a proposal to scale back the growth of Medicare, by encouraging beneficiaries to enroll in health maintenance organizations and other private, managed health care systems. Rallied by their militant partisan brethren in the House, Republican leaders sought to pressure Clinton to accept their priorities on the budget by twice shutting down government offices and even threatening to force the U.S. Treasury into default. These confrontation tactics backfired. Clinton's veto of a sweeping budget bill in December 1995, which would not only overhaul Medicare but also remake decades of federal social policy, roused popular support for the administration. Most important, Clinton's budgetary stand, signaling his growing willingness to draw sharp differences between his priorities and those of the Republican Congress, appeared to preserve the major programs of the New Deal and its successor, the Great Society. In attacking Medicare and social policies such as environmental programs, the Republicans' militant assault on programmatic liberalism went beyond what was

promised by the Contract With America, thus giving Clinton the opportunity
to take a political stand that was supported by most of the country.

When Congress returned for the second session of the 104th Congress in
January 1996, it was not to Speaker Gingrich's agenda of reducing the role of
Washington in the society and economy, but to the measured tones of Clinton's third State of the Union message. The president addressed many of the
themes of his Republican opponents, boldly declaring, "The era of big government is over."[71] This was not merely rhetoric; withstanding furious criticism from liberal members of Congress and interest group activists, Clinton
signed welfare reform legislation in August which ended the sixty-one-year-
old federal entitlement to cash payments for low-income mothers and their
dependent children. Clinton conceded that the act was flawed, cutting too
deeply into nutritional support for low-income working people and denying
support unfairly to legal immigrants. Nevertheless, by encouraging welfare
recipients to take jobs, it served the fundamental principle Clinton championed in the 1992 campaign of "recreating the Nation's social bargain with the
poor."[72]

Warning that "we cannot go back to the time when our citizens were left
to fend for themselves," however, Clinton also called for a halt to Republican
assaults on basic liberal programs dedicated to providing economic security,
educational opportunity, and environmental protection.[73] Employing Democratic National Committee funds, the White House had orchestrated a
national media blitz toward the end of 1995 which excoriated the Republicans' program to reform Medicare and presented the president as a figure of
national reconciliation who favored welfare reform and a balanced budget
but who also would protect middle-class entitlements, education, and the
environment.[74] Clinton's carefully modulated State of the Union message
underscored this media campaign, revealing the president as a would-be
healer anxious to bring all sides together.

Clinton's annual message appeared to depart from weeks of venomous
dialogue between the White House and Republican leaders over a balanced
budget plan. But the surface calm, as Senate majority leader Robert Dole
acknowledged in the Republican response to the president's speech, barely
hid "starkly different philosophies of government and profoundly different
visions of America." Setting the tone for the 1996 national campaign, Dole,
the eventual nominee of his party for president, characterized Clinton as the
"rear guard of the welfare state" and the "chief obstacle to a balanced-budget
amendment." Far more pragmatic than his partisan brethren in the House,

Dole had opposed the use of government shutdowns and holding the debt ceiling hostage to Republican demands during the first session of the 104th Congress. But he now proclaimed that there were times "when even practical statesmen must refuse to bend or yield." That time, apparently, had come for Senator Dole, who now sought to position himself as the leader not only of his party but also of the conservative movement.[75] Indeed, frustrated by the responsibilities of leading the Senate in petty and mean-spirited skirmishes with the White House, Dole resigned his seat in June, hoping he could better lead a charge against the liberal establishment as a private citizen than he could as a Washington insider.

Dole's hope proved to be a chimera. Clinton held firmly to the centrist ground he had staked out after the 1994 election, campaigning on the same "New" Democratic themes of "opportunity, responsibility, and community" which had served him well during his first run for the White House. He won 49 percent of the popular vote to Dole's 41 percent and Perot's 8 percent, along with 379 electoral votes to Dole's 159.

Clinton thus became the first Democratic president to be elected to a second term since FDR. But his candidate-centered campaign, abetted by a strong economy, did little to help his party. The Democrats lost two seats in the Senate and gained but a modest nine seats in the House, thus failing to regain control of either legislative body. In truth, Clinton's campaign testified to the fragility of the nationalized party system that arose during the 1980s. The president's remarkable political comeback in 1995 was supported by so-called soft money that was designated for party-building activities and thus was not covered by campaign finance laws.[76] But these expenditures were used overwhelmingly to mount television advertising campaigns, such as the media blast of the Republicans during the 1995 budget battles, which championed the president's independence from partisan squabbles. Indeed, Clinton scarcely endorsed the election of a Democratic Congress; moreover, his fund-raising efforts for the party supported congressional candidates only late in the campaign. Adding insult to injury, the administration's questionable fund-raising methods led to revelations during the final days of the election which may have reduced Clinton's margin of victory and thus undermined the Democrats' effort to retake the House.[77]

Clinton's Legacy for the Presidency and the Party System

In the final analysis, Clinton's success in forging "a third way" between Republican conservatism and Democratic liberalism will determine his legacy for the presidency and political parties. The disjuncture between the bitter partisanship within the capital and the weakening of partisan affiliation outside it has given Clinton, and his skill in combining doctrines, a certain appeal in the country.[78] This gift for forging compromise was displayed in May 1997 as the White House and Republican leadership reached a compromise on a tentative plan to balance the budget by 2002. In part, this uneasy agreement was made possible by a revenue windfall caused by the robust economy, thus enabling Clinton and GOP leaders to avoid the sort of hard choices over program cuts and taxes which had animated the bitter struggles of the 104th Congress.[79] Even so, this rapprochement, which brought about the first balanced budget in three decades, testifies to the potential of modern presidents to advance principles and pursue policies that defy the sharp cleavages characteristic of the nationalized party system.

The "extraordinary isolation" of the modern presidency has its limits, however.[80] Since FDR, the president has been freed from the constraints of party, only to be enslaved by a fractious political environment that can rapidly undercut popular support. Thus, even after his triumphant reelection, Clinton still faced the profound challenge of establishing the boundaries within which his party and domestic policy could be reformed. Toward the end of 1997, the great majority of House Democrats refused to support legislation that would give Clinton fast track trade-negotiating authority, the very same power that Democratic Congresses gave Republican presidents Ford, Reagan, and Bush. The House Democrats' revolt against free trade underscored the continuing split between Clinton and his party; just as significant, it suggested that leading Democratic opponents of the bill, such as Minority Leader Richard Gephardt, would pose hard challenges to Clinton-style centrism for the remainder of the president's term. This estrangement made it difficult for Democrats to find common ground for the 1998 elections; it may also fracture the party during the presidential campaign of 2000, allowing candidates who stand for traditional Democratic constituencies, such as African Americans and labor unions, to exploit the political vulnerability of Clinton's heir apparent, Vice President Al Gore.[81] As Al From, head of the Democratic Leadership Council, cautioned, "On welfare reform, the balanced budget, and trade—three of the most defining New Democratic issues—powerful Democratic party interest groups and their key congressional allies have opposed President Clinton. . . . [That] is the biggest obstacle to perpetuating New Democratic politics into the next century."[82]

An investigation into Clinton's personal affairs posed a far greater threat to his standing. In early January 1998, Independent Counsel Kenneth Starr was authorized to expand the scope of the Whitewater inquiry to pursue allegations that the president had an affair with a White House intern, Monica Lewinsky, and that he and his intimate Vernon Jordan had encouraged her to lie under oath about it.[83] Predictably, most Democratic members of Congress, still smarting from the president's seeming indifference to their programmatic commitments and election prospects, maintained a deafening silence as the Republicans sought to exploit the scandal.[84] The Clinton administration's response was to accuse Starr, a prominent Republican, and his supporters in Congress of orchestrating a slanderous, partisan campaign to weaken the president. Clinton's rapid counterattack proved effective in the court of public opinion: the president's popular support remained high in the face of the scandal, as voters remained focused on his record of "peace, prosperity, and moderation."[85] But Starr's relentless investigation eventually uncovered evidence that forced Clinton to admit that he had an "improper relationship" with Lewinsky. In September, the independent counsel's report compiling a potentially devastating chronicle of the president's adulterous affair and his months of subsequent lies proposed eleven possible grounds for impeachment to the Congress, including charges of perjury and obstruction of justice. Soon thereafter, the House of Representatives, voting largely along party lines, approved a resolution to begin a full-scale, open-ended inquiry into possible grounds for impeachment of the president.[86]

Remarkably, the public continued to express overwhelming approval of Clinton's performance in office. This expression of support reflected not only approbation for the president's management of the economy but also general disapproval of Starr's tenacious investigation into Clinton's peccadilloes as well as the eagerness with which the Republican-controlled Congress exploited its results. So high was the public's regard for the job Clinton was doing as president that Republican congressional candidates shied away from making impeachment an issue in the 1998 midterm elections, for fear of alienating voters. Nonetheless, Clinton paid dearly in the coin of public trust; the people, although sympathetic, appeared to lose confidence in his ability to lead. More ominously, few Democrats came to the president's defense, underscoring that while Clinton may have allies in Congress, he had few close friends there.[87] Most Democrats did oppose a full impeachment inquiry, but this stance represented their disdain for the Republican majority rather than support for the president. In fact, as the *New York Times* reported, "it is the people who know [Clinton] best—from his own former aides to his wary fellow Democrats in Congress—who have been most disappointed and angry about his handling of the Monica Lewinsky matter, and who have held it against him more harshly than a detached and distant public."[88]

With the decline of Clinton's personal stature, nearly every political expert predicted that the Republicans would emerge from the 1998 elections with a tighter grip on Congress and, by implication, on the president's political fate.[89] But having been preoccupied by the Lewinsky scandal for the entire year, the Republicans were left without an appealing campaign issue. They were unable to increase their 55–45 margin in the Senate and lost five seats in the House, leaving them a slim 223–211 margin. Indeed, for the first time since 1934, the president's party gained seats in a midterm election. Bitterly disappointed by the results, the Republicans fell into soul-searching and recriminations, and the hero of their 1994 ascent to power, Speaker Newt Gingrich, was forced to announce soon after the elections that he was giving up not only his leadership position but also his seat in Congress.[90]

The 1998 elections and their aftermath appeared to take the steam out of the House's impeachment inquiry. But as the president gathered with friends and aides to celebrate what seemed to be another remarkable political resurrection, the Republicans prepared to move forward with the impeachment inquiry. A centrist, poll-driven politician, Clinton, as well as most pundits, underestimated the willingness of Republicans in Congress to defy the survey-tested will of the people.[91] In December, after a year of dramatic and tawdry politics, Clinton was impeached on charges of perjury and obstruction of justice by a bitterly divided House of Representatives, which recommended virtually along party lines that the Senate remove the nation's forty-second president. Hoping to become a great president in the tradition of Franklin Roosevelt, Clinton now became only the second president in American history to face an impeachment trial in the Senate.

Even impeachment did not undermine the president's popular support. Soon after the House's historic action, large majorities of Americans expressed approval of Clinton's handling of his job, opposed a Senate trial, and proclaimed Republican members of Congress as "out of touch with most Americans."[92] The public's support of the president and the small Republican majority in the Senate encouraged discussion among senators about the possibility of substituting a motion of censure for a protracted, agonizing impeachment trial. But Republican leaders were determined not to abort the constitutional process, even though acquittal of the president on the articles of impeachment seemed foreordained. After a five-week-long Senate trial, the president's accusers failed to gain even a majority vote on either of the charges

against Clinton: on February 12, 1999, the Senate rejected the charge of perjury, 55–45, with 10 Republicans voting against conviction; then, with five
Republicans breaking ranks, the Senate split 50–50 on a second article accus-
ing the president of obstruction of justice. Clinton's job was safe. Yet whatever
moral authority Clinton may have had at the beginning of his administration
to establish a new covenant of rights and responsibilities between citizens and
their government was shattered by public disrespect for his morality. Voters
distinguished sharply between Clinton the chief executive, of whom they
approved, and Clinton the man, whom they regarded as immoral and untrust-
worthy. Thus, even though he avoided Senate conviction on the impeachment charges, Clinton faced an erosion of credibility which weakened
severely his ability to command the nation.

Yet the current miasma suggests strongly that it may be unreasonable,
indeed, dangerous, to rely so heavily on presidents to determine the contours
of political action. As the sensational media treatment of the Monica Lewinsky scandal revealed, the modern presidency operates in a political arena that
is seldom congenial to meaningful political debate and which all too often is
guilty of deflecting attention from the painful struggles about the relative merits of contemporary liberalism and conservatism. With the liberation of the
executive from many of the constraints of party leadership and the rise of the
mass media, presidents have resorted to rhetoric and administration, tools
with which they have sought to forge new, more personal ties with the public.
But, as the nation has witnessed all too clearly during the past thirty years, this
form of "populist" presidential politics can all too readily degenerate into rank
opportunism. Moreover, it risks exposing the people to the kind of public figures who will exploit citizens' impatience with the difficult tasks involved in
sustaining a healthy constitutional democracy.

Presidents who enjoy prominent places in history have justified their
reform programs in constitutional terms, claiming to restore the proper understanding of first principles, even as they have attempted to transfuse the Declaration of Independence and Constitution with new meaning. But they have
done so as great party leaders, in the midst of major partisan realignments.
Critical partisan elections have enabled each generation to claim its right to
redefine the Constitution's principles and reorganize its institutions. The
New Deal continued this unending task to ensure that each generation could
affirm its attachment to constitutional government. The burden of the new
century is to hold the modern presidency to account, to recapture the understanding of democracy which has made such momentous deliberation and
choice central to the pursuit of America's political destiny.

Political Parties,
Progressive Democracy, and the
Future of Politics in America

Current political developments in the United States appear profoundly paradoxical. As the country approaches the millennium, it has much to celebrate—an enduring constitutional heritage, a prosperous economy, and a preeminent position in world affairs. Still, in the wake of America's triumph in the Cold War, in the midst of the most prosperous times in three decades, many Americans remain uncertain about the nation's political future. As Joel Silbey has written, "the nation's political commentary is awash in unremitting, harsh, and despairing assertions about institutional and leadership inadequacies; about sleaze, corruption, scandal, and selfishness; about system incoherence, unresponsiveness, drift, and ineffectiveness."[1] Bill Clinton's tempestuous second term, which saw him become the first elected president to be impeached while Americans expressed overwhelming approval of his presidency, underscored the strange nature of our present discontents.

This book has sought to explain the estrangement of the people from their government by revisiting the origins and history of political parties. Parties were formed in the early part of the nineteenth century as a means of engaging the participation of ordinary citizens, and with localistic foundations that were critical for the maintenance of an engaged citizenry. Yet economic and political dynamics have transformed the United States from a decentralized republic to a mass democracy, in which the principles and political associations that sustained civic attachments in the United States have been undermined.

The weak foundation of modern political engagement in the United States is not new, of course; indeed, it prompts us to revisit longstanding issues about the limited attention to civic virtue in the American Constitution—an "extended republic" that attempts to employ institutional arrangements and the constructive use of interests to compensate for the defects of virtuous motives in political life.

For much of our history, the private order was uneasily allied to public life by the American tradition of self-government. The obsession with rights and inherent fractiousness of American government were "checked by a politics—and a press—rooted in locality," Wilson Carey McWilliams has argued, "the kind of 'retail,' face-to-face encounter that personalizes public life, conveys dignity, and encourages participation."[2] Localized democracy was remarkably resilient, expressing a distinct American hostility to centralized administration. Tocqueville believed that the celebration of equality in democratic society required centralization of authority, but he noticed that certain "peculiar and accidental" causes in the American case, especially the lack of a feudal tradition, "diverted" the United States from centralized power. "The American destiny is unusual," he wrote. "They have taken from the English aristocracy the idea of individual rights and a taste for local freedom, and they have been able to keep both these things because they have no aristocracy to fight."[3] Given the commitment to decentralized administration in the United States, it was no good looking for "uniformity and permanence of outlook, minute care of details, or perfection of administrative procedures." What one did find, Tocqueville reported, was a vital political life, "somewhat wild perhaps, but robust," a "life liable to mishaps but full of striving and animation."[4]

Political parties transformed this frenetic activity into contests of opinion which both enlarged and made effective political participation. Through the "art of political association," Tocqueville observed, individuals were drawn "out of their own circle; however much difference in their age, intelligence, or wealth may naturally keep them apart," political associations bring "them together and [put] them in contact. Once they have met, they always know how to meet again." Thus, even when American political parties appeared to be relatively indifferent to broad moral questions, Tocqueville found them to be valuable political associations in which individuals learned the art of cooperation and became citizens. Political parties, he suggested, might be considered the "great free schools to which all citizens come to be taught the general theory of association."[5]

Indeed, as Chapter 2 shows, the party system was formed to guarantee that the authority of republican government in the United States would reside ultimately, as Jefferson put it, "with the people in mass."[6] It was born of a deliberate program of constitutional reform to ensure that the space the Founders created between the cup of power and the lips of the people would not become so great as to make representation impractical. The Constitution's politics, the Antifederalists warned, "would become intricate and perplexed," and thus too "mysterious" for the average citizen to understand. As such, the Framers' idea of republican government was a recipe for "consolidation," for a political life that would rely so heavily on the "enlightened" counsel of the executive as to render the public voice silent.[7] James Madison himself, the principal author of the Constitution, would soon acknowledge the legitimacy of the Antifederalists' concerns. That he joined Jefferson in founding the Republican party, dedicated to unifying public sentiments against government centralization, testified to his recognition by the 1790s that the Constitution's critics were far more prescient than he had thought at the time of the Founding. By the 1830s, political parties had become part of the "living Constitution," and national administrative power was constrained not only by the decentralized organizational structure of these parties but also by the hallowed doctrine of local self-government to which they adhered.

Dedicated to the doctrine of local self-government, shaped by decentralized organizations that found their principal strength in the states and localities, party politics "paralleled Anti-federalist ideas of representation."[8] With the rise of Jacksonian democracy, political parties became so decentralized and dependent on patronage as to risk moral indifference. But they found a compensating source of strength in the political combat of national elections which, particularly during national crises, drew the country into great contests of opinion. As Michael McGerr has observed, the popular politics aroused by national, but decentralized, parties "fused thought and emotion in a single style accessible to all—a rich unity of reason and passion" which allied presidential politics to public philosophy.[9] Shaped by a competitive party system, critical elections exposed constitutional principles and institutional arrangements to mass contests of opinion. Yet in the heat of these popular campaigns the Constitution would find its vital connection to popular sovereignty. As Martin Van Buren, the leading proponent of what Richard Hofstadter has called the "idea of a party system," argued, when "the principles of contending parties are supported with candor, fairness, and moderation, the very discord which is thus produced, may in a government like ours, be conducive to the public good."[10] By making the principles and institutions of the Constitution itself an object of popular struggle, the party system helped ameliorate republican government's gravest vulnerability—public indifference.

In effect, the strength of party organizations in the United States can be explained by the role they performed in making the Constitution safe for democracy, by allying constitutional forms to a "highly mobilized, highly competitive, and locally oriented democracy."[11] By the end of the nineteenth century, however, the fabric of civic attachments was loosened by the emergence of laissez-faire capitalism, which celebrated economic opportunity and industrial development to the detriment of local community. The Progressive movement that arose to challenge industrial capitalism sought to create a national citizenship, to transfer "our sense of security in ourselves as citizens . . . . from the state and local governments where it originated to the federal government."[12] In truth, progressive reformers were ambivalent about using the federal government to reform the society and economy. But, as noted in Chapter 3, they hoped to free state and local governments from what they took to be the parochial, often corrupt influence of political parties. Attempting to reform government by establishing a system of direct popular rule on a national scale, progressive democracy further corroded the vital contact between the populace in local communities and the national government.

Although conservatives claimed that progressives threatened the republican character of the regime, many reformers defined their task as conservative rather than radical, a claim that spoke to the longstanding controversy over the role of states and localities, as well as political parties, in the work of constitutional government. Chapter 3 shows that many reformers claimed that their objective was to build a democracy on a grand scale, just as the original Constitution prescribed—to emancipate Jeffersonian democracy from its perversion, a decrepit version of popular rule sustained by corrupt and corrupting machines. New Nationalists, in particular, whose political ambitions were advanced by the Progressive party campaign of 1912, hoped to renew the debate over issues that had divided the Federalists and Antifederalists, as well as the Hamiltonians and Jeffersonians—indeed, the New Nationalists consciously and deliberately saw themselves involved in a "neo-Hamiltonian" project. To be sure, Progressives defended the People with an enthusiasm that Hamilton might have found dangerous. But in their celebration of "pure democracy," they claimed that they were merely following Lincoln, whose legacy they believed was desecrated by the Republican party of the early twentieth century.

Still, the Progressives' invocation of Lincoln overlooked his support for local self-government and the two-party system that sustained it. As noted in Chapter 2, to the dismay of reformers such as Herbert Croly, Lincoln and the Republicans embraced the system of partisan organization and discipline which was formed during the 1830s. As such, the realignment of 1860 preserved the foundation of decentralized government, even as it required the elimination of forced servitude. The shift from ideological to patronage politics during the 1870s, signaling the failure of Reconstruction, showed how the wheelwork of party politics continued to constrain national administrative power during the later part of the nineteenth century. The failure of the Republicans to remake American politics was doomed from the start, Croly insisted, for they attempted to accomplish the purposes of a "humanized democracy with the machinery" of a provincial democracy. Localized parties allowed for a certain institutional harmony among national institutions, to be sure, but at the cost of preventing the formation of an administrative organization that was equal to the tasks of modern political life.[13] Dedicated to restoring the national character of the Constitution which was preempted by the rise of the two-party system, Progressives sought to create a national democracy, reconcile the tensions between nationalism and democracy, and form a government under the control of "We, the People," just as they believed the preamble of the Constitution prescribed.

In seeking to close the distance between the government and public opinion, Progressive reformers posed fundamental challenges to the American constitutional order. Whereas Lincoln had sought to preserve the country's reverence for the Founding by removing the stain of slavery from it, militant Progressive reformers sought to emancipate American individualism from an emotive attachment to the Constitution, especially the designated guardian of the fundamental law—the judiciary. Just as the realignment of 1860 restored the Declaration's preeminent place in American political life, so Progressives hoped to give birth to a more novel understanding of freedom. As Croly wrote in *The Promise of American Life*:

> The idea of a constructive relation between American nationality and American democracy is in truth equivalent to a new Declaration of Independence. It affirms the American people as free to organize their political, economic, and social life in the service of a comprehensive, a lofty,

and far-reaching democratic purpose. At the present time there is a strong, almost a dominant, tendency to regard the existing Constitution with superstitious awe, and to shrink with horror from modifying it even in the smallest detail; and it is the superstitious fear of changing the most trivial parts of the fundamental legal fabric which brings to pass the great bondage of the American spirit. If such an abject worship of legal precedent for its own sake should continue, the American people will have to be fitted to the rigid and narrow lines of a few legal formulas; and the ruler of the American spirit, like the ruler of the Jewish spirit of old, will become a lawyer. But it will not continue, in case Americans can be brought to understand and believe that the American national political organization should be constructively related to their democratic purpose.[14]

Little wonder that Croly championed Theodore Roosevelt's 1912 Progressive party campaign, which, in contrast to Woodrow Wilson's defense of a New Freedom, truly advocated a new sense of national destiny for the individualism of the past. Just as TR excoriated the "malefactors of great wealth," so he challenged the country to temper its celebration of rights with a proper sense of responsibility. "We can just as little afford to follow the doctrinaires of an extreme individualism as the doctrinaires of an extreme socialism," he declared in a 1910 address. "Individual initiative, so far from being discouraged, should be stimulated; and yet we should remember that, as society develops and grows more complex, we continually find that things which once it was desirable to leave to individual initiative can, under the changed conditions, be performed with better results by common effort."[15]

Conservative critics of TR's defense of the People, such as William Howard Taft and Elihu Root, were surprised and alarmed to learn how much his assault on settled law resonated with the American public. Those who attacked TR's defense of direct popular government as a radical assault on the American political tradition failed to understand, John Dewey observed, how the people were tempted to invest their faith in a leader who flattered them so, who appealed to them as the ultimate guardians of the American heritage (see Chapter 3). At the same time, Dewey feared that TR's defense of national democracy threatened the dignity of the democratic individual, the cornerstone of self-government. As Dewey would argue during the 1920s, progressivism could have a profound effect on the American polity only insofar as it could be transformed into a new liberal tradition—one that did not celebrate a rugged individualism that abhorred state interference with private property, but instead emphasized a new concept of individualism which viewed the state as a guarantor of social and economic welfare. In the commitment of Progressives such as Jane Addams to advance a national program of reform in ways that did not impair the institutions of self-government, Dewey spied an alternative to laissez-faire liberalism which might "break down the idea that freedom is something that individuals have as a ready-made possession" and which might "instill the idea that it is something to be achieved," even "while the possibility of the achievement was shown to be conditioned by the institutional medium in which individuals live." As Dewey wrote in his influential *Liberalism and Social Action*, a book he dedicated to Jane Addams' memory, "These new liberals fostered the idea that the state has the responsibility for creating institutions under which individuals can effectively realize the potentialities that are theirs."[16]

Although the hope of many social reformers that the Progressive party would serve as an instrument for unifying disparate advocacy groups and causes came unraveled, Dewey's celebration of a new conception of liberalism underscores the important ties between the Progressive party of 1912 and the New Deal's programmatic and institutional aspirations. Indeed, the New Deal realignment marks the consolidation of changes begun by the Progressive campaign of 1912. The "purge" campaign of 1938 and other partisan practices during the New Deal period suggest that Franklin Roosevelt and his political allies intended to create a national programmatic two-party system. The system of party responsibility, FDR argued, "required that one of its parties be the liberal party and the other be the conservative party."[17] Ultimately, however, as Chapter 4 shows, Roosevelt and his fellow New Dealers, some of whom were erstwhile Bull Moosers, took actions and pursued procedural reforms that extended the personal and nonpartisan responsibility of the president, to the detriment of collective and partisan responsibility. Like his cousin, FDR conceived of a party program as an assault on party politics. But he presided over a full-scale realignment, the first in American history to place an independent executive at the heart of its approach to politics and government. Understood within the context of the progressive tradition, the New Deal is appropriately viewed as the completion of a realignment that makes future *partisan* realignments unnecessary. As the Brownlow Committee report put it, "Our national will must be expressed not merely in a brief, exultant moment of electoral decision, but in persistent, determined, competent administration of what the nation has decided to do.[18]

But, as Eldon Eisenach has argued, the expansion of national administrative power which followed the New Deal realignment did not result in the kind of national state for which progressive reformers like Croly and Dewey had hoped, one that established regulation and social welfare policy as expressions of national unity and commitment.[19] Eisenach suggests that this failure followed from the New Deal's compromise with the natural rights tradition in American politics. FDR's economic constitutional order—the economic bill of rights he championed—perverted Dewey's idea of new individualism, subordinating enlightened administration to group entitlements. Whereas Dewey had expressed support for reformed local communities as forums of educated political inquiry, the New Deal defended entitlements that were insulated from public opinion. Particular programs such as Social Security and Medicare achieved popular support, but programmatic liberalism was never defined and defended in a form that could withstand the rights claims of favored constituencies.

Indeed, the hallmark of administrative politics in the United States is the virtual absence of a state that can impose its will on the economy and society. The limits of administrative centralization in the American context were revealed clearly enough by the fact that strong opposition to the growth of the central government continued to have force in American politics, especially during times of frenetic government activism. The Great Society, which represented an effort to expand and radicalize the New Deal, as well as the culmination of the progressive assault on the two-party system, was widely perceived as "excessive statism," giving rise to a movement that would pose hard challenges to liberal reforms. With Ronald Reagan's ascent to the White House, it seemed, "government was not the solution to our problems; government was the problem."[20]

But, as noted in the previous chapter, the Reagan "revolution" did not mark a revival of local self-government. The Reagan administration became committed to programmatic innovations in defense and foreign policy which required the expanding, rather than the rolling back, of the national government's responsibilities. Furthermore, the moral imperatives of the modern conservative movement, which Reagan identified as that movement's most fundamental calling, were animated by a missionary zeal that appeared to want to abolish, rather than restore, the distinction between state and society. The spectacle of Patrick Buchanan, who challenged President Bush in the 1992 Republican primaries, speaking at the GOP national convention in Houston before a prime-time television audience, while Ronald Reagan waited offstage until after 11 P.M., was striking evidence of just how powerful new right fundamentalist groups had become in the party.[21] Buchanan likened his party's quarrels with liberalism to a "religious war," a dark tale that testified to the decrepitude of the Reagan "revolution." Conservatives, it seemed, did not want to dismantle the state forged on the New Deal realignment; instead, they desired to put it to new uses—fighting enemies abroad, protecting the domestic economy, and preserving "family values."[22]

Notwithstanding the continuing expansion of national administrative power, our current politics does not confidently presume the existence of a national state. As Barry Karl has argued, Americans continue to abhor, even as they embrace, national administrative power. The surprising Republican victories in the 1994 elections, in which the GOP achieved majority control of the House and Senate for the first time in forty years, testified to growing public concern with "big government" and its cumbersome regulatory structures. This concern found expression in the rejection of national health care reform and the devolution of responsibility for welfare to the states. Even so, as the 1996 presidential election confirmed, the public's persistent commitment to middle-class entitlements, such as Social Security and Medicare, and its strong support for regulatory initiatives dedicated to environmental and consumer protection make unlikely the revival of local self-government.[23]

In truth, Americans have formed a love-hate relationship with the national state, a profound ambivalence that seeks refuge in progressive democracy—the *direct* form of democracy Americans have adopted to ease their anxiety about the expansion of national administrative power. As noted in Chapter 5, the direct form of popular rule championed by the Progressive party of 1912 became newly relevant in the 1960s and 1970s, as reformers attempted to recast the administrative state as an agent of democracy. For all the failures these reformers experienced, their call for "participatory democracy" would have an enduring influence on politics and government in the United States. Unwilling to embrace or reject the state, we have increasingly sought to give the "people" more control over it. Consequently, "pure" democracy has evolved, or degenerated, into a plebiscitary form of politics which mocks the progressive concept of "enlightened administration" and exposes citizens to the sort of public figures who will exploit their impatience with the difficult tasks involved in sustaining a healthy democracy. Bill Clinton's unsteady leadership is not merely attributable to his personal failings; nor are his political problems the creation of a right-wing conspiracy to savage his presidency. More penetratingly, the shifting fortunes of Clinton's two terms as president have dramatically illustrated how progressive democracy has freed the executive from party politics, only to enslave it to a demanding and fractious public.

The displacement of localized parties by progressive democracy has not meant the end of party conflict. As the trials and tribulations of the Clinton years suggest, with respect to a whole range of social and international issues, the Congress may be as polarized as at any time since Reconstruction in the late 1860s, the only other time an American president, Andrew Johnson, was impeached.[24] In effect, the erosion of old-style partisan politics has allowed a more national and issue-oriented party system to develop, one that is potentially more compatible with the "nationalized" electorate created by progressive reforms and the mass media. But the emergence of more centralized parties has strengthened the national party organizations and allowed for more partisan discipline in Congress, only to weaken further partisan loyalties in the electorate. Increasingly, parties seem to be "centralized bureaucracies," writes McWilliams, "less mediators *between* rulers and ruled than a *part* of the government tier."[25]

The insurgency of H. Ross Perot in the 1992 presidential campaign, the most significant assault on the two-party system since TR's Bull Moose campaign, revealed at once the triumph and disappointment of progressive democracy. TR's campaign foretold not only of the emergence of an active and expansive national government but also of presidential campaigns conducted less by parties than by individual candidates. Perot's campaign suggested just how far presidential politics had been emancipated from the constraints of party. Disdaining the importunities of those interested in party renewal that he form a third party, Perot launched his campaign without the formality of a nominating convention—his supporters were summoned to Armageddon on "Larry King Live." Just as significant, the broad appeal of Perot's call for electronic town meetings as a principal vehicle to solve the nation's political and economic problems testifies to the resonance of simple-minded notions of direct democracy—and to the threat this politics of instant gratification poses to constitutional forms.

Although Perot's personal popularity had abated by 1996, the direct plebiscitary politics he championed did not. Indeed, President Clinton and his Republican challenger, Robert Dole, openly imitated Perot's personalistic politics, even as they exploited campaign funds—so-called soft money—

which, ostensibly, were designated for party-building activities. With Perot's politics, if not Perot himself, still having strong support in the nation as the country approached the millennium, the Progressive idea of "direct government" might be destined to play a more important and disturbing part in American political life.[26]

Political parties were first formed and defended in the United States to confront the dangers of administrative aggrandizement. But we must not allow the present discontents of the American people to blind us to the shortcomings of the nineteenth-century polity—certainly, there was no "golden age" of parties. Progressive reformers had good reasons for viewing political parties and the provincial liberties they upheld as an obstacle to economic and political justice. But they failed to appreciate the purpose these parties served as effective channels of democratic participation. Representative government is essentially fostered by public speech, by political discussion that most effectively occurs in the legislature and local community. Civic involvement is enervated by a political process dominated by executive action, which can strengthen and lead but cannot replace the decentralizing institutions as the home of representative government. The benefit of a strong executive, as Hamilton noted in *Federalist* 70, is "promptitude of decision," which does not allow for the "differences of opinion and the jarring of parties" which promote popular rule.[27] Consequently, the advent of progressive democracy strengthened the national purpose, but public debate and legislative authorization, activities that are the essence of popular rule, were displaced as the center of government activity. The involvement of Congress and the courts in the details of administration since the 1970s has tended to relinquish the energy and responsibility of the executive formed on the foundation of the New Deal for a fragmented administrative politics that further insulates the affairs of state from the understanding and control of the rank-and-file citizenry.

Amid the crisis of citizenship which emerged by the late 1970s, scholars and pundits have called repeatedly for reforms that would strengthen the party system. Advocates of party government, of a more "responsible" party system, consider the decline of party an opportunity to build a new kind of party, one that could assemble and register the will of programmatic and disciplined majorities. Indeed, many political scientists question whether the decline of party is a symptom of fundamental flaws in the Constitution and the philosophy that informed its creation. According to Walter Dean Burnham, the forlorn state of parties points overwhelmingly to the conclusion that the American polity has entered the most profound turning point in history. In his seminal 1970 volume, *Critical Elections and the Mainsprings of American Politics*, Burnham argues that the task confronting the United States today is no less than the "construction of instrumentalities of domestic sovereignty to limit individual freedom in the name of collective necessity." This would require "an entirely new structure of parties and of mass behavior, one in which political parties would be instrumentalities of democratic collective purpose." But, Burnham concludes, "this in turn seems inconceivable without a preexisting revolution in social values."[28]

Indeed, for the most part, such calls for fundamental reorganization of political parties and their relationship to politics and government have fallen on deaf ears. "Although policy minded reformers now call for the revitalization of parties almost as a matter of course," Robert Wiebe has written, "their drastic remedies—eliminate primaries, stop ticket-splitting, monopolize campaign funds—suggest a doctor eyeing the artificial respirator."[29]

One suspects that the solution to America's present discontents involves a more conventional, if no less challenging, project—a recognition of the limits of national administrative power to solve the nation's problems. In such a recognition comes hope for the renewal of political associations. Part of the task will require taking the American people to school on the need to restore the balance between rights and interests, as well as between the central and local governments. In the wake of the Roosevelt revolution, nearly every important public policy has been propounded as a right, purporting to confer constitutional status on programs like Social Security, Medicare, welfare, and food stamps. Conservatives no less than liberals have championed new rights, calling for rights of the unborn and a novel interpretation of the "Takings Clause" which would protect property against local land use planning. Thus, with the advent of the New Deal political order, an understanding of rights dedicated to limiting government gradually gave way to a more expansive understanding of rights, requiring a relentless government identification of problems and the search for methods by which these problems might be solved.[30] Invariably, the rights revolution required national administrative solutions; just as important, in routinely conferring constitutional status on policies, the new social contract drained partisan debate and resolution of real meaning. As noted in the previous chapter, a politics of entitlement had arisen by the end of the 1980s which belittled efforts of Democrats and Republicans alike to define a collective purpose with a past and a future. Instead, partisanship was joined to an administrative politics that relegated electoral contests to the intractable demands of policy advocates.

The vitality of the American Constitution has come from its alliance with democratic debate about its meaning. Critical elections have been, so to speak, surrogate constitutional conventions, in which the American people have been drawn into partisan disputes about the proper understanding of their fundamental principles and institutional arrangements. In this way, partisan conflict has enabled each generation to claim its right to redefine the Constitution's principles and reorganize its government. This right, exalting the dignity of democratic individualism, has been lost amid the petty, virulent partisanship that has racked the nation's capital during the past thirty years. In its rediscovery might come the recognition that liberty requires the art of political association no less than the demand for rights. With this recognition, we would have reason to expect a true renewal of party.

NOTES

Chapter 1 Parties and American Democracy

1. Wilson Carey McWilliams, "Parties as Civic Associations," in *Party Renewal in America: Theory and Practice*, ed. Gerald M. Pomper (New York: Praeger, 1980), 51.

2. Rejecting the classical view that democracy required a small homogeneous society, Madison prescribed a large and diverse territory that would "make it less probable that a majority of the whole [would] have a common motive to invade the rights of other citizens." Alexander Hamilton argued in *Federalist* 12 that commerce would be the engine that cultivated a multitude of diverse interests. Alexander Hamilton, James Madison, and John Jay, *The Federalist Papers* (New York: New American Library, 1961), 83, 91. The honor Americans accorded individual self-interest ("the love of wealth"), Alexis de Tocqueville observed, encouraged economic activity that would transform the rural character of the country into a thriving commercial society. Alexis de Tocqueville, *Democracy in America*, ed. J. P. Mayer (Garden City, N.Y.: Doubleday, 1969), 621.

3. Richard Hofstadter, *The Idea of a Party System: The Rise of Legitimate Opposition in the United States, 1780–1840* (Berkeley: University of California Press, 1969), 40–121.

4. Harvey Mansfield, "Political Parties and American Constitutionalism," in *American Political Parties and Constitutional Politics*, ed. Peter W. Schramm and Bradford P. Wilson (Lanham, Md.: Rowman and Littlefield, 1993), 6.

5. Ibid., 3.

6. E. E. Schattschneider, *Party Government* (New York: Farrar and Rinehart, 1942), 1.

7. Tocqueville, *Democracy in America*, 174–78.

8. In making this argument, I attempt to build on the suggestive work of Bruce Ackerman and Walter Dean Burnham, who identify important episodes in our history such as the Civil War and the New Deal as "constitutional moments." See Bruce Ackerman, *We the People: Foundations* (Cambridge: Harvard University Press, 1991), and Walter Dean Burnham, "Dialectics of a System of Change: The 1990s Crisis as a Case in Point" (paper delivered at the annual meeting of the American Political Science Association, San Francisco, August 29–31, 1996).

9. "Letters of Cato," in *The Complete Anti-federalist*, ed. Herbert J. Storing, 7 vols. (Chicago: University of Chicago Press, 1981), 2:112.

10. Wilson Carey McWilliams, "The Anti-federalists, Representation, and Party," *Northwestern University Law Review* 84, no. 1 (Fall 1989): 32–38.

11. Joel Silbey, *The Partisan Imperative* (New York: Oxford University Press, 1985), 36.

12. Herbert Croly, *The Promise of American Life* (New York: Macmillan, 1909; reprint, New York: Dutton, 1963), 169.

13. This phrase comes from Roosevelt's 1909 "New Nationalism" address, given in Osawatomie, Kansas. See Theodore Roosevelt, *The Works of Theodore Roosevelt*, 20 vols. (New York: Scribner's, 1926), 17:349.

14. I make this argument in *The President and the Parties: The Transformation of the American Party System since the New Deal* (New York: Oxford University Press, 1993).

15. For the most widely discussed take on the crisis of citizenship in the United States, see Robert Putnam, "Tuning In, Tuning Out: The Strange Disappearance of Social Capital in America," *PS: Political Science and Politics* 28, no. 4 (December 1995): 664–83. For a detailed account of the contemporary state of civic participation in the United States, see Sidney Verba, Kay Lehman Schlozman, and Henry E. Brady, *Voice and Equality: Civic Voluntarism in American Politics* (Cambridge: Harvard University Press, 1995).

16. Wilson Carey McWilliams, "Conclusion: The Meaning of the Election," in *The Election of 1996: Reports and Interpretations*, ed. Gerald M. Pomper et al. (Chatham, N.J.: Chatham House, 1997), 255–61.

17. See Michael McGerr, *The Decline of Popular Politics: The American North, 1865–1928* (New York: Oxford University Press, 1986), 40.

18. Mary Kingsbury Simkhovitch, "Friendship and Politics," *Political Science Quarterly* 17, no. 2 (June 1902): 199–201.

19. Herbert Croly, *Progressive Democracy* (New York: Macmillan, 1914), 346–47.

20. McWilliams, "Anti-federalists, Representation, and Party," 33.

21. Barry Karl, *The Uneasy State: The United States from 1915 to 1945* (Chicago: University of Chicago Press, 1993), 234–35.

22. Ibid., 236

23. Ibid., 238.

24. Samuel Beer, "In Search of a New Public Philosophy," in *The New American Political System*, ed. Anthony King (Washington, D.C.: American Enterprise Institute, 1979), 27–28.

25. James Ceaser, *Presidential Selection: Theory and Development* (Princeton: Princeton University Press, 1979), 283.

26. Transcript of President Carter's "Address to the Country on Energy Problems," *New York Times*, July 16, 1979.

27. For example, see Walter Dean Burnham, "Realignment Lives: The 1994 Election Earthquake and Its Implications," in *The Clinton Presidency: First Appraisals*, ed. Colin Campbell and Bert A. Rockman (Chatham, N.J.: Chatham House, 1995).

28. Everett Carll Ladd, "1996 Vote: The No Majority Coalition Continues," *Political Science Quarterly* 112, no. 1 (Spring 1997): 17.

29. Joel H. Silbey, "Foundation Stones of Present Discontents: The American Political Nation, 1776–1945," in *Present Discontents: American Politics in the Very Late Twentieth Century*, ed. Byron Shafer (Chatham, N.J.: Chatham House, 1997), 25.

Chapter 2 Localism, Political Parties, and Democratic Participation

1. Robert H. Wiebe, *Self-Rule: A Cultural History of American Democracy* (Chicago: University of Chicago Press, 1995), 264.

2. Alexis de Tocqueville, *Democracy in America*, ed. J. P. Mayer (Garden City, N.Y.: Doubleday, 1969), 68, 82, 95.

3. As George Wilson Pierson argues, Tocqueville failed to notice the growing significance of the two-party system in the work of American constitutional government. See Pierson, *Tocqueville and Beaumont in America* (New York: Oxford University Press, 1938), 765.

4. Tocqueville, *Democracy in America*, 174–79, 189–95, 509–13, 520–24.

5. Wilson Carey McWilliams, "Tocqueville and Responsible Parties: Individualism, Partisanship, and Citizenship in America," in *Challenges to Party Government*, ed. John Kenneth White and Jerome Mileur (Carbondale: Southern Illinois University Press, 1992), 195.

6. Thomas Jefferson to Samuel Kercheval, July 12, 1816, in *The Portable Thomas Jefferson*, ed. Merrill D. Peterson (New York: Viking Press, 1975), 557.

7. Frequently, the historical literature will refer to the Jeffersonian party as the "Democratic-Republicans." The use of this term may help us distinguish the Jeffersonian Republican party from the Republicans that formed in the 1850s in response to the slavery controversy. But the name most frequently, almost exclusively, used by Jefferson and his supporters is Republican, not Democratic-Republican. More to the point, as noted in this chapter, the link between the Jeffersonian Republicans and the Republican party of the 1850s is deliberate. The founders of the latter meant to indicate that they—and not the Jacksonian Democrats—were the loyal followers of the Jeffersonian tradition.

8. Tocqueville, *Democracy in America*, 508; Wilson Carey McWilliams, "Parties as Civic Associations," in *Party Renewal in America: Theory and Practice*, ed. Gerald Pomper (New York: Praeger, 1980), 59.

9. Advisory Commission on Intergovernmental Relations, *The Transformation of American Politics: Implications for Federalism* (Washington, D.C.: Advisory Commission on Intergovernmental Relations, 1986), 45.

10. V. O. Key Jr., *Politics, Parties, and Pressure Groups* (New York: Crowell, 1964), 334 (my emphasis).

11. Wilson Carey McWilliams, "Democracy and Citizen: Community, Dignity, and the Crisis of Contemporary Politics in America," in *How Democratic Is the Constitution?* ed. Robert Goldwin and William A. Schambra (Washington, D.C.: American Enterprise Institute, 1981), 91.

12. Donald R. Brand, "Reformers of the 1960s and 1970s: Modern Anti-Federalists?" in

Remaking American Politics, ed. Richard A. Harris and Sidney M. Milkis (Boulder, Colo.: Westview Press, 1989), 50 n. 50.

13. James Madison to Thomas Jefferson, October 24, 1787, in *Writings of James Madison*, ed. Gaillard Hunt, 9 vols. (New York: Putnam's, 1904), 5:31.

14. Alexander Hamilton, James Madison, and John Jay, *The Federalist Papers* (New York: New American Library, 1961), 325.

15. Ibid., Number 85, 526.

16. Ibid., 323 (emphasis in original).

17. Marvin Meyers, ed., *Sources of the Political Thought of James Madison* (Indianapolis: Bobbs-Merrill, 1973), 236.

18. James Madison to Thomas Jefferson, June 13, 1793, in Hunt, *Writings of James Madison*, 6:131.

19. *Letters of Pacificus and Helvidius on the Proclamation of Neutrality of 1793* (Washington, D.C.: Gideon, 1845), 5–15.

20. Thomas Jefferson to James Madison, July 7, 1793, in *The Writings of Thomas Jefferson*, ed. Paul Leicester Ford, 10 vols. (New York: Putnam's, 1895), 6:338.

21. *Letters of Pacificus and Helvidius*, 53–64.

22. The Jeffersonian scholar Lance Banning challenges the proposition that Madison's thought changed dramatically from the time he coauthored the *Federalist Papers* to the time he wrote the *National Gazette* essays. Madison was never as committed to nationalism as was Hamilton, Banning argues. He became a leader of the Republican opposition to support his longstanding view of the Constitution as "that middle ground . . . between state sovereignty and an excessive concentration of authority in distant, unresponsive hands." *The Sacred Fire of Liberty: James Madison and the Founding of the Federal Republic* (Ithaca, N.Y.: Cornell University Press, 1995), esp. chaps. 1, 10–11. Without denying that Madison favored a *federal* republic, it seems clear that he became doubtful that the original Constitution sustained such a vital "mean" between national and state sovereignty. Moreover, Madison came to believe that minority rather than majority factionalism posed the greatest threat to liberty and that this threat called for the creation of a political party to assert the will of the people. This concern to awaken a vigorous and active public represented a significant revision, if not a direct contradiction, of Madison's position in the *Federalist Papers*. As Stanley Elkins and Eric McKitrick write of Madison's revised understanding of factions, "Parties are still a necessary evil. But in Madison's mind the emphasis is now mainly on the 'necessary.'" See Elkins and McKitrick, *The Age of Federalism* (New York: Oxford University Press, 1993), 267.

23. This discussion draws on two essays that have called attention to Madison's party papers and to the importance of the debate about party government. See James Piereson, "Party Government," *Political Science Reviewer* 12 (Fall 1982): 2–52, and Harry Jaffa, "A Phoenix from the Ashes: The Death of James Madison's Constitution (Killed by James Madison) and the Birth of Party Government" (prepared for delivery at the annual meeting of the American Political Science Association, Washington, D.C., 1977).

24. "Consolidation," *National Gazette*, December 5, 1791, in Hunt, *Writings of James Madison*, 6:68–69.

25. "A Candid State of the Parties," *National Gazette*, September 26, 1792, in Hunt, *Writings of James Madison*, 6:119.

26. "Report on the Resolutions," House of Delegates, Virginia, Session 1799–1800, in Hunt, *Writings of James Madison*, 6:405.

27. Ibid., 402–3.

28. See, for example, Madison's essay "Universal Peace," which invokes Rousseau in arguing that the "will of the government . . . must be made subordinate to, or rather the same with, the will of the community." *National Gazette*, February 2, 1792, in Hunt, *Writings of James Madison*, 6:89.

29. Thomas Jefferson, "First Inaugural Address," March 4, 1801, in Peterson, *Portable Thomas Jefferson*, 293.

30. Piereson, "Party Government," 51.

31. Jefferson to James Sullivan, February 9, 1797, in Ford, *Writings of Thomas Jefferson*, 7:118.

32. James Madison to Richard Henry Lee, June 25, 1824, in Hunt, *Writings of James Madison*, 9:190–91.

33. James Roger Sharp, *American Politics in the Early Republic* (New Haven: Yale University Press, 1993), 288.

34. Thomas Jefferson to William Duane, March 28, 1811, in Ford, *Writings of Thomas Jefferson*, 9:313 (emphasis in original).

35. Sharp, *American Politics in the Early Republic*, 284.

36. Martin Van Buren, *Inquiry into the Origin and Course of Political Parties in the United States* (New York: Hudson and Houghton, 1867), 4–6. In the face of these developments, Jefferson endorsed Van Buren's plan to reintroduce party competition. See Ford, *Writings of Thomas Jefferson*, 10:316. For an excellent discussion of Van Buren and the critical part he played in renewing party competition, see James Ceaser, *Presidential Selection: Theory and Development* (Princeton: Princeton University Press, 1979), chap. 3.

37. Martin Van Buren to Thomas Ritchie, July 13, 1827, Martin Van Buren Papers, Library of Congress, Washington, D.C.

38. Van Buren, *Inquiry into the Origin and Course of Political Parties in the United States*, 4–6.

39. Van Buren to Ritchie, January 13, 1827, Van Buren Papers.

40. Ibid.

41. "Political Proscription," *United States Magazine and Democratic Review* 9, no. 60 (October 1841): 345.

42. Ceaser, *Presidential Selection*, 149.

43. Marvin Meyers, *The Jacksonian Persuasion: Politics and Belief* (Stanford, Calif.: Stanford University Press, 1957), 28.

44. Andrew Jackson, "Veto Message," July 10, 1832, in James D. Richardson, ed., *Mes-*

sages and Papers of the Presidents, 20 vols. (New York: Bureau of National Literature, 1897), 3:1153.

45. Wiebe, *Self-Rule*, 28.

46. John C. Spencer to Thurlow Weed, "Jacksonian Democracy and the Rise of the Nominating Convention," in *Essays on Jacksonian America*, ed. Frank Otto Gatell (New York: Holt, Rinehart, and Winston, 1970), 88.

47. Tocqueville, *Democracy in America*, 63; Edward Everett, "On the *Democracy in America*, Alexis de Tocqueville," *North American Review* 43 (July 1836): 197–99 (emphasis in original).

48. Banning, *Sacred Fire of Liberty*, 393.

49. Richardson, *Messages and Papers of the Presidents*, 3:1206.

50. Major L. Wilson, *The Presidency of Martin Van Buren* (Lawrence: University Press of Kansas, 1984), 13.

51. Andrew Jackson, Farewell Address, March 4, 1837, in *The Meaning of Jacksonian Democracy*, ed. Edwin C. Rozwenc (Lexington, Mass.: D. C. Heath, 1963), 6–7.

52. Andrew Jackson to James Gwin, February 23, 1835, *Niles' Register*, April 4, 1835, 80.

53. Joel Silbey, *The Partisan Imperative: The Dynamics of American Politics before the Civil War* (New York: Oxford University Press, 1985), 35–40.

54. *Niles' Register*, November 17, 1832, 177. On the 1832 election, see Richard Remini, *Andrew Jackson and the Course of American Freedom, 1822–1832* (New York: Harper and Row, 1981), chap. 23.

55. Tocqueville, *Democracy in America*, 82.

56. Governor Horatio Seymour, "The Democratic Theory of Government," July 4, 1856, in *Seymour and Blair: Their Lives and Services*, ed. David G. Croly (New York: Richardson and Co., 1868), 49, 52.

57. Jabez D. Hammond, *Life and Times of Silas Wright* (Syracuse, N.Y.: Hall and Dickson, 1848), 670. For an overview of constitutional reform in the states during the Jacksonian era, see George P. Parkinson Jr., "Antebellum State Constitution-Making: Retention, Circumvention, Revision" (Ph.D. diss., Department of History, University of Wisconsin, 1972).

58. Van Buren, *Inquiry into the Origin and Course of Political Parties*, 11; *Reports of the Proceedings of the New York Constitutional Convention, 1821* (New York: Da Capo Press, 1970), 341, 353–54. For an excellent discussion of Van Buren's struggle to balance party organization and direct election of local officials, see J. A. Casais, "The New York State Constitutional Convention of 1821 and Its Aftermath" (Ph.D. diss., Department of History, Columbia University, 1970), esp. chap. 9.

59. Casais, "New York State Constitutional Convention of 1821," 295. Whether Van Buren truly understood Rousseau is debatable; but, clearly, he viewed the party system as corrective to what he understood to be the constitution's inadequate regard for self-government. As such, I would take issue with Ceaser's observation that Van Buren and his allies were "less concerned with . . . abstract considerations of democratic theory than with cer-

tain immediate problems in the presidential selection process." Ceaser, *Presidential Selection*, 132. Like the Madison of the 1790s, Van Buren was struggling to find an institutional solution to the original Constitution's failure to resist the centralizing ambitions of those like Hamilton who hoped to transform a regime of checks and balances into an administrative republic.

60. "Amendments to the Constitution of 1821," ratified September 1826, in *The Federal and State Constitutions*, ed. Francis Newton Thorpe, 7 vols. (Washington, D.C.: Government Printing Office, 1909), 5:2651.

61. "Responsibility of the Ballot Box; with an Illustration," *American Whig Review* 4, no. 5 (November 1846): 440.

62. Tocqueville, *Democracy in America*, 262–76; 392–93 (emphasis in original).

63. John O'Sullivan, "European Views of American Democracy—Number II. (M. De Tocqueville)," *United States Magazine and Democratic Review* 2, no. 8 (July 1838): 355.

64. Thomas Hart Benton, *Thirty Years View; or, A History of the Working of the American Government for Thirty Years, from 1820 to 1850* (New York: Appleton and Co., 1854), 224.

65. John O'Sullivan, "European Views of American Democracy (M. De Tocqueville)," *United States Magazine and Democratic Review* 1, no. 1 (October 1837): 97–98. Had O'Sullivan had the opportunity to read the second volume of *Democracy in America* before writing his review, he would have seen that Tocqueville did indeed grasp the *vis inertia* that underlay the rapid innovation of American society. As Tocqueville wrote in his brilliant chapter "Why Great Revolutions Will Become More Rare": "I am not making out that the inhabitants of democratic communities are by nature stationary; on the contrary, I think that such a society is always on the move and that none of its members knows what rest is; but I think that all bestir themselves within certain limits which they hardly ever pass. Daily they change, alter, and renew things of secondary importance; but they are very careful not to touch fundamentals. They love change, but they are afraid of revolutions. . . . Although the Americans are constantly modifying or repealing some of their laws, they are far from showing any revolutionary passions." Tocqueville, *Democracy in America*, 638.

66. Jackson, Farewell Address, 12.

67. Seymour, "Democratic Theory of Government," 51.

68. Tocqueville, *Democracy in America*, 175. Jean Elshtain and Christopher Beem apply this distinction to the 1996 election. See their essay "Issues and Themes: Economics, Culture, and 'Small-Party' Politics," in *The Elections of 1996*, ed. Michael Nelson (Washington, D.C.: Congressional Quarterly, 1997).

69. Pierson, *Tocqueville and Beaumont in America*, 765.

70. Wiebe, *Self-Rule*, 6.

71. Stephen Skowronek, *Building a New American State: The Expansion of National Administrative Capacities, 1877–1920* (New York: Cambridge University Press, 1982), 40.

72. Robert W. Johannsen, ed., *The Lincoln-Douglas Debates of 1858* (New York: Oxford University Press, 1965), 126–27.

73. Richardson, *Messages and Papers of the Presidents*, 7:3206.

74. Undated fragment, written in late 1860 or early 1861, in *New Letters and Papers of Lincoln*, ed. Paul N. Angle (Boston: Houghton Mifflin, 1930), 241–42. Lincoln's reference was to Prov. 25:11.

75. Garry Wills, *Lincoln at Gettysburg: The Words That Remade America* (New York: Simon and Schuster, 1992), 121–33, and David Herbert Donald, *Lincoln* (London: Jonathan Cape, 1995), 462.

76. Bovay cited in Frank A. Flower, *History of the Republican Party: Its Origin, Growth, and Mission* (Springfield, Ill.: Union Publishing Co., 1884), 151.

77. Abraham Lincoln, "Speech at Columbus, Ohio," September 16, 1859, in *The Collected Works of Abraham Lincoln*, ed. Roy Basler, 9 vols. (New Brunswick, N.J.: Rutgers University Press, 1953), 3:423.

78. Ibid., 423–24.

79. Richard Hofstadter, *The Idea of a Party System: The Rise of Legitimate Opposition in the United States, 1780–1840* (Berkeley: University of California Press, 1969), 268 (emphasis in original).

80. George E. Baker, ed., *The Works of William H. Seward*, 5 vols. (Boston: Houghton Mifflin, 1889), 4:243, 278.

81. McWilliams, "Tocqueville and Responsible Parties," 196.

82. Hofstadter, *Idea of a Party System*, 270.

83. Phillip Shaw Paludan, *The Presidency of Abraham Lincoln* (Lawrence: University Press of Kansas, 1994), 297–302. Of course, as it had been sixty-one years since the last constitutional amendment (the Twelfth Amendment was added to the Constitution in 1804), Congress was out of practice.

84. Ibid., 300.

85. James M. McPherson, *Abraham Lincoln and the Second American Revolution* (New York: Oxford University Press, 1991), 138.

86. Abraham Lincoln, Address to a Special Session of Congress, July 4, 1861, in *The Political Thought of Abraham Lincoln*, ed. Richard N. Current (Indianapolis: Bobbs-Merrill, 1967), 187–88.

87. Herbert Croly, *Progressive Democracy* (New York: Macmillan, 1914), 99, 347.

88. Michael McGerr, *The Decline of Popular Politics: The American North, 1865–1928* (New York: Oxford University Press, 1986), chap. 3.

89. Henry Adams, "The Independents in the Canvas," *North American Review* 123 (October 1876): 463.

90. Henry Adams, *Democracy* (New York: New American Library, 1961), 183, 191.

91. Adams, "Independents in the Canvas," 464. See also McGerr, *Decline of Popular Politics*, 53–54.

Chapter 3 Progressivism and Direct Democracy

1. "Abraham Lincoln: The Democratic Spirit and the Poets of the People," *Arena* 41 (July 1909): 480.

2. Charles Merz, "Progressivism: Old and New," *Atlantic Monthly* 132 (July 1923): 106 (emphasis in original).

3. Barry Karl, *The Uneasy State: The United States from 1915 to 1945* (Chicago: University of Chicago Press, 1993), 234–35.

4. Herbert Croly, *Progressive Democracy* (New York: Macmillan, 1914), 1.

5. Arthur S. Link and Richard L. McCormick, *Progressivism* (Arlington Heights, Ill.: Harlan Davidson, 1983), 43–44.

6. Peter Filene, "An Obituary for the Progressive Movement," *American Quarterly* 22 (1970): 20–34.

7. Daniel T. Rogers, "In Search of Progressivism," *Reviews of American History* 10, no. 4 (December 1982): 114–23.

8. For a more complete discussion of the Progressive party and its legacy, see Sidney M. Milkis and Daniel J. Tichenor, "'Direct Democracy' and Social Justice: The Progressive Party Campaign of 1912," *Studies in American Political Development* 8 (Fall 1994): 282–340.

9. Martin Shefter, *Political Parties and the State: The American Historical Experience* (Princeton: Princeton University Press, 1994), 77. Also see Eldon Eisenach, *The Lost Promise of Progressivism* (Lawrence: University Press of Kansas, 1994), chaps. 1, 4.

10. Woodrow Wilson, "Constitutional Government in the United States," in *The Papers of Woodrow Wilson*, ed. Arthur S. Link, 69 vols. (Princeton: Princeton University Press, 1974), 18:197–98.

11. Ibid., 213–14.

12. Louis Brandeis to Walter Roger, July 30, 1914, microfilm reel 37, Louis Brandeis Papers, University of Louisville, Louisville, Ky.

13. James Montague, "Morgan, Belmont, and Ryan Ordered to Keep Hands off Convention," *San Francisco Examiner*, June 28, 1912, 1, and "Convention in All-Night Session; Now Hearing Nominating Speeches; Bryan Pledge against the Interests," *New York Times*, June 28, 1912, 1. Ironically, it was Speaker Champ Clark, and not Wilson, who gained the most support in the Democratic primaries. But Bryan claimed that Clark's progressive credentials were tarnished by his willingness to accept the support of party "bosses" such as Charles Murphy. For a good source on Bryan's influence on the Democratic party, see Louis W. Koenig, *Bryan: A Political Biography of William Jennings Bryan* (New York: Putnam's, 1971).

14. Woodrow Wilson to Alexander Mitchell Palmer, February 5, 1913, in Link, *Papers of Woodrow Wilson*, 27:98–102. See also Daniel Stid, *The President as Statesman: Woodrow Wilson and the Constitution* (Lawrence: University Press of Kansas, 1998), 103–4.

15. Wilson, "Constitutional Government in the United States," 18:114, 123.

16. George M. Forbes, "Buttressing the Foundations of Democracy," *Survey*, November 18, 1911, 1231–35. The social centers movement championed principles and practices that closely resemble the prescriptions of contemporary advocates of community forums. For example, see Benjamin Barber, *Strong Democracy* (Berkeley: University of California

Press, 1984). For an instructive account of the social centers movement and what it can teach us about the crisis of democracy in contemporary America, see Kevin Mattson, *Creating a Democratic Public: The Struggle for Urban Participatory Democracy during the Progressive Era* (University Park: Pennsylvania State University Press, 1998).

17. Mary Parker Follett, *The New State: Group Organization of Popular Government* (New York: Longmans, Green, and Co., 1918; reprint, Gloucester, Mass.: Peter Smith Publishers, 1965).

18. Forbes, "Buttressing the Foundations of Democracy," 1232.

19. Edward J. Ward, *The Social Center* (New York: Appleton and Co., 1913), 87.

20. William Hemstreet, "Theory and Practice of the New Primary Law," *Arena* 28 (December 1902): 592 (emphasis in original).

21. Editorial, "The Political Use of School Buildings," *Outlook*, September 14, 1912.

22. Benjamin Park Dewitt, *The Progressive Movement* (Seattle: University of Washington Press, 1915), 215.

23. "Let the People Rule," *Nation*, September 26, 1912, 276–77. TR also spoke of his willingness to have the recall extended to the presidency in a speech in Denver, Colorado. See "Roosevelt Favors the Recall of the President," *New York Times*, September 20, 1912, 1.

24. John Dewey, "Theodore Roosevelt," in *John Dewey: The Middle Works, 1899–1924*, ed. Jo Ann Boydston (Carbondale: Southern Illinois University Press, 1982), 2:146. H. L. Mencken's "autopsy" of Roosevelt argued that TR only *thought* he believed in democracy. His real creed was enlightened government. Although Roosevelt might have been "carried away by the emotional storms of the moment," by the "quasi-religious monkey-shines" that marked the Progressive party's creation, Mencken avers, TR's "remedy for all the great pangs and longings of existence was not a dispersion of authority, but a hard concentration of authority." Mencken, "Roosevelt: An Autopsy," in *Prejudices: A Selection*, ed. James T. Farrell (New York: Vintage Books, 1958), 61. In truth, TR embodied the hope of New Nationalists that democracy and administrative efficiency could be combined. Arguably, this hope revealed a basic contradiction in their thinking. But, as this chapter argues, the concept of forming a national democracy, with a dominant and dominating executive at its head, had deep roots in American political life. The quest for enlightened administration had its origins in the Federalists' interpretation of the Constitution, in their ambition to create self-government on a grand scale.

25. Elmer E. Cornwell Jr., *Presidential Leadership of Public Opinion* (Bloomington: Indiana University Press, 1965), 10 (emphasis in original).

26. Beveridge cited in David Thelen, *Robert M. La Follette and the Insurgent Spirit* (Boston: Little, Brown, 1976), 76.

27. Roosevelt derived the term *muckraker* from the description in John Bunyan's *Pilgrim's Progress* of the man with the "Muck-Rack."

Address at the laying of the cornerstone of the office building of the House of Representatives, Washington, D.C., April 14, 1906, found in Willis Fletcher Johnson, ed., *Theodore Roosevelt: Addresses and Papers* (New York: Sun Dial Classics, 1908), 311.

28. Mark Sullivan, *Our Times: The United States, 1900–1925*, 6 vols. (New York: Scribner's, 1926–35), 3:83–84.

29. Eisenach, *Lost Promise of Progressivism*, 241.

30. James Montague, "Roosevelt and Johnson Nominated; Moose Lift Voices in Hymn Singing," *San Francisco Examiner*, August 8, 1912, 1.

31. In accepting the Progressive party's nomination in person, Roosevelt followed the example of previous third-party candidates who scorned the two-party system. But TR's popularity and the significant support of his newly formed party highlighted his acceptance of the nomination at the Progressive party convention as a pathbreaking event. "Marking a new departure in the proceedings of national conventions," reported the *San Francisco Examiner*, "the two candidates were notified of their nominations, and in the midst of deafening cheers they appeared before the delegates to voice their acceptance and to pledge their best efforts in the coming campaign." August 8, 1912, 1. See also John Allen Gable, *The Bull Moose Years: Theodore Roosevelt and the Progressive Party* (Port Washington, N.Y.: Kennikat Press, 1978), 108.

32. Editorial, "What Roosevelt Believes in 1912," *San Francisco Examiner*, August 8, 1912, 22.

33. William Kittle, "The Making of Public Opinion," *Arena* 41 (July 1909): 449.

34. Croly, *Progressive Democracy*, 5.

35. Eisenach, *Lost Promise of Progressivism*, 239.

36. William Howard Taft to L. O'Brien, January 21, 1910, William Howard Taft Papers, Manuscript Division, Library of Congress, Washington, D.C.

37. Ibid.; Taft to Frank P. Flint, February 15, 1911, Taft Papers.

38. William Howard Taft, "The Sign of the Times" (address given before the Electoral Manufacturers Club, Hot Springs, Va., November 6, 1913), Taft Papers.

39. Statement dictated by the president for Harry Dunlap, for publication in the *New York World*, November 14, 1912, Taft Papers.

40. For example, see George Bancroft, "An Oration Delivered before the Democracy of Springfield and neighboring Towns," July 4, 1836. Reprinted in Leon Stein and Philip Taft, eds., *Labor Politics: Collected Pamphlets*, 2 vols. (New York: Arno Press, 1971), 1:4.

41. Eltweed Pomeroy, "Needed Political Reforms: Direct Legislation; Or, The Initiative and the Referendum, and the Recall," *Arena* 28 (November 1902): 465–66.

42. Forbes, "Buttressing the Foundations of Democracy," 1235.

43. Hemstreet, "Theory and Practice of the New Primary Law," 592.

44. On the limits of progressive democracy, see Robert H. Wiebe, *Self-Rule: A Cultural History of American Democracy* (Chicago: University of Chicago Press, 1995), chap. 7.

45. Shefter, *Political Parties and the State*, 75–81.

46. Louis Galambos and Joseph Pratt, *The Rise of the Corporate Commonwealth: United States Business and Public Policy in the Twentieth Century* (New York: Basic Books, 1988).

47. Herbert Croly, *The Promise of American Life* (New York: Macmillan, 1909; reprint, New York: Dutton, 1963), 338. On the progressives' commitment to strengthening executive

administration, see Peri Arnold, *Making the Managerial Presidency* (Princeton: Princeton University Press, 1986), chap. 2.

48. Theodore Roosevelt, *The Works of Theodore Roosevelt*, 20 vols. (New York: Scribner's, 1926), 20:347.

49. Paul Van Riper, *History of the United States Civil Service* (Evanston, Ill.: Row Peterson, 1958), 189.

50. Stephen Skowronek, *Building a New American State: The Expansion of National Administrative Capacities, 1877–1920* (New York: Cambridge University Press, 1982), 176.

51. Transcript of story from *Chicago Record Herald*, November 21, 1912, in Charles McCarthy Papers, Wisconsin Historical Society, Madison.

52. Walter Weyl, *The New Democracy* (New York: Macmillan, 1912), 5.

53. Delos F. Wilcox, *Government by All the People: The Initiative, Referendum, and the Recall as Instruments of Democracy* (New York: Macmillan, 1912; reprint, New York: Da Capo Press, 1972), 9–10.

54. Croly, *Progressive Democracy*, 341.

55. George Mowry, "The Election of 1912," in *History of American Presidential Elections*, ed. Arthur Schlesinger Jr. and Fred L. Israel (New York: Chelsea, 1971), 2160.

56. George Mowry, *Theodore Roosevelt and the Progressive Movement* (Madison: University of Wisconsin Press, 1947), 217.

57. William Howard Taft, Address at the Republican Club of New York City, February 12, 1912, Taft Papers.

58. William Howard Taft, Address at the Republican Club, New York City, January 4, 1913, Taft Papers.

59. Address of William Howard Taft, 62d Cong., 2d sess., April 25, 1912, S. Doc. 615 (62–2, vol. 38, 2), 3–4.

60. Taft, Address at the Republican Club, February 12, 1912.

61. Theodore Gilman, "The Progressive Party Comes Not to Destroy, but to Fulfill, the Constitution" (address delivered at a public rally in Yonkers, N.Y., September 27, 1912), Progressive Party Publications, 1912–16, Theodore Roosevelt Collection, Harvard University, Cambridge, Mass., 4.

62. Croly, *Progressive Democracy*, 54–55.

63. Gilman, "Progressive Party Comes Not to Destroy, but to Fulfill, the Constitution," 5–6.

64. Debs cited in "The New Party Gets Itself Born," *Current Literature* (September 1912): 256.

65. Letter to the Editor, *Social Democratic Herald*, November 19, 1898, Eugene V. Debs Papers, Indiana State University, Terre Haute, Ind.

66. Eugene V. Debs, "The Greatest Political Campaign in American History" (St. Louis Campaign Opening Speech, July 6, 1912), Debs Papers.

67. Learned Hand to Felix Frankfurter, April 4, 1912, Learned Hand Papers, Harvard University Law School.

68. Roosevelt to Sydney Brooks, June 4, 1912, in *The Letters of Theodore Roosevelt*, ed. Elting Morison, 8 vols. (Cambridge: Harvard University Press, 1952), 7:552–53 (my emphasis).

69. Croly, *Progressive Democracy*, 281–82.

70. Jane Addams, "Social Justice through National Action" (speech delivered at the Second Annual Lincoln Day Dinner of the Progressive party, New York City, February 12, 1914), printed manuscript, located in Jane Addams Papers, Swarthmore College, Swarthmore, Pa., file 136, reel 42.

71. Croly, *Progressive Democracy*, 336.

72. Editorial, "The Democrats as Legislators," *New Republic*, September 2, 1916, 103.

73. Kenneth Campbell, "The Progressive Movement of 1924" (Ph.D. diss., Columbia University, 1947).

74. Sidney M. Milkis and Michael Nelson, *The American Presidency: Origins and Development, 1776–1999*, 3d ed. (Washington, D.C.: Congressional Quarterly, 1999), 250–54.

75. For example, see Michael E. McGerr, *The Decline of Popular Politics: The American North, 1865–1928* (New York: Oxford University Press, 1986).

76. Morton Keller, "Social and Economic Regulation in the Progressive Era," in *Progressivism and the New Democracy*, ed. Jerome Mileur and Sidney M. Milkis (Amherst: University of Massachusetts Press, 1999).

77. Gerald Rusk argues that registration requirements and the Australian ballot advanced the progressive cause of emancipating the voter from the corrupt influence of machine politics. See Rusk, "The American Electoral Universe: Speculation and Evidence," *American Political Science Review* 68, no. 3 (September 1974): 1033. Walter Dean Burnham dissents from this position, arguing that the ballot reforms were part of an antidemocratic movement at the end of the nineteenth century. See Burnham, "Theory and Voting Research: Some Reflections on Converse's 'Change in the American Electorate,'" ibid., 1002–23. For an analysis of voting laws which complements the argument of this chapter, see Robert Wiebe's essay "Sinking the Lower Class," which argues that these reforms unintentionally disenfranchised lower-class men: "Voting, once a loyalty-affirming public action, became an individualized private act. Instead of crowding to the polls and waving the party's ballot as they went to vote, lower-class men, one by one, ran the gauntlet of electoral officials, perhaps only to discover that they could not decipher the procedures." Wiebe, *Self-Rule*, 137.

78. Arthur S. Link, "What Happened to the Progressive Movement in the 1920s," *American Historical Review* 64, no. 4 (July 1959): 848.

79. Joel H. Silbey, "Foundation Stones of Present Discontents: The American Political Nation, 1776–1945," in *Present Discontents: American Politics in the Very Late Twentieth Century*, ed. Byron Shafer (Chatham, N.J.: Chatham House, 1997), 24.

80. Wilson Carey McWilliams, "Standing at Armageddon: Morality and Religion in Progressive Thought," in Mileur and Milkis, *Progressivism and the New Democracy*.

81. Ibid.

82. John Dewey, *The Public and Its Problems* (New York: Henry Holt, 1927), 109.

83. Ibid., 208, 211.

84. Wiebe, *Self-Rule*, 176.

85. Hemstreet, "Theory and Practice of the New Primary Law," 589–90 (emphasis in the original).

86. Alexis de Tocqueville, *Democracy in America*, ed. J. P. Mayer (Garden City, N.Y.: Doubleday, 1969), 525–28.

87. Alexander Hamilton to James Bayard, April 6, 1802, in *The Papers of Alexander Hamilton*, 25 vols. (New York: Columbia University Press, 1977), 25:587–89.

88. Harvey Flaumenhaft, "Hamilton's Administrative Republic and the American Presidency," in *The Presidency in the Constitutional Order*, ed. Joseph M. Bessette and Jeffrey Tulis (Baton Rouge: Louisiana State University Press, 1981).

89. There were some notable exceptions, of course. For example, see Jane Addams, "Why the Ward Boss Rules," *Outlook*, April 2, 1898, reprinted in William L. Riordan, *Plunkitt of Tammany Hall*, ed. Terrence J. McDonald (Boston: Bedford Books, 1994), 122. Mary Simkhovitch had similar advice for the New York reformer. "True reform and lasting reform will come about when public opinion will sustain it," she wrote. "When the reformer understands men as well as the politician friend understands them, he too will have his day." "Friendship and Politics," *Political Science Quarterly* 17, no. 2 (June 1902): 204.

90. See McGerr, *Decline of Popular Politics*, esp. chap. 2.

91. Tocqueville, *Democracy in America*, 162. Although Tocqueville criticized political parties in the United States for being relatively indifferent to broad moral questions and dedicated to the personal ambitions of their members, he also suggested that they might be considered valuable political associations, as "great free schools to which all citizens come to be taught the general theory of association." See esp. 189–95, 509–13, 520–24.

92. Wilson describes the "extraordinary isolation" of the president in "Constitutional Government in the United States," 18:114–15.

Chapter 4　The New Deal Liberalism and the Doctrine of Responsible Party Government

1. Herbert Knox Smith, "The Progressive Party," *Yale Review* 2 (1912–13): 18–32.

2. Progressive National Committee, "First Quarterly Report of the Progressive National Service," March 31, 1913, Jane Addams Papers, Swarthmore College, Swarthmore, Pa., file 136, reel 42.

3. George Perkins to Albert J. Beveridge, November 11, 1913, and attached letter to Frances Kellor, same date; Perkins to Beveridge, December 6, 1913, Albert J. Beveridge Papers, Manuscript Division, Library of Congress, Washington, D.C.

4. John Allen Gable, *The Bull Moose Years: Theodore Roosevelt and the Progressive Party* (Port Washington, N.Y.: Kennikat Press, 1978), 187–88.

5. Roosevelt to Gifford Pinchot, November 13, 1912, in *The Letters of Theodore Roosevelt*, ed. Elting E. Morison, 8 vols. (Cambridge: Harvard University Press, 1952), 7:640–45.

6. Victor Murdock to George Perkins, March 21, 1914, Correspondence of the Progressive Party National Committee, Theodore Roosevelt Collection, Harvard University.

7. Alice Carpenter to George Perkins, July 28, 1914, Correspondence of the Progressive Party National Committee.

8. Committee on Political Parties, *Toward a More Responsible Two Party System* (New York: Rinehart, 1950), 24–25.

9. E. E. Schattschneider, *Party Government* (New York: Farrar and Rinehart, 1942), 163.

10. Franklin D. Roosevelt, *Public Papers and Addresses*, 13 vols., ed. Samuel I. Rosenman (New York: Random House, 1938–50), 7:xxxi.

11. Ibid., xxviii–xxix.

12. Woodrow Wilson, "Constitutional Government in the United States," in *The Papers of Woodrow Wilson*, ed. Arthur S. Link, 69 vols. (Princeton: Princeton University Press, 1974), 18:214.

13. Woodrow Wilson, "Cabinet Government in the United States," *International Review* 7 (August 1879): 146–63, 150–51.

14. Wilson to Alexander Mitchell Palmer, February 5, 1913, in Link, *Papers of Woodrow Wilson*, 27:100.

15. Quoted in David Lawrence, *The True Story of Woodrow Wilson* (New York: Doran, 1924), 39.

16. Wilson, "Constitutional Government in the United States," 18:115.

17. Ibid., 116.

18. On the tension between Wilson party leadership and progressive reform, see Sidney M. Milkis, *The President and the Parties: The Transformation of the American Party System since the New Deal* (New York: Oxford University Press, 1993), chap. 2, and Daniel Stid, *The President as Statesman: Woodrow Wilson and the Constitution* (Lawrence: University Press of Kansas, 1998).

19. Stephen Skowronek, *Building a New American State: The Expansion of National Administrative Capacities, 1877–1920* (New York: Cambridge University Press, 1982), 40.

20. Woodrow Wilson, "Monopoly or Opportunity," in *The Growth of Presidential Power: A Documented History*, ed. William M. Goldsmith, 3 vols. (New York: Chelsea, 1974), 3:1341.

21. Herbert Croly, *Progressive Democracy* (New York: Macmillan, 1914), 15.

22. Stid, *President as Statesman*, chap. 8.

23. Roosevelt, *Public Papers and Addresses*, 1:751–52.

24. "Democratic Platform of 1936," in *National Party Platforms*, ed. Donald Bruce Johnson (Urbana: University of Illinois Press, 1978), 360.

25. Roosevelt, *Public Papers and Addresses*, 13:40.

26. John Dewey, "Individualism, Old and New," reprinted in *John Dewey: The Later*

Works, 1925–1953, ed. Jo Ann Boydston, 17 vols. (Carbondale: Southern Illinois University Press, 1984), 5:41–123 (my emphasis).

27. Ibid., 68.

28. H. M. Kallen, "Salvation by Intelligence," a review of Dewey's *Liberalism and Social Action, Saturday Review,* December 14, 1935, 7.

29. Josephus Daniels to FDR, December 15, 1932, Ray Stannard Baker Collection, Franklin D. Roosevelt File, Princeton University Library.

30. Personal and Political Diary of Homer Cummings, January 5, 1933, box 234, no. 2, 90, Homer Cummings Papers (9973), Manuscripts Department, University of Virginia Library, Charlottesville.

31. Edward J. Flynn, *You're the Boss* (New York: Viking Press, 1948), 153.

32. Paul Van Riper, *History of the United States Civil Service* (Evanston, Ill.: Row Peterson, 1958), 327.

33. Lindsay Rogers, "Reorganization: Post-Mortem Notes," *Political Science Quarterly* 53, no. 2 (June 1938): 170.

34. Phillips to FDR, June 9, 1937, and FDR to Phillips, June 16, 1937, Presidential Personal File 2666, Franklin D. Roosevelt Papers, Hyde Park, N.Y.

35. Stanley High, "Whose Party Is It?" *Saturday Evening Post,* February 6, 1937, 34.

36. Thomas Stokes, *Chip off My Shoulder* (Princeton: Princeton University Press, 1940), 503.

37. For an account of the debate over the two-thirds rule as it took shape during the 1930s, see Frank Clarkin, "Two-Thirds Rule Facing Abolition," *New York Times,* January 5, 1936, sec. 4, 10.

38. Bailey to R. R. King, August 10, 1936, Josiah Bailey Papers, Senatorial Series, Political National Papers, box 475, Manuscript Department, William R. Perkins Library, Duke University, Durham, N.C.

39. Ralph M. Goldman, *Search for Consensus: The Story of the Democratic Party* (Philadelphia: Temple University Press, 1979), 326.

40. The "solid South" enabled Democrats from below the Mason-Dixon line to benefit disproportionately from the seniority rule—many southerners, as a result, held key committee positions. Moreover, the South was important to party finances; owing to the effectiveness of Farley's organization there, more than 37 percent of all Democratic contributions of one hundred dollars or more in 1936 came from the South. See Louise Overacker, "Campaign Funds in the Presidential Election of 1936," *American Political Science Review* 31, no. 3 (June 1937): 496.

41. Personal and Political Diary of Homer Cummings, August 1, 1937, box 235, no. 9, 119.

42. Ronald D. Rotunda, "The Liberal Label: Roosevelt's Capture of a Symbol," in *Public Policy,* ed. John D. Montgomery and Albert O. Hirschman (Cambridge: Harvard University Press, 1968), 17:399. *New York Times,* September 3, 1938, 1.

43. James A. Farley, *Jim Farley's Story* (New York: McGraw-Hill, 1948), 146.

44. Ernest Cuneo, "The Eve of the Purge," 24, unpublished manuscript found in the Ernest Cuneo Papers, box 111, Franklin D. Roosevelt Library, Hyde Park, N.Y.

45. Raymond Clapper, "Roosevelt Tries the Primaries," *Current History* 76, no. 2 (October 1938): 17.

46. Charles Merriam, "Recent Tendencies in Primary Election Systems," published in *The Direct Primary*, National Municipal League, New York City, 1926, Theodore Roosevelt Collection, Houghton Library, Harvard University.

47. Bryant Putney, "Nomination by Primary," *Electoral Research Reports* 2, no. 7 (August 19, 1938): 127–28.

48. William H. Meier to James Farley, December 23, 1938, Official File 300 (Democratic National Committee), Roosevelt Papers.

49. Roosevelt, *Public Papers and Addresses*, 7:397–98.

50. Felix Frankfurter to FDR, August 9, 1937, box 210, folder: Franklin D. Roosevelt, 1937, Corcoran Papers, Manuscript Division, Library of Congress, Washington, D.C.; and FDR to Frankfurter, August 12, 1937, microfilm reel 60, Felix Frankfurter Papers, Library of Congress, Washington, D.C.

51. Roosevelt, *Public Papers and Addresses*, 7:398–99.

52. Ibid., 395.

53. Glass to Jack Dionne, October 17, 1938, Carter Glass Papers, accession no. 2913, box 383, University of Virginia Library.

54. Transcript of tape done by James Farley, January 27, 1976, 77, Cuneo Papers.

55. Roosevelt, *Public Papers and Addresses*, 7:xxxi–xxxii.

56. Clapper, "Roosevelt Tries the Primaries," 16.

57. Morton J. Frisch, *Franklin D. Roosevelt: The Contribution of the New Deal to American Political Thought and Practice* (Boston: Twayne, 1975), 79.

58. Croly, *Progressive Democracy*, 345–46, 348.

59. Committee on Political Parties, *Toward a More Responsible Two Party System*, 14.

60. Ray Stannard Baker to Roosevelt, September 26, 1936, and FDR to Baker, September 30, 1936, President's Personal File, 2332, Roosevelt Library.

61. Turner Catledge, "The New Deal Councils Split over Choice of Foes for Purge," *New York Times*, June 29, 1938, 1, 6.

62. Clapper, "Roosevelt Tries the Primaries," 18.

63. *Time*, October 3, 1938, 9.

64. Frank Freidel, *Franklin D. Roosevelt: Rendezvous with Destiny* (Boston: Little, Brown, 1990), 286.

65. Schattschneider, *Party Government*, 163–69; also see John Edward Hopper, "The Purge: Franklin D. Roosevelt and the 1938 Democratic Nominations" (Ph.D. diss., University of Chicago, 1966), 220–21.

66. Philip La Follette, Elmer Bensen, and Frank Murphy, "Why We Lost," *Nation*,

December 3, 1938. In the general election, the Democrats lost eighty-one seats in the House and eight in the Senate, as well as thirteen governorships. See Milton Plesur, "The Republican Congressional Comeback of 1938," *Review of Politics* 24 (1962): 525–62.

67. E. E. Schattschneider, "The Struggle for Party Government," originally published in 1948, reprinted in *The Party Battle* (New York: Arno Press, 1974), 40.

68. On the limits of party government in the United States, see James Sterling Young and Russell L. Riley, "Party Government and Political Culture" (paper presented at the annual meeting of the American Political Science Association, San Francisco, September 1990). Also see Milkis, *President and the Parties*, 228–38.

69. "Outline for a New York Conference," April 8, 1936, Papers of the President's Committee on Administrative Management, Roosevelt Library.

70. The President's Committee on Administrative Management, headed by Louis Brownlow, played a central role in the planning and politics of institutional reform, 1936–40.

71. Luther Gulick, "Politics, Administration, and the New Deal," *Annals* 169 (September 1933): 64.

72. Louis Brownlow, "Perfect Union," January 27, 1943, Appendix to Official Files 101 and 101b, 38–39, Roosevelt Papers (my emphasis).

73. *Congressional Record*, 75th Cong., 3d sess., April 8, 1938, 83, pt. 5:5121.

74. *Humphrey's Executor v. U.S.*, 295 U.S. 602 (1935); *A. L. A. Schechter Poultry Corp. et al. v. United States*, 295 U.S. 553 (1935).

75. *Myers v. United States*, 272 U.S. 53 (1926).

76. Ernest Cuneo, "The FDR Drama," unpublished manuscript found in Cuneo Papers, folder: JAF, pre–1932.

77. *Report of the President's Committee on Administrative Management* (Washington, D.C.: Government Printing Office, 1937), 53.

78. The Ramspeck Act authorized the extension by the president of the merit system rules to nearly two hundred thousand positions previously exempted by law. Roosevelt took early advantage of this authorization in 1941 and by executive order extended the coverage of civil service protection to the point where about 95 percent of the permanent service was included. Leonard White, "Franklin Roosevelt and the Public Service," *Public Personnel Review* 6 (July 1945): 142.

79. Charles Edward Merriam, "The Written and Unwritten Constitution," in *Party Battle*, 85.

80. Martha Derthick, *Policymaking for Social Security* (Washington, D.C.: Brookings Institution, 1983), 417.

Chapter 5 Remaking American Politics

1. Richard Rovere, "A Man for This Age Too," *New York Times Magazine*, April 11, 1965, 118.

2. An account of Leuchtenburg's interview with Johnson is given in Leuchtenburg, "A Visit with LBJ," *American Heritage* 41, no. 4 (May/June 1990): 47–64.

3. William E. Leuchtenburg, *In the Shadow of FDR: From Harry Truman to Ronald Reagan*, rev. ed. (Ithaca, N.Y.: Cornell University Press, 1985), 142.

4. Hugh Heclo, "The Sixties' False Dawn: Awakenings, Movements, and Post-modern Policy-making," *Journal of Policy History* 8, no. 1 (1996): 56.

5. Jeffrey Berry, *The Interest Group Society* (Boston: Little, Brown, 1984), 28.

6. Harry McPherson, *A Political Education* (Boston: Little, Brown, 1972), 301.

7. Anthony King, "The American Polity in the Late 1970s: Building Coalitions in the Sand," in *The New American Political System*, ed. Anthony King (Washington, D.C.: American Enterprise Institute, 1978), 372–73.

8. See Chapter 3.

9. Daniel P. Moynihan, *Maximum Feasible Misunderstanding: Community Action and the War on Poverty* (New York: Free Press, 1970).

10. Alexis de Tocqueville, *Democracy in America* (Garden City, N.Y.: Doubleday, 1969), 263.

11. George E. Reedy, *The Twilight of the Modern Presidency* (New York: New American Library, 1970), xv.

12. Harry McPherson, interview with the author, Washington, D.C., July 30, 1985.

13. Michael R. Bechloss, ed., *Taking Charge: The Johnson White House Tapes, 1963–1964* (New York: Simon and Schuster, 1997), 326.

14. *Public Papers of the Presidents of the United States: Lyndon Baines Johnson, 1963–64*, 2 vols. (Washington, D.C.: Government Printing Office, 1965), 1:704. On the origins and significance of the Great Society speech, see Richard Goodwin, *Remembering America* (Boston: Little, Brown, 1988), 274, 276.

15. *Public Papers of the Presidents of the United States: Lyndon Baines Johnson, 1966*, 2 vols. (Washington, D.C.: Government Printing Office, 1967), 1:3–7.

16. Horace Busby to LBJ, July 13, 1964, and attached memorandum, "The Democratic Party and the Presidency in the Twentieth Century, 1900–1960," Office Files of Horace Busby, box 52, folder: Memos to Mr. Johnson, July 1964, Lyndon Baines Johnson Library, Austin, Tex.

17. Goodwin, *Remembering America*, 275.

18. Students for a Democratic Society, "Port Huron Statement," printed in *The New Left: A Documentary History*, ed. Missimo Teodori (Indianapolis: Bobbs-Merrill, 1969), 165 (emphasis in original). See also Goodwin, *Remembering America*, 276.

19. Goodwin, *Remembering America*, 274.

20. Lyndon Baines Johnson, *The Vantage Point: Perspectives on the Presidency, 1963–1969* (New York: Holt, Rinehart, and Winston, 1971), 73.

21. John Dewey, "The Future of Liberalism," *Journal of Philosophy* 32, no. 9 (April 25, 1935): 230.

22. John Dewey, *Liberalism and Social Action* (New York: Putnam's, 1935), 26.

23. *Public Papers of the Presidents of the United States: Lyndon Baines Johnson*, 1966, 1:6.

24. Fred I. Greenstein, "Nine Presidents in Search of a Modern Presidency," in *Leadership in the Modern Presidency*, ed. Fred I. Greenstein (Cambridge: Harvard University Press, 1988), 329.

25. William Leuchtenburg, "The Genesis of the Great Society," *Reporter*, April 21, 1966, 38.

26. Donald Horowitz, "Is the Presidency Failing?" *Public Interest* 88 (Summer 1987): 25.

27. Alan Otten, "The Incumbent's Edge," *Wall Street Journal*, December 28, 1967.

28. David B. Truman, "Party Reform, Party Atrophy, and Constitutional Change," *Political Science Quarterly* 99, no. 4 (Winter 1984–85): 639; see also Byron E. Shafer, *The Quiet Revolution: The Struggle for the Democratic Party and the Shaping of Post-reform Politics* (New York: Russell Sage Foundation, 1983).

29. James Ceaser, *Presidential Selection: Theory and Development* (Princeton: Princeton University Press, 1979), 283.

30. Samuel Beer, "In Search of a New Public Philosophy," in *The New American Political System*, ed. Anthony King (Washington, D.C.: American Enterprise Institute, 1979), 16–17.

31. Moynihan, *Maximum Feasible Misunderstanding*, chap. 5.

32. James Morone, *The Democratic Wish: Popular Participation and the Limits of American Government*, rev. ed. (New Haven: Yale University Press, 1998), 226.

33. Johnson, *Vantage Point*, 74.

34. Peter Skerry, "The Charmed Life of Head Start," *Public Interest* 73 (Fall 1983): 35.

35. W. W. Rostow, Memorandum of Conversation, participants: the president; the vice president; Charles Murphy; W. W. Rostow, April 5, 1968, White House Famous Names, box 6, folder: Robert F. Kennedy, 1968 Campaign, Johnson Library.

36. Richard Goodwin, "Sources of Public Unhappiness," *New Yorker*, January 4, 1969, 40.

37. Stephen E. Ambrose, *Nixon*, vol. 3: *Ruin and Recovery, 1973–1990* (New York: Simon and Schuster, 1991).

38. *United States v. Nixon*, 418 U.S. 683 (1974).

39. Greenstein, "Nine Presidents in Search of a Modern Presidency," 334.

40. On the House Study Group, see Mark F. Ferber, "The Formation of the Democratic Study Group," in *Congressional Behavior*, ed. Nelson W. Polsby (New York: Random House, 1971).

41. R. Shep Melnick, *Between the Lines: Interpreting Welfare Rights* (Washington, D.C.: Brookings Institution, 1994), 196–200.

42. Benjamin Ginsberg and Martin Shefter, *Politics by Other Means: The Declining Importance of Elections in America* (New York: Basic Books, 1990), 16.

43. A. James Reichley, *Conservatives in an Age of Change* (Washington, D.C.: Brookings Institution, 1981), 259.

44. R. Shep Melnick, "The Politics of Partnership," *Public Administration Review* 45 (November 1985): 653–60.

45. Walter A. Rosenbaum, "Public Involvement as Reform and Ritual: The Political Development of Federal Participation Programs," in *Citizen Participation in America: Essays on the State of the Art*, ed. Stuart Langton (Lexington, Mass.: Lexington Books, 1978).

46. For a more detailed discussion of the meaning and significance of social regulation, see Richard A. Harris and Sidney M. Milkis, *The Politics of Regulatory Change: A Tale of Two Agencies*, 2d ed. (New York: Oxford University Press, 1996), esp. chaps. 1 and 3.

47. Falk cited in Berry, *The Interest Group Society*, 36.

48. Ralph Nader, "The Case for Federal Chartering," in *The Consumer and Corporate Accountability* (New York: Harcourt Brace Jovanovich, 1973), 365.

49. On the role of auxiliary party organizations in New Deal party politics, see Milkis, *President and the Parties*, 76–77.

50. Michael W. McCann, "Public Interest Liberalism and the Modern Regulatory State," *Polity* 21, no. 2 (Winter 1988): 389, 394.

51. Richard Ayres, interview with Richard A. Harris and Sidney M. Milkis, Washington, D.C., July 11, 1986.

52. Rosenbaum, "Public Involvement as Reform and Ritual," 81.

53. Ibid., 83.

54. Joan B. Aron, "Citizen Participation at Government Expense," *Public Administration Review* 39, no. 5 (September/October 1979): 477–85.

55. Max D. Peglin and Edgar Shore, "Regulatory Agency Responses to the Development of Public Participation," *Public Administration Review* 37, no. 2 (March/April 1977): 142.

56. For a list of grants made under the FTC public-intervenor funding program, see Hearings, Subcommittee for Consumers, Committee on Commerce, "Oversight to Examine the Enforcement and Administrative Authority of the FTC to Regulate Unfair and Deceptive Trade Practices," 96th Cong., 1st sess., September 18, 19, 27, 28; October 4, 5, 10 1979, 158–60.

57. Barry Boyer, "Funding Public Participation in Agency Proceedings: The Federal Trade Commission Experience," *Georgetown Law Journal* 70, no. 1 (1980): 71.

58. On this development, see Melnick, *Between the Lines*.

59. Martin Shapiro, "APA: Past, Present, and Future," *Virginia Law Review* 72 (1986): 461–62.

60. Richard B. Stewart, "The Reformation of Administrative Law," *Harvard Law Review* 88 (June 1975): 1712.

61. James Q. Wilson, "The Politics of Regulation," in *The Politics of Regulation*, ed. James Q. Wilson (New York: Basic Books, 1980), 370–71.

62. Michael Pertschuk, *Revolt against Regulation: The Rise and Pause of the Consumer Movement* (Berkeley: University of California Press, 1982), 130.

63. Jeremy Rabkin, "The Judiciary in the Administrative State," *Public Interest* 71 (Spring 1983): 63.

64. Hugh Heclo, "Issue Networks and the Executive Establishment," in King, *New American Political System*, 124.

65. Ralph Nader, "A Citizen's Guide to the American Economy," in Nader, *Consumer and Corporate Accountability*, 4.

66. McCann, "Public Interest Liberalism and the Modern Regulatory State," 392.

67. John Coleman argues that Carter did successfully defy Congress to pursue a policy of restraint during the recession of 1980. See Coleman, *Party Decline in America: Policy, Politics, and the Fiscal State* (Princeton: Princeton University Press, 1996), 174–75. Still, Carter's command was severely challenged by Senator Edward Kennedy, the champion of orthodox liberals, who came very close to denying the incumbent president the Democratic nomination in 1980. Indeed, Kennedy's insurgency forced Carter to run on a party platform that repudiated his own economic program. See Stephen Skowronek, *The Politics Presidents Make: Leadership from John Adams to Bill Clinton* (Cambridge: Harvard University Press, 1997), 405.

68. R. Shep Melnick, "The Politics of Partnership: Institutional Coalitions and Statutory Rights," Occasional Paper No. 84-3, Center for American Political Studies, Harvard University, 8.

69. For a review of these institutional developments and how they were modified during the Reagan years, see Harris and Milkis, *Politics of Regulatory Change*, chap. 4.

70. Charles Jones, *The Trusteeship Presidency* (Baton Rouge: Louisiana State University Press, 1988).

71. Jimmy Carter, *Keeping Faith: Memoirs of a President* (New York: Bantam Books, 1982), 80.

72. Erwin Hargrove, *Jimmy Carter as President: Leadership and the Politics of the Public Good* (Baton Rouge: Louisiana State University Press, 1988), 192.

73. Patrick Caddell, "Of Crisis and Opportunity," April 23, 1979, "Memoranda: President Carter 1/10/79–4/23/79 [CF, O/A 519]," box 40, Jody Powell Files, Jimmy Carter Library, Atlanta, Ga.

74. "The Scramble Starts," editorial, *Los Angeles Times*, July 17, 1979, pt. 2, 4. See also Robert Shogan, "Carter Returns to Moralistic Themes," ibid., pt. 1, 1, 15; "Winning Neither Confidence nor More Oil," editorial, *Chicago Tribune*, July 17, 1979, sec. 3, p. 2; "Riding Casually to War," editorial, *New York Times*, July 17, 1979, A16; "President Carter's Directive," editorial, *Boston Globe*, July 17, 1979, 10.

75. Transcript of President Carter's "Address to the Country on Energy Problems," *New York Times*, July 16, 1979.

76. Hargrove, *Jimmy Carter as President*, 192–93; see also William E. Leuchtenburg, "Jimmy Carter and the Post–New Deal Presidency," in *The Carter Presidency: Policy Choices in the Post–New Deal Era*, ed. Gary M. Mink and Hugh Davis Graham (Lawrence: University Press of Kansas, 1998).

77. Wilson Carey McWilliams, "Conclusion: The Meaning of the Election," in *The Election of 1996: Reports and Interpretations*, ed. Gerald M. Pomper et al. (Chatham, N.J.: Chatham House, 1997), 258–59.

Chapter 6 Divided Government and Beltway Partisanship

1. Gerald Ford, "Imperiled, Not Imperial," *Time*, November 10, 1980, 30.

2. Theodore White, *America in Search of Itself: The Making of the President, 1956–1980* (New York: Harper and Row, 1982), 124.

3. Benjamin Ginsberg and Martin Shefter, *Politics by Other Means: The Declining Importance of Elections in America* (New York: Basic Books, 1990), and Benjamin Ginsberg, Walter R. Mebane Jr., and Martin Shefter, "The Presidency and Interest Groups: Why Presidents Cannot Govern," in *The Presidency and the Political System*, ed. Michael Nelson, 4th ed. (Washington, D.C.: Congressional Quarterly, 1995). In contrast, David Mayhew showed that laws were passed with equal frequency under divided and unified forms of party control. His conclusion is that divided control makes no important difference to government performance. See Mayhew, *Divided We Govern: Party Control, Lawmaking, and Investigations, 1946–1990* (New Haven: Yale University Press, 1991). I agree with Mayhew that divided party control has not caused "gridlock"; but I would not go so far as to say it does not make a difference. As suggested in this essay, divided government is a symptom of, if not a solution to, Americans' "love-hate" relationship with the "state."

4. Alfred H. Kelly, Winfred A. Harbison, and Herman Belz, *The American Constitution: Its Origins and Development*, 7th ed. (New York: Norton, 1991), 705.

5. William Schneider, "A Loud Vote for Change," *National Journal*, November 7, 1992, 2544.

6. For example, see Phil Duncan and Steve Langdon, "When Congress Had to Choose, It Voted to Back Clinton," *Congressional Quarterly Weekly Report*, December 18, 1993, 3427–34.

7. Michael J. Malbin, "Was Divided Government Really Such a Big Problem?" in *Separation of Powers and Good Government*, ed. Bradford P. Wilson and Peter W. Schramm (Lanham, Md.: Rowman and Littlefield, 1994), 233.

8. Ronald Reagan, "A Time for Choosing," October 27, 1964. Printed in *Ronald Reagan Talks to America*, ed. Richard M. Scaife (Old Greenwich, Conn.: Devin Adair, 1983), 4–5. On Reagan's rhetoric, see William Muir Jr., *The Bully Pulpit: The Presidential Leadership of Ronald Reagan* (San Francisco: Institute for Contemporary Studies, 1992).

9. "Inaugural Address of Ronald Reagan," January 20, 1981. Printed in Richard Nathan, *The Administrative Presidency* (New York: Wiley, 1983), 159.

10. *New York Times,* July 20, 1980, E20.

11. William E. Leuchtenburg, *In the Shadow of FDR: From Harry Truman to Ronald Reagan,* rev. ed. (Ithaca, N.Y.: Cornell University Press, 1985), 210.

12. Congressman Dana Rohrabacher, former speech writer, Reagan administration, interview with the author, Washington, D.C., July 31, 1989. On Coolidge's presidency, see Sidney M. Milkis and Michael Nelson, *The American Presidency: Origins and Development, 1776–1999,* 3d ed. (Washington, D.C.: Congressional Quarterly, 1999), 250–54.

13. *Public Papers of the Presidents of the United States: Ronald Reagan, 1983,* 2 vols. (Washington, D.C.: Government Printing Office, 1984), 1:364; see also Muir, *Bully Pulpit,* 74–78.

14. Thomas Paine, *Common Sense* (New York: Penguin Books, 1976), 120.

15. Wilson Carey McWilliams, *The Idea of Fraternity in America* (Berkeley: University of California Press, 1973), 180–85.

16. Paine, *Common Sense,* 65 (emphasis in original).

17. Ibid., 120.

18. A. James Reichley, "The Rise of National Parties," in *The New Direction in American Politics,* ed. John E. Chubb and Paul E. Peterson (Washington, D.C.: Brookings Institution, 1985). By the end of the 1980s, Reichley was much less hopeful that the emergent national parties were well suited to perform the parties' historical function of mobilizing public support for political values and substantive government approaches and policies. See his *The Life of the Parties: A History of American Political Parties* (New York: Free Press, 1992), chaps. 18–21.

19. Rhodes Cook, "Reagan Nurtures His Adopted Party to Strength," *Congressional Quarterly Weekly Report,* September 18, 1985, 14, and Mitch Daniels, assistant to the president for political and governmental affairs, interview with the author, Washington, D.C., June 5, 1986.

20. Thomas E. Cavanaugh and James L. Sundquist, "The New Two Party System," in Chubb and Peterson, *New Direction in American Politics.*

21. Frank Fahrenkopf, interview with the author, Washington, D.C., July 27, 1987.

22. Representative Price as quoted in Rhodes Cook, "Pressed by Jackson Demands, Dukakis Yields on Party Rules," *Congressional Quarterly Weekly Report,* July 2, 1988, 179. In September 1989 the Democratic National Committee voted to rescind the part of the Jackson-Dukakis agreement concerning the cutback in "superdelegate" seats, but the proportional requirement was retained. See Rhodes Cook, "Democratic Party Rules Changes Readied for '92 Campaign," *Congressional Quarterly Weekly Report,* March 17, 1990, 847–49.

23. Loren Smith, interview with the author, Washington, D.C., June 23, 1987.

24. Senator Richard Lugar, phone interview with the author, August 7, 1987.

25. *Report of the Congressional Committees Investigating the Iran-Contra Affair,* with supplemental, minority, and additional views, 100th Cong., 1st sess., November 13, 1987, H. Rept. 100-433, S. Rept. 100-216, 515.

26. Richard A. Harris and Sidney M. Milkis, *The Politics of Regulatory Change: A Tale of Two Agencies*, 2d ed. (New York: Oxford University Press, 1996).

27. Sidney Blumenthal, *The Rise of the Counter-establishment: From Conservative Ideology to Political Power* (New York: Times Books, 1986), 9.

28. William E. Brock, interview with the author, Washington, D.C., August 12, 1987.

29. David Stockman, *The Triumph of Politics: Why the Reagan Revolution Failed* (New York: Harper and Row, 1986), 159.

30. Jeffrey Tulis, *The Rhetorical Presidency* (Princeton: Princeton University Press, 1983), 197.

31. William Greider, *The Education of David Stockman and Other Americans* (New York: Dutton, 1982), 23.

32. On the "neo-Keynesian" philosophy of supply-side economists, see James D. Savage, *Balanced Budgets and American Politics* (Ithaca, N.Y.: Cornell University Press, 1988), 205–6.

33. Alan Ehrenhalt, "Failed Campaign Cost Republicans the Senate," *Congressional Quarterly Weekly Report*, November 8, 1986, 2803.

34. Background information for the discussion of the 1986 campaign was obtained through a number of interviews with RNC staff, as well as GOP members of Congress. Many of those interviewed requested anonymity.

35. Vin Weber, interview with the author, Washington, D.C., July 28, 1987.

36. Ronald Reagan, "Remarks at a Rally for Senator James T. Broyhill," October 28, 1986, *Weekly Compilation of Presidential Documents* 22, no. 44, 1476. "When a house is messy, its residents welcome a cleanup crew," Ehrenhalt observed about the president's campaign speeches. "When the place is clean again, they thank the crew, pay them, and let them leave. If the crew wants to stay, it has to offer reasons why it is still needed." Ehrenhalt, "Failed Campaign Cost Republicans the Senate," 2803, 2871.

37. Ronald Reagan, "Remarks to Administration Officials on Domestic Policy," December 13, 1988, *Weekly Compilation of Presidential Documents* 24, no. 50, 1619. The phrase *iron triangle* had been used by practitioners and scholars since the advent of the New Deal to describe an alliance of executive bureaus, congressional committees, and interest groups, all linked together in a sort of closed-door conspiracy to maintain and expand particular programs. Reagan's use of the term was the first to elevate the press to full triangularity. The importance of the media's role in Reagan's analysis testifies to both the reformation of administrative politics in the late 1960s and 1970s and the president's failure to come to terms with this change.

38. The "gag rule," first issued by the Reagan administration's Department of Health and Human Services in 1988, declared that a program that received federal funds "may not provide counseling concerning the use of abortion as a method of family planning or provide referral for abortion as a method of family planning." The Reagan administration was thwarted in this policy by the lower courts, delaying the regulation for three years. But in late May 1991 the Supreme Court upheld the "gag rule" in *Rust v. Sullivan*, 500 U.S. 173

(1991), and the Bush administration prepared to carry it out. Congress quickly passed legislation that would stop the administration from enforcing the rules; however, the House failed by a dozen votes to override Bush's veto of the legislation. Soon after his inauguration, President Clinton issued an executive order reversing Reagan's and Bush's policy of forbidding abortion counseling at federally funded clinics.

39. David M. O'Brien, "The Reagan Judges: His Most Enduring Legacy?" in *The Reagan Legacy*, ed. Charles Jones (Chatham, N.J.: Chatham House, 1989).

40. John Marini, "The Political Conditions of Legislative-Bureaucratic Supremacy," *Claremont Review of Books* (Spring 1988). See also William Kristol, "The Judiciary: Conservatism's Lost Branch," *Harvard Journal of Law and Public Policy* 17, no. 1 (Winter 1994): 131–36.

41. In *Grove City* the Court ruled 6–3 that when an institution receives federal aid, only the "program or activity" actually getting the aid—not the entire institution—was covered by the laws. The civil rights restoration law passed over President Reagan's veto stated that federal antidiscrimination statutes apply to an institution in its entirety if it accepts federal aid for as little as one program. *Grove City College v. Bell*, 79 L. Ed. 2d 516 (1984); Mark Willen, "Congress Overrides Reagan's *Grove City* Veto," *Congressional Quarterly Weekly Report*, March 26, 1988, 774–76.

42. The Civil Rights Act of 1991 restored the legal standard established by the Supreme Court's 1971 ruling in *Griggs v. Duke Power Company*, 401 U.S. 424 (1971), which held employers responsible for justifying employment practices that were seemingly fair but had an "adverse impact" on women and minorities. A 1989 ruling, *Wards Cove Packing Company v. Atonio*, 490 U.S. 642 (1989), had shifted the burden, saying workers had to show that companies had no legitimate need for the challenged practices. The new legislation instructed the courts to follow the standard of *Griggs* and related rulings prior to *Ward's Cove*. Bush agreed to sign the bill, but he proclaimed that documents introduced by Senate minority leader Robert Dole, which offered a narrow understanding of the statute, would "be treated as authoritative interpretive guidance by all officials in the executive branch with respect to the law of disparate impact as well as the other matters covered in the document." On the controversy aroused by Bush's interpretation of the law, see Joan Biscupic, "Bush Signs Anti-job Bias Bill amid Furor over Preferences," *Congressional Quarterly Weekly Report*, November 23, 1991, 3463.

43. David Shribman, "Tsongas Suggests Third Party, Sees Powell as a Candidate," *Boston Globe*, December 13, 1994, 1, 28.

44. See, for example, Malbin, "Was Divided Government Really Such a Big Problem?"; Mayhew, *Divided We Govern*; and Richard M. Vallely, "Divided They Govern," in *The American Prospect: Reader in American Politics*, ed. Walter Dean Burnham (Chatham, N.J.: Chatham House, 1995).

45. William Clinton, "The New Covenant: Responsibility and Rebuilding the American Community," Washington, D.C., October 23, 1991.

46. Similar ideas and attendant policy proposals are spelled out in detail in Will Mar-

shall and Martin Schramm, eds., *Mandate for Change* (New York: Berkeley Books, 1993).

47. "Champions of the People," *Esquire* (December 1984): 447.

48. Will Marshall, president, Progressive Policy Institute, and Al From, president, Democratic Leadership Council, interviews with the author, Washington, D.C., May 20, 1997.

49. Dan Balz, "Democrats' Perennial Rising Star Wants to Put a New Face on the Party," *Washington Post*, June 25, 1991, A4; E. J. Dionne, "Democratic Hopefuls Play for Solidarity," ibid., March 15, 1992, A21; Helen Dewar and Kenneth Cooper, "Clinton Seeks Partnership for Change on Hill," ibid., April 30, 1992, A16; and David Von Drehle, "Clinton's Movers and Shapers," ibid., March 23, 1992, A1.

50. Sidney Blumenthal, "Bob Dole's First Strike," *New Yorker*, May 3, 1993, 40–46; Douglas Jehl, "Rejoicing Is Muted for the President in Budget Victory," *New York Times*, August 8, 1993, 1, 23; David Shribman, "Budget Battle a Hollow One for President," *Boston Globe*, August 8, 1993, 1, 24.

51. "Democratic Chiefs Apply Brake to Spending-Cut Juggernaut," *Congressional Quarterly Weekly Report*, November 23, 1993, 3186. For a discussion of the political damage Clinton suffered in the budget battles of 1993, see Paul Pierson, "The Deficit and the Politics of Domestic Reform," in *The Social Divide: Political Parties and the Future of Activist Government*, ed. Margaret Weir (Washington, D.C.: Brookings Institution, 1998), 148–52.

52. Penny cited in Fred Barnes, "Gored," *New Republic*, September 20 and 27, 1993, 12.

53. William Clinton, "Address before a Joint Session of Congress on Administration Goals," *Weekly Compilation of Presidential Documents* 29, no. 7, 215–24; Jill Zuckerman, "Pared Funding Speeds Passage of National Service," *Congressional Quarterly Weekly Report*, August 7, 1993, 2160–61.

54. Indeed, during the early days of his presidency, Clinton sought to identify with his party's leadership in Congress and the national committee—partly, one suspects, to avoid the political isolation from which Carter suffered. The White House lobbying efforts on Capitol Hill focused almost exclusively on the Democratic caucus; and the administration relied heavily on the Democratic National Committee to marshal public support for its domestic programs. White House staffer, interview with the author, November 3, 1994, not for attribution; David Wilhelm, chairman, Democratic National Committee, interview with the author, Washington, D.C., October 18, 1993; and Craig Smith, political director, Democratic National Committee, interview with the author, Washington, D.C., October 19, 1993. Also see Rhodes Cook, "DNC under Wilhelm Seeking a New Role," *Congressional Quarterly Weekly Report*, March 13, 1993, 634.

55. Al From and Will Marshall, *The Road to Realignment: Democrats and the Perot Voters* (Washington, D.C.: Democratic Leadership Council, 1993), 1-3–1-5.

56. David Shribman, "A New Brand of D.C. Politics," *Boston Globe*, November 18, 1993, 15; Gwen Ifill, "Fifty-six Long Days of Coordinated Persuasion," *New York Times*, November 19, 1993, A27.

57. Address to Congress on Health Care Plan, printed in *Congressional Quarterly*

Weekly Report, September 25, 1993, 2582–86; Robin Toner, "Alliance to Buy Health Care: Bureaucrat or Public Servant?" *New York Times*, December 5, 1993, 1, 38.

58. For a fuller account of the health care reform battle, see Haynes Johnson and David S. Broder, *The System: The American Way of Politics at the Breaking Point* (Boston: Little, Brown, 1996), and Theda Skocpol, *Boomerang: Clinton's Health Security Effort and the Turn against Government* (New York: Norton, 1996).

59. Adam Clymer, "National Health Program, President's Greatest Goal, Declared Dead in Congress," *New York Times*, September 27, 1994, A1, B10.

60. Alan Brinkley, "The 43 Percent President," *New York Times Magazine*, July 4, 1993, 22.

61. William Schneider, "Clinton: The Reason Why," *National Journal*, November 12, 1994, 2630–32.

62. Dan Balz and Ronald Brownstein, *Storming the Gates: Protest Politics and the Republican Revival* (Boston: Little Brown, 1996), 205–6.

63. Alan Ehrenhalt, "Changing South Perils Conservative Coalition," *Congressional Quarterly Weekly Report*, August 1, 1987, 1704.

64. Balz and Brownstein, *Storming the Gates*, 207.

65. Remarks of William Galston, lecture at Harvard University, December 2, 1994.

66. Steven Gettinger, "'94 Elections: Real Revolution or Blip on Political Radar?" *Congressional Quarterly Weekly Report*, November 5, 1994, 3127–32; Richard L. Berke, "Epic Political Realignments Often Aren't," *New York Times*, January 1, 1995, sec. 4, 3.

67. Michael Wines, "Republicans Seek Sweeping Changes in the House's Rules," *New York Times*, December 8, 1994, A1, B21; Michael Wines, "Moderate Republicans Seek an Identity for Gingrich Era," ibid., December 26, 1994, 1, 22.

68. Although many pundits were quick to view the 1994 election results as the end of the New Deal, neither Democrats nor Republicans were proposing to make changes in the largest entitlement program, Social Security, or to end the entitlement status of Medicare. See Robert Pear, "Welfare Debate Will Re-examine Core Assumptions," *New York Times*, January 2, 1995, 1, 9.

69. Peter Baker and John F. Harris, "Clinton Seeks to Shift Focus by Using Executive Powers," *Washington Post*, April 11, 1997, A1; John H. Cushman, "Clinton Sharply Tightens Air Pollution Regulations despite Concerns over Costs," *New York Times*, A1; Allan Freedman, "Oversight: Lack of Focus Leaves GOP Stuck in the Learning Curve," *Congressional Quarterly Weekly Report*, November 1, 1997, 2649–55.

70. Kathy Harriger, "Independent Justice: The Office of the Independent Counsel," in *Government Lawyers: The Federal Legal Bureaucracy and Presidential Politics*, ed. Cornell W. Clayton (Lawrence: University Press of Kansas, 1995), 86; see also "A Case against Independent Counsel," *Chicago Tribune*, May 26, 1996, C20.

71. William Clinton, "Address before a Joint Session of Congress on the State of the Union," January 23, 1996, printed in *Congressional Quarterly Weekly Report*, January 27, 1996, 258–62.

72. William Clinton, "Remarks on Signing the Personal Responsibility and Opportunity Reconciliation Act," August 22, 1996, *Weekly Compilation of Presidential Documents* 32, no. 34, 1484–89.

73. Clinton, State of the Union Address, January 23, 1996.

74. Bob Woodward, *The Choice* (New York: Simon and Schuster, 1996), 344.

75. Robert Dole, "Republican Response to President Clinton's State of the Union Message," *Congressional Quarterly Weekly Report*, January 27, 1996, 262–63.

76. Anthony Corrado, "Financing the 1996 Elections," in *The Election of 1996: Reports and Interpretations*, ed. Gerald M. Pomper et al. (Chatham, N.J.: Chatham House, 1997). "Soft money" was provided for in the 1979 amendments to the campaign finance legislation of 1974, as part of the broader effort to strengthen national party organizations. By 1992, both Democrats and Republicans had come to depend on it to finance the expensive media campaigns that dominated national elections. As such, the parties violated the spirit of the 1979 amendments, which were dedicated to increasing party spending on traditional grassroots boosterism and get-out-the-vote drives rather than mass media campaigns. More to the point, the institutional separation between the president and parties allowed, indeed encouraged, the exploitation of these funds by presidential candidates. See Beth Donovan, "Much-Maligned 'Soft Money' Is Precious to Both Parties," *National Journal*, May 15, 1993, 1195–1200.

77. Michael Nelson, "The Election: Turbulence and Tranquility in Contemporary American Politics," in *The Elections of 1996*, ed. Michael Nelson (Washington, D.C.: Congressional Quarterly Press, 1997), 52, and Gary Jacobson, "The 105th Congress: Unprecedented and Unsurprising," in ibid., 161.

78. Clinton's "third way" politics is placed in historical perspective and carefully analyzed in Stephen Skowronek, *The Politics Presidents Make: Leadership from John Adams to Bill Clinton* (Cambridge: Harvard University Press, 1997), 447–64.

79. Richard Stevenson, "After Year of Wrangling, Accord Is Reached on Plan to Balance the Budget by 2002," *New York Times*, May 3, 1997, 1.

80. The term "extraordinary isolation" is Woodrow Wilson's. See "Constitutional Government in the United States," in *The Papers of Woodrow Wilson*, ed. Arthur S. Link, 69 vols. (Princeton: Princeton University Press, 1974), 18:114.

81. James A. Barnes and Richard E. Cohen, "Divided Democrats," *National Journal*, November 13, 1997, 2304–7; Ronald D. Elving, "Early Task for '98 Candidates Is to Find New Political Footing," *Congressional Quarterly Weekly Report*, February 14, 1998, 353–57.

82. Al From, "Securing Our Gains," *New Democrat* 9 (November/December 1997): 35.

83. Michael Kelly, "At the White House, a Theory of Containment," *National Journal*, January 31, 1998, 204–5.

84. Jeffrey L. Katz and Dan Carney, "Clinton's Latest, Worst Troubles Put His Whole Agenda on Hold," *Congressional Quarterly Weekly Report*, January 24, 1998, 164–65;

Richard L. Berke, "Republicans End Silence on Troubles of President," *New York Times*, March 1, 1998, 20.

85. John R. Zaller, "Monica Lewinsky's Contribution to Political Science," *PS: Political Science and Politics* 31, no. 2 (June 1998): 182–89.

86. R. W. Apple Jr., "House, in a Partisan 258–176 Vote, Approves a Broad, Open-Ended Impeachment Inquiry," *New York Times*, October 9, 1998, A1. Thirty-one Democrats, many of them from southern and border states, voted for the resolution.

87. Katz and Carney, "Clinton's Latest, Worst Troubles Put His Whole Agenda on Hold," 164–65.

88. Todd S. Purdum, "Clinton Most Charming at a Distance," *New York Times*, September 27, 1998, 18.

89. Janny Scott, "'Talking Heads' Post-Mortem: 'All Wrong, All the Time,'" *New York Times*, November 8, 1998, A22.

90. "Gingrich Will Step Down as Speaker," *New York Times*, November 6, 1998.

91. "How Republican Determination Upset Clinton's Backing at Polls," *New York Times*, December 1, 1998.

92. "Early Views after Impeachment: The Public Supports Clinton," *New York Times*, December 1, 1998.

Chapter 7 Political Parties, Progressive Democracy, and the Future of Politics in America

1. Joel H. Silbey, "Foundation Stones of Present Discontents: The American Political Nation, 1776–1945," in *Present Discontents: American Politics in the Very Late Twentieth Century*, ed. Byron Shafer (Chatham, N.J.: Chatham House, 1997), 2. Also see Katherine Q. Seelye, "Americans Take a Dim View of Government, Survey Finds," *New York Times*, March 10, 1998, A15.

2. Wilson Carey McWilliams, "Conclusion: The Meaning of the Election," in *The Election of 1996: Reports and Interpretations*, ed. Gerald M. Pomper et al. (Chatham, N.J.: Chatham House, 1997), 255.

3. Alexis de Tocqueville, *Democracy in America*, ed. J. P. Mayer (Garden City, N.Y.: Doubleday, 1969), 676.

4. Ibid., 92–93.

5. Ibid., 521–22.

6. Thomas Jefferson to Spencer Roane, September 6, 1819, in *The Portable Thomas Jefferson*, ed. Merrill D. Peterson (New York: Viking Press, 1975), 563.

7. "Letters of Cato," in *The Complete Anti-federalist*, ed. Herbert J. Storing, 7 vols. (Chicago: University of Chicago Press, 1981), 2:111.

8. Wilson Carey McWilliams, "The Anti-federalists, Representation, and Party," *Northwestern University Law Review* 84, no. 1 (Fall 1989): 37.

9. Michael McGerr, *The Decline of Popular Politics: The American North, 1865–1928* (New York: Oxford University Press, 1986), 41.

10. Van Buren as cited in McWilliams, "The Anti-federalists, Representation, and Party," 37 n. 133. Richard Hofstadter, *The Idea of a Party System: The Rise of Legitimate Opposition in the United States, 1780–1840* (Berkeley: University of California Press, 1969).

11. Stephen Skowronek, *Building a New American State: The Expansion of National Administrative Capacities, 1877–1920* (New York: Cambridge University Press, 1982), 40.

12. Barry Karl, *The Uneasy State: The United States from 1915 to 1945* (Chicago: University of Chicago Press, 1993), 238.

13. Herbert Croly, *Progressive Democracy* (New York: Macmillan, 1914), 88, 101.

14. Herbert Croly, *The Promise of American Life* (New York: Macmillan, 1909; reprint, New York: Dutton, 1963), 278–79.

15. Theodore Roosevelt, *Citizenship in a Republic*, address delivered at the Sorbonne, Paris, April 23, 1910 (New York: Review of Books, 1910), 2204.

16. John Dewey, *Liberalism and Social Action* (New York: Putnam's, 1935), 26.

17. Franklin D. Roosevelt, *Public Papers and Addresses*, 13 vols., ed. Samuel I. Rosenman (New York: Random House, 1938–50), 7:xxviii–xxxii.

18. *Report of the President's Committee on Administrative Management* (Washington, D.C.: Government Printing Office, 1937), 53. I am not taking issue here with Otis Graham's argument that many Progressives opposed the New Deal. See Graham, *An Encore for Reform: The Old Progressives and the New Deal* (New York: Oxford University Press, 1967). It is the case, however, that the New Deal political program was very much inspired by TR's Bull Moose campaign. On the link between progressivism and the New Deal, see Sidney M. Milkis, *The President and the Parties: The Transformation of the American Party System since the New Deal* (New York: Oxford University Press, 1993), esp. chap. 2.

19. Eldon Eisenach, *The Lost Promise of Progressivism* (Lawrence: University Press of Kansas, 1994).

20. Alonzo Hamby, *Liberalism and Its Challengers: FDR to Reagan* (New York: Oxford University Press, 1985), esp. chap. 6, epilogue.

21. Scott Shepard, "Reagan Rouses the GOP Faithful," *Atlanta Constitution*, August 18, 1992, A1.

22. Many editorials around the country warned that Buchanan's speech risked splintering the Republican party. As the *Atlanta Constitution* averred, "The dominance of hardliners at the convention has left many mainstream Republicans uncomfortable. . . . The Republicans ought to know better. They have spent the past two decades deriding the Democrats for the reputation they established with a 1972 party platform that went too far in accommodating the radical fringe. . . . It has taken the Democrats 20 years to recover. How long will it take the Republicans to get over what they have wrought in Houston this week?" Editorial, "GOP Moves Past the Middle," August 20, 1992, A18.

23. In fact, as Melissa Buis has shown, the Personal Responsibility and Work Opportu-

nity Reconciliation Act of 1996, although giving states more discretion to tailor their individual welfare programs, imposes important new national standards to determine eligibility, to attack illegitimacy and teen pregnancy, and to establish work requirements. See C. Melissa Buis, "Devolution Then and Now: Redefining the Federal Role in Welfare Policy" (paper presented at the Northeastern Political Science Annual Meeting, Boston, 1996).

24. Jackie Calmes, "Why Congress Hews to the Party Lines on Impeachment," *Wall Street Journal*, December 16, 1998, 1.

25. Wilson Carey McWilliams, "Two-Tier Politics and the Problem of Public Policy," in *The New Politics of Public Policy*, ed. Marc K. Landy and Martin A. Levin (Baltimore: Johns Hopkins University Press, 1995), 275 (emphasis in the original). See also A. James Reichley, "Party Politics in a Federal Polity," in *Challenges to Party Government*, ed. John Kenneth White and Jerome Mileur (Carbondale: Southern Illinois University Press, 1992), and Milkis, *President and the Parties*, chaps. 10–12.

26. Scot Lehigh, "Right Idea, Wrong Leader? Third Party Favored by Many, but Perot Presents a Problem," *Boston Globe*, October 1, 1995, A33. On the cultural and institutional factors that abet "outsiderism" in contemporary politics, see James W. Ceaser and Andrew Busch, *Losing to Win: The 1996 Elections and American Politics* (Lanham, Md.: Rowman and Littlefield, 1997), esp. chap. 6. Perot's promise in 1996 to subordinate his personal ambitions to a collective organization—the Reform party—was not kept; indeed, as Ceaser and Busch point out, the Reform party's nomination process "only served to accentuate [Perot's] control and to deepen the split between those who were primarily Perot supporters and those who wanted to depersonalize" the movement he represented (112).

27. Alexander Hamilton, James Madison, and John Jay, *The Federalist Papers* (New York: New American Library, 1961), 426–27.

28. Walter Dean Burnham, *Critical Elections and the Mainsprings of American Politics* (New York: Norton, 1970), 188–89.

29. Robert H. Wiebe, *Self-Rule: A Cultural History of American Democracy* (Chicago: University of Chicago Press, 1995), 249.

30. On the "rights revolution" and its legacy for governing institutions, see R. Shep Melnick, *Between the Lines: Interpreting Welfare Rights* (Washington, D.C.: Brookings Institution, 1994), and Landy and Levin, *New Politics of Public Policy*.

INDEX

Library of Congress Cataloging-in-Publication Data

Milkis, Sidney M.
    Political parties and constitutional government : remaking
American democracy / Sidney M. Milkis.
        p.   cm. — (Interpreting American politics)
    Includes bibliographical references.
    ISBN 0-8018-6194-2 (alk. paper). — ISBN 0-8018-6195-0 (pbk. :
alk. paper)
        1. Political parties—United States.   2. Democracy—United States.
3. United States—Politics and government.   I. Title.   II. Series.
JK2261.M53 1999
324.273'09—dc21   99-14370
                                                          CIP